THE BITCOIN STANDARD

THE BITCOIN STANDARD

The Decentralized Alternative to Central Banking

Saifedean Ammous

WILEY

Published by John Wiley & Sons, Inc., Hoboken, New Jersey.
Published simultaneously in Canada.

For general information on our other products and services or for technical support, please contact our Customer Care Department within the United States at (800) 762–2974, outside the United States at (317) 572–3993, or fax (317) 572–4002.

Wiley publishes in a variety of print and electronic formats and by print-on-demand. Some material included with standard print versions of this book may not be included in e-books or in print-on-demand. If this book refers to media such as a CD or DVD that is not included in the version you purchased, you may download this material at http://booksupport.wiley.com. For more information about Wiley products, visit www.wiley.com.

Library of Congress Cataloging-in-Publication Data is Available:

ISBN 9781119473862 (Hardcover)
ISBN 9781119473893 (ePDF)
ISBN 9781119473916 (ePub)

Cover Design: Wiley
Cover Images: REI stone © Danita Delimont/Getty Images; gold bars © Grassetto/Getty Images; QR code/Courtesy of Saifedean Ammous

Printed in the United States of America

SKY10031161_110321

To my wife and daughter, who give me a reason to write.
And to Satoshi Nakamoto, who gave me something worth writing
about.

Contents

About the Author   viii
Author's Preface to 2021 Update   ix
Foreword   xi
Prologue   xiv

Chapter 1   **Money**   1

Chapter 2   **Primitive Moneys**   11

Chapter 3   **Monetary Metals**   17
                 Why Gold?   19
                 Roman Golden Age and Decline   25
                 Byzantium and the Bezant   28
                 The Renaissance   29
                 La Belle Époque   34

Chapter 4   **Government Money**   41
                 Monetary Nationalism and the End of the Free
                    World   43
                 The Interwar Era   47
                 World War II and Bretton Woods   53
                 Government Money's Track Record   60

Chapter 5   **Money and Time Preference**   73
                 Monetary Inflation   81

	Saving and Capital Accumulation	90
	Innovations: "Zero to One" versus "One to Many"	96
	Artistic Flourishing	98
Chapter 6	**Capitalism's Information System**	**105**
	Capital Market Socialism	109
	Business Cycles and Financial Crises	113
	Sound Basis for Trade	126
Chapter 7	**Sound Money and Individual Freedom**	**135**
	Should Government Manage the Money Supply?	136
	Unsound Money and Perpetual War	145
	Limited versus Omnipotent Government	149
	The Bezzle	155
Chapter 8	**Digital Money**	**167**
	Bitcoin as Digital Cash	168
	Supply, Value, and Transactions	177
	Appendix to Chapter 8	191
Chapter 9	**What Is Bitcoin Good For?**	**193**
	Store of Value	193
	Individual Sovereignty	200
	International and Online Settlement	205
	Global Unit of Account	212
Chapter 10	**Bitcoin Questions**	**217**
	Is Bitcoin Mining a Waste?	217
	Out of Control: Why Nobody Can Change Bitcoin	222
	Antifragility	230
	Can Bitcoin Scale?	232
	Is Bitcoin for Criminals?	238
	How to Kill Bitcoin: A Beginners' Guide	241
	Altcoins	251
	Blockchain Technology	257
Acknowledgments		273
Bibliography		275
List of Figures		282
List of Tables		284
Index		285

About the Author

S aifedean Ammous is an independent scholar researching and teaching bitcoin and economics in the Austrian school tradition on his website: www.saifedean.com.

Author's Preface to 2021 Update

Three years after the initial publication of *The Bitcoin Standard* in 2018, interest in the book has continued to grow steadily, with each of the first three months of 2021 registering a record in monthly sales, and translations rights sold for 25 languages. The growing demand made me consider publishing a second edition of the book, correcting some unfortunate errors, updating the book with the data and developments of the intervening three years, and adding two new chapters to discuss bitcoin's scaling and energy consumption in more depth. But a lot has changed in the world of bitcoin over the last three years, and introducing the data and developments of these years would require significant edits to the text. *The Bitcoin Standard*, and its analysis and conclusions, was the product of its time, a snapshot of a specific point in bitcoin's history, after the contentious hard fork wars were decisively resolved in a way that cemented bitcoin's value proposition of an immutable hard monetary policy, when the total value of the bitcoin network had settled around the milestone of $100 billion, just before the network was to enter its second decade and mature into an investment-grade asset class attracting the attention of the world's major financial institutions and corporations. While the events of the last three years do not invalidate the analysis and conclusions of the book, including them would change the book significantly from the original text, popular with readers around the world, and result in the creation of a different book, a product of a different time in bitcoin's life.

Instead of a significantly altered second edition, and in consultation with my editor, I decided to let The Bitcoin Standard live on in its original form, with only some minor adjustments to correct a few obvious mistakes, some of which were glaring, though inconsequential to the substance and arguments of the book. I will instead include new developments and analysis in a sequel, *The Fiat Standard: The Debt Slavery Alternative to Human Civilization*. The sequel will analyze the rise of bitcoin by analyzing the workings of the fiat monetary system using the same approach, methods, and terminology used in studying bitcoin in *The Bitcoin Standard*.

Unexpected to me at the time of writing, *The Bitcoin Standard* has proven popular among corporations and financial institutions entering the bitcoin space. The most astonishing compliment the book received was when Michael Saylor, CEO of publicly traded software intelligence firm Microstrategy, decided to put his company on a bitcoin standard, making bitcoin its prime treasury reserve asset. Mr. Saylor has not only backed his conviction in bitcoin by putting significant amounts of his personal wealth and company treasury in bitcoin, but he has, in a very short period of time, become one of the leading thinkers and analysts of bitcoin, as well as one of its most effective communicators. The conviction, courage, and clarity of Mr. Saylor in pursuing a bitcoin standard has been an inspiration, and I am honored he has agreed to write a foreword to include with this reprint, to contextualize the importance of this book for the continued emergence of a global bitcoin standard.

With the revisions complete, and a new foreword to introduce the book from the world's pioneering leader in adopting the bitcoin standard, I hope readers find this version of the book worthy of a place on their bookshelves, and in their recommendations to family, friends, and colleagues, well into the future.

Saifedean Ammous
Amman, Jordan
April 27, 2021

Foreword

by Michael J. Saylor

I n March 2020, the world was struck by a pandemic, which brought entire segments of our economy to a grinding halt, and interrupted patterns of behavior that we had all grown accustomed to over the course of hundreds of years. Offices and schools closed, public gatherings ceased, commercial and recreational travel were stopped, and in-person meetings became impossible or impractical. Stores were closed, factories idled, aircraft were grounded, ships anchored, roads were blocked, and borders closed.

The monetary response of policymakers to this economic shock was unprecedented. The supply of currency expanded at the fastest rate in modern history, with every nation engaged in aggressive asset purchases, fiscal stimulus, deficit spending, and interest rate suppression. The result was a K-shaped recovery—asset-rich firms rapidly bounced back and had their best performing year of the century, while operating companies saw their revenues collapse and their earnings dissipate.

The cognitive dissonance was bewildering, as was the massive wealth redistribution. Purely digital firms saw their demand and revenues explode upwards. Brick-and-mortar retail, travel, hospitality, and entertainment industries struggled to stay solvent. MicroStrategy was positioned in the middle of this economic landscape—and we spent the entire second quarter transforming our operations to become digital first, by rebuilding the sales, marketing, and services operations around our website, and implementing videoconferencing, automation, cloud services, and remote work.

By June, we had done enough work and gained enough information to conclude that the five-hundred-million-dollar war chest that we were saving for a rainy day would be of no use in the new virtual world, and we would probably generate an additional five hundred million in cash flow due to our digital transformation. The good news was that we had plenty of cash and a high prospect of generating more over time. The bad news was that the monetary inflation rate had tripled, and the price of other assets was exploding at the fastest rate in a generation. Our treasury was a rapidly melting ice cube, and we needed to act quickly if we didn't want to see all the value it represented waste away.

This catalyzed a mad scramble for a solution to our problem. How does a modern corporation protect its balance sheet in an environment of monetary inflation where the currency is losing 15% of its purchasing power each year, while the after-tax yields available from traditional treasury instruments are effectively zero? A company generating seventy-five million per year in cash flow, holding five hundred million dollars in treasury balances at a negative real yield of 15% is destroying as much shareholder value as it is creating. In essence, we were running as hard as we could to stand still.

After considering and dismissing cash, bonds, real estate, equity, derivatives, art, commodities, and collectibles as treasury assets, we were left with just precious metals and cryptocurrencies. It was at this point in my search for a solution that I discovered *The Bitcoin Standard* by Saifedean Ammous, and it was this book, more than any other, that provided the holistic economic framework that I needed to interpret the macroeconomic forces reshaping our world, distorting our markets, and buffeting corporations.

The Bitcoin Standard should be required reading for everyone in modern society. It offers a concise, coherent narrative of monetary theory, the history of money, practical economics, and the impact of political policy on business, culture, and the economy. The book contains perhaps one of the best articulations of the virtues of strong money and the dangers of weak currency yet presented in modern business literature. *The Bitcoin Standard* also masterfully debunks the myths of modern monetary theory and the broken ideas that have dominated the fiat economic school of thought since the early twentieth century.

In May 2020, this book was critical in leading me to conclude that bitcoin was the solution to our corporate treasury problem. Our firm elected to invest our cash assets in bitcoin in August 2020, eventually adopting it as our primary treasury reserve asset and purchasing $2.2 billion in BTC over the following six months. *The Bitcoin Standard* helped us realize that the best business strategy for our firm was to hold just a small working capital balance in fiat currencies, sweeping the rest of our cash flows into our treasury and converting those sums into bitcoin as soon as practical. As I write these words, 99% of our assets are stored in bitcoin, with the remaining 1% stored in the local currencies required to do business in various markets. In essence, MicroStrategy has adopted the bitcoin standard.

The Bitcoin Standard is my first recommendation for those seeking a holistic appreciation of the economic theory, political history, and technological developments that have driven the growth of the bitcoin network and define its future trajectory. It is suitable for individuals, investors, executives, technologists, politicians, journalists, and academics alike, regardless of their agenda. Bitcoin is the world's first digital monetary network. Bitcoin is also the world's first engineered monetary asset. Together, these traits represent the most disruptive technology in the world, the greatest opportunity currently available to those who wish to create something new and wonderful, and the solution to the store-of-value problem faced by 7.8 billion people, 100+ million companies, and hundreds of trillions of dollars of investor capital.

I hope you enjoy this book as much as I did, and benefit from ideas contained within these pages.

Michael J. Saylor
Chairman & CEO
MicroStrategy
Miami Beach, FL
24 March 2021

Prologue

O n October 31, 2008, a computer programmer going by the pseudonym Satoshi Nakamoto sent an email to a cryptography mailing list to announce that he had produced a "new electronic cash system that's fully peer-to-peer, with no trusted third party."[1] He copied the abstract of the paper explaining the design, and a link to it online. In essence, bitcoin offered a payment network with its own native currency, and used a sophisticated method for members to verify all transactions without having to trust in any single member of the network. The currency was issued at a predetermined rate to reward the members who spent their processing power on verifying the transactions, thus providing a reward for their work. The startling thing about this invention was that, contrary to many other previous attempts at setting up a digital cash, it actually worked.

While a clever and neat design, there wasn't much to suggest that such a quirky experiment would interest anyone outside the circles of cryptography geeks. For months this was the case, as barely a few dozen users worldwide were joining the network and engaging in mining and

---

[1] The full email can be found on the Satoshi Nakamoto Institute archive of all known Satoshi Nakamoto writings, available at www.nakamotoinstitute.org. "Re: Bitcoin P2P e-cash paper." Received by The Cryptography Mailing List, 31 Oct. 2008.

sending each other coins that began to acquire the status of collectibles, albeit in digital form.

But in October 2009, an Internet exchange[2] sold 5,050 bitcoins for $5.02, at a price of $1 for 1,006 bitcoins, to register the first purchase of a bitcoin with money.[3] The price was calculated by measuring the value of the electricity needed to produce a bitcoin. In economic terms, this seminal moment was arguably the most significant in bitcoin's life. Bitcoin was no longer just a digital game being played within a fringe community of programmers; it had now become a market good with a price, indicating that someone somewhere had developed a positive valuation for it. On May 22, 2010, someone else paid 10,000 bitcoins to buy two pizza pies worth $25, representing the first time that bitcoin was used as a medium of exchange. The token had needed seven months to transition from being a market good to being a medium of exchange.

Since then, the bitcoin network has grown in the number of users and transactions, and the processing power dedicated to it, while the value of its currency has risen quickly, exceeding $7,000 per bitcoin as of November 2017.[4] After eight years, it is clear that this invention is no longer just an online game, but a technology that has passed the market test and is being used by many for real-world purposes, with its exchange rate being regularly featured on TV, in newspapers, and on websites along with the exchange rates of national currencies.

Bitcoin can be best understood as distributed software that allows for transfer of value using a currency protected from unexpected inflation without relying on trusted third parties. In other words, bitcoin automates the functions of a modern central bank and makes them predictable and virtually immutable by programming them into code decentralized among thousands of network members, none of whom can alter the code without the consent of the rest. This makes bitcoin the first demonstrably reliable operational example of *digital cash* and *digital hard money*. While bitcoin is a new invention of the digital age, the problems it purports to solve—namely, providing a form of money that is

---

[2] The now-defunct *New Liberty Standard*, newlibertystandard.wikifoundry.com/.

[3] Popper, Nathaniel. *Digital Gold: Bitcoin and the Inside Story of the Misfits and Millionaires Trying to Reinvent Money*. HarperCollins, 2015.

[4] In other words, in the eight years it has been a market commodity, a bitcoin has appreciated around almost eight million-fold, or, precisely 793,513,944% from its first price of $0.000994 to its all-time high at the time of writing, $7,888.

under the full command of its owner and likely to hold its value in the long run—are as old as human society itself. This book presents a conception of these problems based on years of studying this technology and the economic problems it solves, and how societies have previously found solutions for them throughout history. My conclusion may surprise those who label bitcoin a scam or ruse of speculators and promoters out to make a quick buck. Indeed, bitcoin improves on earlier "store of value" solutions, and bitcoin's suitability as the sound money of a digital age may catch naysayers by surprise.

History can foreshadow what's to come, particularly when examined closely. And time will tell just how sound the case made in this book is. As it must, the first part of the book explains money, its function and properties. As an economist with an engineering background, I have always sought to understand a technology in terms of the problems it purports to solve, which allows for the identification of its functional essence and its separation from incidental, cosmetic, and insignificant characteristics. By understanding the problems money attempts to solve, it becomes possible to elucidate what makes for sound and unsound money, and to apply that conceptual framework to understand how and why various goods, such as seashells, beads, metals, and government money, have served the function of money, and how and why they may have failed at it or served society's purposes to store value and exchange it.

The second part of the book discusses the individual, social, and global implications of sound and unsound forms of money throughout history. Sound money allows people to think about the long term and to save and invest more for the future. Saving and investing for the long run are the key to capital accumulation and the advance of human civilization. Money is the information and measurement system of an economy, and sound money is what allows trade, investment, and entrepreneurship to proceed on a solid basis, whereas unsound money throws these processes into disarray. Sound money is also an essential element of a free society as it provides for an effective bulwark against despotic government.

The third section of the book explains the operation of the bitcoin network and its most salient economic characteristics, and analyzes the possible uses of bitcoin as a form of sound money, discussing some use cases which bitcoin does not serve well, as well as addressing some of the most common misunderstandings and misconceptions surrounding it.

This book is written to help the reader understand the economics of bitcoin and how it serves as the digital iteration of the many technologies used to fulfill the functions of money throughout history. This book is not an advertisement or invitation to buy into the bitcoin currency. Far from it. The value of bitcoin is likely to remain volatile, at least for a while; the bitcoin network may yet succeed or fail, for whatever foreseeable or unforeseeable reasons; and using it requires technical competence and carries risks that make it unsuited for many people. This book does not offer investment advice, but aims at helping elucidate the economic properties of the network and its operation, to provide readers an informed understanding of bitcoin before deciding whether they want to use it.

Only with such an understanding, and only after extensive and thorough research into the practical operational aspects of owning and storing bitcoins, should anyone consider holding value in bitcoin. While bitcoin's rise in market value may make it appear like a no-brainer as an investment, a closer look at the myriad hacks, attacks, scams, and security failures that have cost people their bitcoins provides a sobering warning to anyone who thinks that owning bitcoins provides a guaranteed profit. Should you come out of reading this book thinking that the bitcoin currency is something worth owning, your first investment should not be in buying bitcoins, but in time spent understanding how to buy, store, and own bitcoins securely. It is the inherent nature of bitcoin that such knowledge cannot be delegated or outsourced. There is no alternative to personal responsibility for anyone interested in using this network, and that is the real investment that needs to be made to get into bitcoin.

Chapter 1

Money

Bitcoin is the newest technology to serve the function of money—an invention leveraging the technological possibilities of the digital age to solve a problem that has persisted for all of humanity's existence: how to move economic value across time and space. In order to understand bitcoin, one must first understand money, and to understand money, there is no alternative to the study of the function and history of money.

The simplest way for people to exchange value is to exchange valuable goods with one another. This process of *direct exchange* is referred to as barter, but is only practical in small circles with only a few goods and services produced. In a hypothetical economy of a dozen people isolated from the world, there is not much scope for specialization and trade, and it would be possible for individuals to each engage in the production of the most basic essentials of survival and exchange them among themselves directly. Barter has always existed in human society and continues to this day, but it is highly impractical and remains only in use in exceptional circumstances, usually involving people with extensive familiarity with one another.

In a more sophisticated and larger economy, the opportunity arises for individuals to specialize in the production of more goods and to exchange them with many more people—people with whom they have no personal relationships, strangers with whom it is utterly impractical to keep a running tally of goods, services, and favors. The larger the market, the more the opportunities for specialization and exchange, but also the bigger the problem of *coincidence of wants*—what you want to acquire is produced by someone who doesn't want what you have to sell. The problem is deeper than different requirements for different goods, as there are three distinct dimensions to the problem.

First, there is the lack of coincidence in scales: what you want may not be equal in value to what you have and dividing one of them into smaller units may not be practical. Imagine wanting to sell shoes for a house; you cannot buy the house in small pieces each equivalent in value to a pair of shoes, nor does the homeowner want to own all the shoes whose value is equivalent to that of the house. Second, there is the lack of coincidence in time frames: what you want to sell may be perishable but what you want to buy is more durable and valuable, making it hard to accumulate enough of your perishable good to exchange for the durable good at one point in time. It is not easy to accumulate enough apples to be exchanged for a car at once, because they will rot before the deal can be completed. Third, there is the lack of coincidence of locations: you may want to sell a house in one place to buy a house in another location, and (most) houses aren't transportable. These three problems make direct exchange highly impractical and result in people needing to resort to performing more layers of exchange to satisfy their economic needs.

The only way around this is through *indirect exchange*: you try to find some other good that another person would want and find someone who will exchange it with you for what you want to sell. That intermediary good is a *medium of exchange*, and while any good could serve as the medium of exchange, as the scope and size of the economy grows it becomes impractical for people to constantly search for different goods that their counterparty is looking for, carrying out several exchanges for each exchange they want to conduct. A far more efficient solution will naturally emerge, if only because those who chance upon it will be far more productive than those who do not: a single medium of exchange (or at most a small number of media of exchange) emerges for everyone to trade their goods for. A good that assumes the role of a widely accepted medium of exchange is called money.

Being a medium of exchange is the quintessential function that defines money—in other words, it is a good purchased not to be consumed (a consumption good), nor to be employed in the production of other goods (an investment, or capital good), but primarily for the sake of being exchanged for other goods. While investment is also meant to produce income to be exchanged for other goods, it is distinct from money in three respects: first, it offers a return, which money does not offer; second, it always involves a risk of failure, whereas money is supposed to carry the least risk; third, investments are less liquid than money, necessitating significant transaction costs every time they are to be spent. This can help us understand why there will always be demand for money, and why holding investments can never entirely replace money. Human life is lived with uncertainty as a given, and humans cannot know for sure when they will need what amount of money.[1] It is common sense, and age-old wisdom in virtually all human cultures, for individuals to want to store some portion of their wealth in the form of money, because it is the most liquid holding possible, allowing the holder to quickly liquidate if she needs to, and because it involves less risk than any investment. The price for the convenience of holding money comes in the form of the forgone consumption that could have been had with it, and in the form of the forgone returns that could have been made from investing it.

From examining such human choices in market situations, Carl Menger, the father of the Austrian school of economics and founder of marginal analysis in economics, came up with an understanding of the key property that leads to a good being adopted freely as money on the market, and that is *salability*—the ease with which a good can be

---

[1] See Ludwig von Mises' *Human Action,* p. 250, for a discussion of how uncertainty about the future is the key driver of demand for holding money. With no uncertainty of the future, humans could know all their incomes and expenditures ahead of time and plan them optimally so they never have to hold any cash. But as uncertainty is an inevitable part of life, people must continue to hold money so they have the ability to spend without having to know the future.

sold on the market whenever its holder desires, with the least loss in its price.[2]

There is nothing in principle that stipulates what should or should not be used as money. Any person choosing to purchase something not for its own sake, but with the aim of exchanging it for something else, is making it de facto money, and as people vary, so do their opinions on, and choices of, what constitutes money. Throughout human history, many things have served the function of money: gold and silver, most notably, but also copper, seashells, large stones, salt, cattle, government paper, precious stones, and even alcohol and cigarettes in certain conditions. People's choices are subjective, and so there is no "right" and "wrong" choice of money. There are, however, consequences to choices.

The relative salability of goods can be assessed in terms of how well they address the three facets of the problem of the lack of coincidence of wants mentioned earlier: their salability across scales, across space, and across time. A good that is salable across scales can be conveniently divided into smaller units or grouped into larger units, thus allowing the holder to sell it in whichever quantity he desires. Salability across space indicates an ease of transporting the good or carrying it along as a person travels, and this has led to good monetary media generally having high value per unit of weight. Both of these characteristics are not very hard to fulfill by a large number of goods that could potentially serve the function of money. It is the third element, salability across time, which is the most crucial.

A good's salability across time refers to its ability to hold value into the future, allowing the holder to store wealth in it, which is the second function of money: *store of value*. For a good to be salable across time it has to be immune to rot, corrosion, and other types of deterioration. It is safe to say anyone who thought he could store his wealth for the long term in fish, apples, or oranges learned this lesson the hard way, and likely had very little reason to worry about storing wealth for a while. Physical integrity through time, however, is a necessary but insufficient condition for salability across time, as it is possible for a good to lose its value significantly even if its physical condition remains unchanged.

---

[2]Menger, Carl. "On the Origins of Money." Trans. C. A. Foley. *Economic Journal*, vol. 2, 1892, pp. 239–55.

For the good to maintain its value, it is also necessary that the supply of the good not increase too drastically during the period in which the holder owns it. A common characteristic of forms of money throughout history is the presence of some mechanism to restrain the production of new units of the good to maintain the value of the existing units. The relative difficulty of producing new monetary units determines the hardness of money: money whose supply is hard to increase is known as *hard money*, while *easy money* is money whose supply is amenable to large increases.

We can understand money's hardness through understanding two distinct quantities related to the supply of a good: (1) the *stock*, which is its existing supply, consisting of everything that has been produced in the past, minus everything that has been consumed or destroyed; and (2) the *flow*, which is the extra production that will be made in the next time period. The ratio between the stock and flow is a reliable indicator of a good's hardness as money, and how well it is suited to playing a monetary role. A good that has a low ratio of stock-to-flow is one whose existing supply can be increased drastically if people start using it as a store of value. Such a good would be unlikely to maintain value if chosen as a store of value. The higher the ratio of the stock to the flow, the more likely a good is to maintain its value over time and thus be more salable across time.[3]

If people choose a hard money, with a high stock-to-flow ratio, as a store of value, their purchasing of it to store it would increase demand for it, causing a rise in its price, which would incentivize its producers to make more of it. But because the flow is small compared to the existing supply, even a large increase in the new production is unlikely to depress the price significantly. On the other hand, if people chose to store their wealth in an easy money, with a low stock-to-flow ratio, it would be trivial for the producers of this good to create very large quantities of it that depress the price, devaluing the good, expropriating the wealth of the savers, and destroying the good's salability across time.

I like to call this the *easy money trap*: anything used as a store of value will have its supply increased, and anything whose supply can be easily

[3] Fekete, Antal. *Whither Gold?* Winner of the 1996 International Currency Prize, Sponsored by Bank Lips, 1997, www.professorfekete.com/articles/AEFWhitherGold.pdf.

increased will destroy the wealth of those who used it as a store of value. The corollary to this trap is that anything that is successfully used as money will have some natural or artificial mechanism that restricts the new flow of the good into the market, maintaining its value across time. It therefore follows that for something to assume a monetary role, it has to be costly to produce, otherwise the temptation to make money on the cheap will destroy the wealth of the savers, and destroy the incentive anyone has to save in this medium.

Whenever a natural, technological, or political development resulted in quickly increasing the new supply of a monetary good, the good would lose its monetary status and be replaced by other media of exchange with a more reliably high stock-to-flow ratio, as will be discussed in the next chapter. Seashells were used as money when they were hard to find, loose cigarettes are used as money in prisons because they are hard to procure or produce, and with national currencies, the lower the rate of increase of the supply, the more likely the currency is to be held by individuals and maintain its value over time.

When modern technology made the importation and catching of seashells easy, societies that used them switched to metal or paper money, and when a government increases its currency's supply, its citizens shift to holding foreign currencies, gold, or other more reliable monetary assets. The twentieth century provided us an unfortunately enormous number of such tragic examples, particularly from developing countries. The monetary media that survived the longest are the ones that had very reliable mechanisms for restricting their supply growth—in other words, *hard money*. Competition is at all times alive between monetary media, and its outcomes are foretold through the effects of technology on the differing stock-to-flow ratio of the competitors, as will be demonstrated in the next chapter.

While people are generally free to use whichever goods they please as their media of exchange, the reality is that over time, the ones who use hard money will benefit most, by losing very little value due to the negligible new supply of their medium of exchange. Those who choose easy money will likely lose value as its supply grows quickly, bringing its market price down. Whether through prospective rational calculation, or the retrospective harsh lessons of reality, the majority of money and wealth will be concentrated with those who choose the hardest and most salable forms of money. But the hardness and salability of goods itself is not something that is static in time. As the technological capabilities of different societies and eras have varied, so has the hardness of various forms of money, and with it their salability. In reality, the choice of what makes the best money has always been determined by the technological realities of societies shaping the salability of different goods. Hence, Austrian economists are rarely dogmatic or objectivist in their definition of sound money. They define it not as a specific good or commodity, but as whichever money emerges on the market, freely chosen by the people who transact with it. It is not imposed by coercive authority, and its value is determined through market interaction, not government imposition.[4] Free-market monetary competition is ruthlessly effective at producing sound money, as it only allows those who choose the right money to maintain considerable wealth over time. There is no need for government to impose the hardest money on society; society will have uncovered it long before it concocted its government, and any governmental imposition, if it were to have any effect, would only serve to hinder the process of monetary competition.

The full individual and societal implications of hard and easy money are far more profound than mere financial loss or gain, and are a central theme of this book, discussed thoroughly in Chapters 5, 6, and 7. Those who are able to save their wealth in a good store of value are likely to plan for the future more than those who have bad stores of value. The soundness of the monetary media, in terms of its ability to hold value over time, is a key determinant of how much individuals value the present over the future, or their *time preference*, a pivotal concept in this book.

Beyond the stock-to-flow ratio, another important aspect of a monetary medium's salability is its acceptability by others. The more people accept a monetary medium, the more liquid it is, and the more likely it is to be bought and sold without too much loss. In social settings with many peer-to-peer interactions, as computing protocols demonstrate, it is natural for a few standards to emerge to dominate exchange, because the gains from joining a network grow exponentially the larger the size of the network. Hence, Facebook and a handful of social media networks

---

[4]Salerno, Joseph. *Money: Sound and Unsound.* Auburn, AL, Ludwig von Mises Institute, 2010, pp. xiv–xv.

dominate the market, when many hundreds of almost identical networks were created and promoted. Similarly, any device that sends emails has to utilize the IMAP/POP3 protocol for receiving email, and the SMTP protocol for sending it. Many other protocols were invented, and they could be used perfectly well, but almost nobody uses them because to do so would preclude a user from interacting with almost everyone who uses email today, because they are on IMAP/POP3 and SMTP. Similarly, with money, it was inevitable that one, or a few, goods would emerge as the main medium of exchange, because the property of being exchanged easily matters the most. A medium of exchange, as mentioned before, is not acquired for its own properties, but for its salability.

Further, wide acceptance of a medium of exchange allows all prices to be expressed in its terms, which allows it to play the third function of money: *unit of account.* In an economy with no recognized medium of exchange, each good will have to be priced in terms of each other good, leading to a large number of prices, making economic calculations exceedingly difficult. In an economy with a medium of exchange, all prices of all goods are expressed in terms of the same unit of account. In this society money serves as a metric with which to measure interpersonal value; it rewards producers to the extent that they contribute value to others, and signifies to consumers how much they need to pay to obtain their desired goods. Only with a uniform medium of exchange acting as a unit of account does complex economic calculation become possible, and with it comes the possibility for specialization into complex tasks, capital accumulation, and large markets. The operation of a market economy is dependent on prices, and prices, to be accurate, are dependent on a common medium of exchange, which reflects the relative scarcity of different goods. If this is easy money, the ability of its issuer to constantly increase its quantity will prevent it from accurately reflecting opportunity costs. Every unpredictable change in the quantity of money would distort its role as a measure of interpersonal value and a conduit for economic information.

Having a single medium of exchange allows the size of the economy to grow as large as the number of people willing to use that medium of exchange. The larger the size of the economy, the larger the opportunities for gains from exchange and specialization, and perhaps more significantly, the longer and more sophisticated the structure of production can become. Producers can specialize in producing capital goods that will only produce final consumer goods after longer intervals, which allows for more productive and superior products. In the primitive small economy, the structure of production of fish consisted of individuals going to the shore and catching fish with their bare hands, with the entire process taking a few hours from start to finish. As the economy grows, more sophisticated tools and capital goods are utilized, and the production of these tools stretches the duration of the production process significantly while also increasing its productivity. In the modern world, fish are caught with highly sophisticated boats that take years to build and are operated for decades. These boats are able to sail to seas that smaller boats cannot reach and thus produce fish that would otherwise not be available. The boats can brave inclement weather and continue production in very difficult conditions where less capital-intensive boats would be docked uselessly. As capital accumulation has made the process longer, it has become more productive per unit of labor, and it can produce superior products that were never possible for the primitive economy with basic tools and no capital accumulation. None of this would be possible without money playing the roles of medium of exchange to allow specialization; store of value to create future-orientation and incentivize individuals to direct resources to investment instead of consumption; and unit of account to allow economic calculation of profits and losses.

The history of money's evolution has seen various goods play the role of money, with varying degrees of hardness and soundness, depending on the technological capabilities of each era. From seashells to salt, cattle, silver, gold, and gold-backed government money, ending with the current almost universal use of government-provided legal tender, every step of technological advance has allowed us to utilize a new form of money with added benefits, but, as always, new pitfalls. By examining the history of the tools and materials that have been employed in the role of money throughout history, we are able to discern the characteristics that make for good money and the ones that make for bad money. Only with this background in place can we then move on to understand how bitcoin functions and what its role as a monetary medium is.

The next chapter examines the history of obscure artifacts and objects that have been used as money throughout history, from the Rai stones of Yap Island, to seashells in the Americas, glass beads in Africa, and cattle and salt in antiquity. Each of these media of exchange served the function of money for a period during which it had one of the best stock-to-flow ratios available to its population, but stopped when it lost that property. Understanding how and why is essential to understanding the future evolution of money and any likely role bitcoin will play. Chapter 3 moves to the analysis of monetary metals and how gold came to be the prime monetary metal in the world during the era of the gold standard at the end of the nineteenth century. Chapter 4 analyzes the move to government money and its track record. After the economic and social implications of different kinds of money are discussed in Chapters 5, 6, and 7, Chapter 8 introduces the invention of bitcoin and its monetary properties.

Chapter 2

Primitive Moneys

O f all the historical forms of money I have come across, the one that most resembles the operation of bitcoin is the ancient system based on Rai stones on Yap Island, today a part of the Federated States of Micronesia. Understanding how the large circular stones carved from limestone functioned as money will help us explain bitcoin's operation in Chapter 8. Understanding the remarkable tale of how the Rai stones lost their monetary role is an object lesson in how money loses its monetary status once it loses its hardness.

The Rai stones that constituted money were of various sizes, rising to large circular disks with a hole in the middle that weighed up to four metric tons. They were not native to Yap, which did not contain any limestone, and all of Yap's stones were brought in from neighboring Palau or Guam. The beauty and rarity of these stones made them desirable and venerable in Yap, but procuring them was very difficult as it involved a laborious process of quarrying and then shipping them with rafts and canoes. Some of these rocks required hundreds of people to transport them, and once they arrived on Yap, they were placed in a prominent

11

location where everyone could see them. The owner of the stone could use it as a payment method without it having to move: all that would happen is that the owner would announce to all townsfolk that the stone's ownership has now moved to the recipient. The whole town would recognize the ownership of the stone and the recipient could then use it to make a payment whenever he so pleased. There was effectively no way of stealing the stone because its ownership was known by everybody.

For centuries, and possibly even millennia, this monetary system worked well for the Yapese. While the stones never moved, they had salability across space, as one could use them for payment anywhere on the island. The different sizes of the different stones provided some degree of salability across scales, as did the possibility of paying with fractions of a single stone. The stones' salability across time was assured for centuries by the difficulty and high cost of acquiring new stones, because they didn't exist in Yap and quarrying and shipping them from Palau was not easy. The very high cost of procuring new stones to Yap meant that the existing supply of stones was always far larger than whatever new supply could be produced at a given period of time, making it prudent to accept them as a form of payment. In other words, Rai stones had a very high stock-to-flow ratio, and no matter how desirable they were, it was not easy for anyone to inflate the supply of stones by bringing in new rocks. Or, at least, that was the case until 1871, when an Irish-American captain by the name of David O'Keefe was shipwrecked on the shores of Yap and revived by the locals.[1]

O'Keefe saw a profit opportunity in taking coconuts from the island and selling them to producers of coconut oil, but he had no means to entice the locals to work for him, because they were very content with their lives as they were, in their tropical paradise, and had no use for whatever foreign forms of money he could offer them. But O'Keefe wouldn't take no for an answer; he sailed to Hong Kong, procured a large boat and explosives, took them to Palau, where he used the explosives and modern tools to quarry several large Rai stones, and set sail to Yap to present the stones to the locals as payment for coconuts. Contrary

---

[1] The story of O'Keefe inspired the writing of a novel named *His Majesty O'Keefe* by Laurence Klingman and Gerald Green in 1952, which was made into a Hollywood blockbuster by the same name starring Burt Lancaster in 1954.

to what O'Keefe expected, the villagers were not keen on receiving his stones, and the village chief banned his townsfolk from working for the stones, decreeing that O'Keefe's stones were not of value, because they were gathered too easily. Only the stones quarried traditionally, with the sweat and blood of the Yapese, were to be accepted in Yap. Others on the island disagreed, and they did supply O'Keefe with the coconuts he sought. This resulted in conflict on the island, and in time the demise of Rai stones as money. Today, the stones serve a more ceremonial and cultural role on the island and modern government money is the most commonly used monetary medium.

While O'Keefe's story is highly symbolic, he was but the harbinger of the inevitable demise of Rai stones' monetary role with the encroachment of modern industrial civilization on Yap and its inhabitants. As modern tools and industrial capabilities reached the region, it was inevitable that the production of the stones would become far less costly than before. There would be many O'Keefes, local and foreign, able to supply Yap with an ever-larger flow of new stones. With modern technology, the stock-to-flow ratio for Rai stones decreased drastically: it was possible to produce far more of these stones every year, significantly devaluing the island's existing stock. It became increasingly unwise for anyone to use these stones as a store of value, and thus they lost their salability across time, and with it, their function as a medium of exchange.

The details may differ, but the underlying dynamic of a drop in stock-to-flow ratio has been the same for every form of money that has lost its monetary role, up to the collapse of the Venezuelan bolivar taking place as these lines are being written.

A similar story happened with the aggry beads used as money for centuries in western Africa. The history of these beads in western Africa is not entirely clear, with suggestions that they were made from meteorite stones, or passed on from Egyptian and Phoenician traders. What is known is that they were precious in an area where glassmaking technology was expensive and not very common, giving them a high stock-to-flow ratio, making them salable across time. Being small and valuable, these beads were salable across scale, because they could be combined into chains, necklaces, or bracelets; though this was far from ideal, because there were many different kinds of beads rather than one standard unit. They were also salable across space as they were easy to move around. In contrast, glass beads were not expensive and had no monetary role in Europe, because the proliferation of glassmaking technology meant that if they were to be utilized as a monetary unit, their producers could flood the market with them—in other words, they had a low stock-to-flow ratio.

When European explorers and traders visited West Africa in the sixteenth century, they noticed the high value given to these beads and so started importing them in mass quantities from Europe. What followed was similar to the story of O'Keefe, but given the tiny size of the beads and the much larger size of the population, it was a slower, more covert process with bigger and more tragic consequences. Slowly but surely, Europeans were able to purchase a lot of the precious resources of Africa for the beads they acquired back home for very little.[2] European incursion into Africa slowly turned beads from hard money to easy money, destroying their salability and causing the erosion of the purchasing power of these beads over time in the hands of the Africans who owned them, impoverishing them by transferring their wealth to the Europeans, who could acquire the beads easily. The aggry beads later came to be known as slave beads for the role they played in fueling the slave trade of Africans to Europeans and North Americans. A one-time collapse in the value of a monetary medium is tragic, but at least it is over quickly and its holders can begin trading, saving, and calculating with a new one. But a slow drain of its monetary value over time will slowly transfer the wealth of its holders to those who can produce the medium at a low cost. This is a lesson worth remembering when we turn to the discussion of the soundness of government money in the later parts of the book.

Seashells are another monetary medium that was widely used in many places around the world, from North America to Africa and Asia. Historical accounts show that the most salable seashells were usually the ones that were scarcer and harder to find, because these would hold value more than the ones that can be found easily.[3] Native Americans and early European settlers used wampum shells extensively, for the

---

[2]To maximize their profits, Europeans used to fill the hulls of their boats with large quantities of these beads, which also served to stabilize the boat on its trip.
[3]Szabo, Nick. "Shelling Out: The Origins of Money." *Satoshi Nakamoto Institute*, 2002, nakamotoinstitute.org/shelling-out/.

same reasons as aggry beads: they were hard to find, giving them a high stock-to-flow ratio, possibly the highest among durable goods available at the time. Seashells also shared with aggry beads the disadvantage of not being uniform units, which meant prices and ratios could not be easily measured and expressed in them uniformly, which creates large obstacles to the growth of the economy and the degree of specialization. European settlers adopted seashells as legal tender from 1636, but as more and more British gold and silver coins started flowing to North America, these were preferred as a medium of exchange due to their uniformity, allowing for better and more uniform price denomination and giving them higher salability. Further, as more advanced boats and technologies were employed to harvest seashells from the sea, their supply was very highly inflated, leading to a drop in their value and a loss of salability across time. By 1661, seashells stopped being legal tender and eventually lost all monetary role.[4]

This was not just the fate of seashell money in North America; whenever societies employing seashells had access to uniform metal coins, they adopted them and benefited from the switch. Also, the arrival of industrial civilization, with fossil-fuel-powered boats, made scouring the sea for seashells easier, increasing the flow of their production and dropping the stock-to-flow ratio quickly.

Other ancient forms of money include cattle, cherished for their nutritional value, as they were one of the most prized possessions anyone could own and were also salable across space due to their mobility. Cattle continue to play a monetary role today, with many societies using them for payments, especially for dowries. Being bulky and not easily divisible, however, meant cattle were not very useful to solve the problems of divisibility across scales, and so another form of money coexisted along with cattle, and that was salt. Salt was easy to keep for long durations and could be easily divided and grouped into whatever weight was necessary. These historical facts are still apparent in the English language, as the word *pecuniary* is derived from *pecus*, the Latin word for cattle, while the word *salary* is derived from *sal*, the Latin word for salt.[5]

---

[4] Ibid: Szabo.
[5] Fekete, Antal. *Whither Gold?* Winner of the 1996 International Currency Prize, Sponsored by Bank Lips, 1997, www.professorfekete.com/articles/AEFWhitherGold.pdf.

As technology advanced, particularly with metallurgy, humans developed superior forms of money to these artifacts, which began to quickly replace them. These metals proved a better medium of exchange than seashells, stones, beads, cattle, and salt because they could be made into uniform, highly valuable small units that could be moved around far more easily. Another nail in the coffin of artifact money came with the mass utilization of hydrocarbon fuel energy, which increased our productive capacity significantly, allowing for a quick increase in the new supply (flow) of these artifacts, meaning that the forms of money that relied on difficulty of production to protect their high stock-to-flow ratio lost it. With modern hydrocarbon fuels, Rai stones could be quarried easily, aggry beads could be made for very little cost, and seashells could be collected en masse by large boats. As soon as these monies lost their hardness, their holders suffered significant wealth expropriation and the entire fabric of their society fell apart as a result. The Yap Island chiefs who refused O'Keefe's cheap Rai stones understood what most modern economists fail to grasp: a money that is easy to produce is no money at all, and easy money does not make a society richer; on the contrary, it makes it poorer by placing all its hard-earned wealth for sale in exchange for something easy to produce.

Chapter 3

Monetary Metals

As human technical capacity for the production of goods became more sophisticated, and our utilization of metals and commodities grew, many metals began to be produced at large enough quantities and were in large enough demand to make them highly salable and suited for being used as monetary media. These metals' density and relatively high value made moving them around easy, easier than salt or cattle, making them highly salable across space. The production of metals was initially not easy, making it hard to increase their supply quickly and giving them good salability across time.

Due to their durability and physical properties, as well as their relative abundance in earth, some metals were more valuable than others. Iron and copper, because of their relatively high abundance and their susceptibility to corrosion, could be produced in increasing quantities. Existing stockpiles, constantly depleting from corrosion and consumption, could be dwarfed by new production, destroying the value in them. These metals developed a relatively low market value and would be used for smaller transactions. Rarer metals such as silver and gold, on the other hand, were more durable and less likely to corrode or ruin, making them more salable across time and useful as a store of value into the future. Gold's virtual indestructibility, in particular, allowed humans to store value across generations, thus allowing us to develop a longer time horizon orientation.

Initially, metals were bought and sold in terms of their weight,[1] but over time, as metallurgy advanced, it became possible to mint them into uniform coins and brand them with their weight, making them far more salable by saving people from having to weigh and assess the metals every time. The three metals most widely used for this role were gold, silver, and copper, and their use as coins was the prime form of money for around 2,500 years, from the time of the Lydian king Croesus, who was the first recorded to have minted gold coins, to the early twentieth century. Gold coins were the goods most salable across time, because they could hold their value over time and resist decay and ruin. They were also the goods most salable across space, because they carried a lot of value in small weights, allowing for easy transportation. Silver coins, on the other hand, had the advantage of being the most salable good across scales, because their lower value per weight unit compared to gold allowed for them to conveniently serve as a medium of exchange for small transactions, while bronze coins would be useful for the least valuable transactions. By standardizing values into easily identifiable units, coins allowed for the creation of large markets, increasing the scope of specialization and trade worldwide. While the best monetary system technologically possible at the time, it still had two major drawbacks: the first was that the existence of two or three metals as the monetary standard created economic problems from the fluctuation of their values over time due to the ebbs of supply and demand, and created problems for owners of these coins, particularly silver, which experienced declines in value due to increases in production and drops in demand. The second, more serious flaw was that governments and counterfeiters could, and frequently did, reduce the precious metal content in these coins, causing their value to decline by transferring a fraction of their purchasing power to the counterfeiters or the government. The reduction in the metal content of the coins compromised the purity and soundness of the money.

---

[1]Szabo, Nick. "Shelling Out: The Origins of Money." *Satoshi Nakamoto Institute*, 2002, nakamotoinstitute.org/shelling-out/.

By the nineteenth century, however, with the development of modern banking and the improvement in methods of communication, individuals could transact with paper money and checks backed by gold in the treasuries of their banks and central banks. This made gold-backed transactions possible at any scale, thus obviating the need for silver's monetary role, and gathering all essential monetary salability properties in the gold standard. The gold standard allowed for unprecedented global capital accumulation and trade by uniting the majority of the planet's economy on one sound market-based choice of money. Its tragic flaw, however, was that by centralizing the gold in the vaults of banks, and later central banks, it made it possible for banks and governments to increase the supply of money beyond the quantity of gold they held, devaluing the money and transferring part of its value from the money's legitimate holders to the governments and banks.

Why Gold?

To understand how commodity money emerges, we return in more detail to the easy money trap we first introduced in Chapter 1, and begin by differentiating between a good's *market demand* (demand for consuming or holding the good for its own sake) and its *monetary demand* (demand for a good as a medium of exchange and store of value). Any time a person chooses a good as a store of value, she is effectively increasing the demand for it beyond the regular market demand, which will cause its price to rise. For example, market demand for copper in its various industrial uses is around 20 million tons per year, at a price of around $5,000 per ton, and a total market valued around $100 billion. Imagine a billionaire deciding he would like to store $10 billion of his wealth in copper. As his bankers run around trying to buy 10% of annual global copper production, they would inevitably cause the price of copper to increase. Initially, this sounds like a vindication of the billionaire's monetary strategy: the asset he decided to buy has already appreciated before he has even completed his purchase. Surely, he reasons, this appreciation will cause more people to buy more copper as a store of value, bringing the price up even more.

But even if more people join him in monetizing copper, our hypothetical copper-obsessed billionaire is in trouble. The rising price makes copper a lucrative business for workers and capital across the world. The quantity of copper under the earth is beyond our ability to even measure, let alone extract through mining, so practically speaking, the only binding restraint on how much copper can be produced is how much labor and capital is dedicated to the job. More copper can always be made with a higher price, and the price and quantity will continue to rise until they satisfy the monetary investors' demand; let's assume that happens at 10 million extra tons and $10,000 per ton. At some point, monetary demand must subside, and some holders of copper will want to offload some of their stockpiles to purchase other goods, because, after all, that was the point of buying copper.

After the monetary demand subsides, all else being equal, the copper market would go back to its original supply-and-demand conditions, with 20 million annual tons selling for $5,000 each. But as the holders begin to sell their accumulated stocks of copper, the price will drop significantly below that. The billionaire will have lost money in this process; as he was driving the price up, he bought most of his stock for more than $5,000 a ton, but now his entire stock is valued below $5,000 a ton. The others who joined him later bought at even higher prices and will have lost even more money than the billionaire himself.

This model is applicable for all consumable commodities such as copper, zinc, nickel, brass, or oil, which are primarily consumed and destroyed, not stockpiled. Global stockpiles of these commodities at any moment in time are around the same order of magnitude as new annual production. New supply is constantly being generated to be consumed. Should savers decide to store their wealth in one of these commodities, their wealth will only buy a fraction of global supply before bidding the price up enough to absorb all their investment, because they are competing with the consumers of this commodity who use it productively in industry. As the revenue to the producers of the good increases, they can then invest in increasing their production, bringing the price crashing down again, robbing the savers of their wealth. The net effect of this entire episode is the transfer of the wealth of the misguided savers to the producers of the commodity they purchased.

This is the anatomy of a market bubble: increased demand causes a sharp rise in prices, which drives further demand, raising prices further, incentivizing increased production and increased supply, which inevitably brings prices down, punishing everyone who bought at a price higher than the usual market price. Investors in the bubble are fleeced while producers of the asset benefit. For copper and almost every other commodity in the world, this dynamic has held true for most of recorded history, consistently punishing those who choose these commodities as money by devaluing their wealth and impoverishing them in the long run, and returning the commodity to its natural role as a market good, and not a medium of exchange.

For anything to function as a good store of value, it has to beat this trap: it has to appreciate when people demand it as a store of value, but its producers have to be constrained from inflating the supply significantly enough to bring the price down. Such an asset will reward those who choose it as their store of value, increasing their wealth in the long run as it becomes the prime store of value, because those who chose other commodities will either reverse course by copying the choice of their more successful peers, or will simply lose their wealth.

The clear winner in this race throughout human history has been gold, which maintains its monetary role due to two unique physical characteristics that differentiate it from other commodities: first, gold is so chemically stable that it is virtually impossible to destroy, and second, gold is impossible to synthesize from other materials (alchemists' claims notwithstanding) and can only be extracted from its unrefined ore, which is extremely rare in our planet.

The chemical stability of gold implies that virtually all of the gold ever mined by humans is still more or less owned by people around the world. Humanity has been accumulating an ever-growing hoard of gold in jewelry, coins, and bars, which is never consumed and never rusts or disintegrates. The impossibility of synthesizing gold from other chemicals means that the only way to increase the supply of gold is by mining gold from the earth, an expensive, toxic, and uncertain process in which humans have been engaged for thousands of years with ever-diminishing returns. This all means that the existing stockpile of gold held by people around the world is the product of thousands of years of gold production, and is orders of magnitude larger than new annual production. Over the

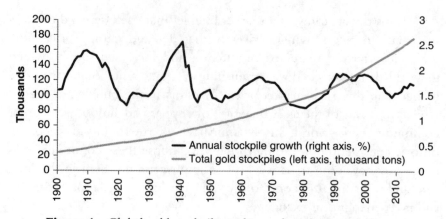

Figure 1   Global gold stockpiles and annual stockpile growth rate.

past seven decades with relatively reliable statistics, this growth rate has always been around 1.5%, never exceeding 2%. (See Figure 1.[2])

To understand the difference between gold and any consumable commodity, imagine the effect of a large increase in demand for it as a store of value that causes the price to spike and annual production to double. For any consumable commodity, this doubling of output will dwarf any existing stockpiles, bringing the price crashing down and hurting the holders. For gold, a price spike that causes a doubling of annual production will be insignificant, increasing stockpiles by 3% rather than 1.5%. If the new increased pace of production is maintained, the stockpiles grow faster, making new increases less significant. It remains practically impossible for goldminers to mine quantities of gold large enough to depress the price significantly.

Only silver comes close to gold in this regard, with an annual supply growth rate historically around 5–10%, rising to around 20% in the modern day. This is higher than that of gold for two reasons: First, silver does corrode and can be consumed in industrial processes, which means the existing stockpiles are not as large relative to annual production as gold's stockpiles are relative to its annual production. Second, silver is less rare than gold in the crust of the earth and easier to refine. Because of having the second highest stock-to-flow ratio, and its lower value per

---

[2] *Source*: US Geological Survey. Global Gold Stockpiles and Annual Stockpile Growth Rate.

unit of weight than gold, silver served for millennia as the main money used for smaller transactions, complementing gold, whose high value meant dividing it into very small units was impractical. The adoption of the international gold standard allowed for payments in paper backed by gold at any scale, as will be discussed in more detail later in this chapter, which obviated silver's monetary role. With silver no longer required for smaller transactions, it soon lost its monetary role and became an industrial metal, losing value compared to gold. Silver may maintain its sporting connotation for second place, but as nineteenth-century technology made payments possible without having to move the monetary unit itself, second place in monetary competition was equivalent to losing out.

This explains why the silver bubble has popped before and will pop again if it ever inflates: as soon as significant monetary investment flows into silver, it is not as difficult for producers to increase the supply significantly and bring the price crashing down, taking the savers' wealth in the process. The best-known example of the easy-money trap comes from silver itself, of all commodities. Back in the late 1970s, the very affluent Hunt brothers decided to bring about the remonetization of silver and started buying enormous quantities of silver, driving the price up. Their rationale was that as the price rose, more people would want to buy, which would keep the price rising, which in turn would lead to people wanting to be paid in silver. Yet, no matter how much the Hunt brothers bought, their wealth was no match for the ability of miners and holders of silver to keep selling silver onto the market. The price of silver eventually crashed and the Hunt brothers lost over $1 billion, probably the highest price ever paid for learning the importance of the stock-to-flow ratio, and why not all that glitters is gold.[3] (See Figure 2.[4])

It is this consistently low rate of supply of gold that is the fundamental reason it has maintained its monetary role throughout human history, a role it continues to hold today as central banks continue to hold significant supplies of gold to protect their paper currencies. Official central bank reserves are at around 33,000 tons, or a sixth of total

[3]Rudolph, Barbara. "Big Bill for a Bullion Binge." *TIME*, 29 Aug. 1988.
[4]*Source*: U.S. Geological Survey data for gold. Silver Institute data for silver, BP.com statistical review for oil. Author's estimates from various media sources for copper.

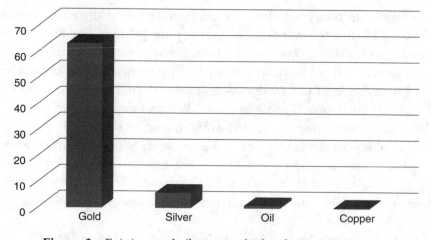

Figure 2   Existing stockpiles as a multiple of annual production.

above-ground gold. The high stock–to–flow ratio of gold makes it the commodity with the lowest *price elasticity of supply*, which is defined as the percentage increase in quantity supplied over the percentage increase in price. Given that the existing supply of gold held by people everywhere is the product of thousands of years of production, an X% increase in price may cause an increase in new mining production, but that increase will be trivial compared to existing stockpiles. For instance, the year 2006 witnessed a 36% rise in the spot price of gold. For any other commodity, this would be expected to increase mining output significantly to flood markets and bring the price down. Instead, annual production in 2006 was 2,370 tons, 100 tons less than in 2005, and it would drop a further 10 tons in 2007. Whereas the new supply was 1.67% of existing stockpiles in 2005, it was 1.58% of existing stockpiles in 2006, and 1.54% of existing stockpiles in 2007. Even a 35% rise in price can lead to no appreciable increase in the supply of new gold onto the market. According to the U.S. Geological Survey, the single biggest annual increase in production was around 15% in the year 1923, which translated to an increase in stockpiles around only 1.5%. Even if production were to double, the likely increase in stockpiles would only be around 3–4%. The highest annual increase in global stockpiles happened in 1940, when stockpiles rose by around 2.6%. Not once has the annual stockpile growth exceeded that number, and not once since 1942 has it exceeded 2%.

As the production of metals began to proliferate, ancient civilizations in China, India, and Egypt began to use copper, and later silver, as money, as these two were relatively hard to manufacture at the time and allowed for good salability across time and space. Gold was highly prized in these civilizations, but its rarity meant its salability for transactions was limited. It was in Lydia, in modern day Turkey, where gold was first minted into regular coins for trade, under King Croesus. This invigorated global trade as gold's global appeal saw the coin spread far and wide. Since then, the turns of human history have been closely intertwined with the soundness of money. Human civilization flourished in times and places where sound money was widely adopted, while unsound money all too frequently coincided with civilizational decline and societal collapse.

Roman Golden Age and Decline

The denarius was the silver coin that traded at the time of the Roman Republic, containing 3.9 grams of silver, while gold became the most valuable money in the civilized areas of the world at the time and gold coins were becoming more widespread. Julius Caesar, the last dictator of the Roman Republic, created the aureus coin, which contained around 8 grams of gold and was widely accepted across Europe and the Mediterranean, increasing the scope of trade and specialization in the Old World. Economic stability reigned for seventy-five years, even through the political upheaval of his assassination, which saw the Republic transformed into an Empire under his chosen successor, Augustus. This continued until the reign of the infamous emperor Nero, who was the first to engage in the Roman habit of "coin clipping," wherein the Emperor would collect the coins of the population and mint them into newer coins with less gold or silver content.

For as long as Rome could conquer new lands with significant wealth, its soldiers and emperors could enjoy spending their loot, and emperors even decided to buy themselves popularity by mandating artificially low prices of grains and other staples, sometimes even granting them for free. Instead of working for a living in the countryside, many peasants would leave their farms to move to Rome, where they could live better lives for free. With time, the Old World no longer had prosperous lands to be conquered, the ever-increasing lavish lifestyle and growing military required some new source of financing, and the number of unproductive citizens living off the emperor's largesse and price controls increased. Nero, who ruled from 54–68 AD, had found the formula to solve this, which was highly similar to Keynes's solution to Britain's and the U.S.'s problems after World War I: devaluing the currency would at once reduce the real wages of workers, reduce the burden of the government in subsidizing staples, and provide increased money for financing other government expenditure.

The aureus coin was reduced from 8 to 7.2 grams, while the denarius's silver content was reduced from 3.9 to 3.41g. This provided some temporary relief, but had set in motion the highly destructive self-reinforcing cycle of popular anger, price controls, coin debasement, and price rises, following one another with the predictable regularity of the four seasons.[5]

Under the reign of Caracalla (AD 211–217), the gold content was further reduced to 6.5 grams, and under Diocletian (AD 284–305) it was further reduced to 5.5g, before he introduced a replacement coin called the solidus, with only 4.5 grams of gold. On Diocletian's watch, the denarius only had traces of silver to cover its bronze core, and the silver would disappear quite quickly with wear and tear, ending the denarius as a silver coin. As inflationism intensified in the third and fourth centuries, with it came the misguided attempts of the emperors to hide their inflation by placing price controls on basic goods. As market forces sought to adjust prices upward in response to the debasement of the currency, price ceilings prevented these price adjustments, making it unprofitable for producers to engage in production. Economic production would come to a standstill until a new edict allowed for the liberalization of prices upward.

With this fall in the value of its money, the long process of terminal decline of the empire resulted in a cycle that might appear familiar to modern readers: coin clipping reduced the aureus's real value, increasing

---

[5]See Robert Schuettinger and Eamonn Butler's highly entertaining *Forty Centuries of Price and Wage Controls: How Not to Fight Inflation.*

the money supply, allowing the emperor to continue imprudent overspending, but eventually resulting in inflation and economic crises, which the misguided emperors would attempt to ameliorate via further coin clipping. Ferdinand Lips summarizes this process with a lesson to modern readers:

> It should be of interest to modern Keynesian economists, as well as to the present generation of investors, that although the emperors of Rome frantically tried to "manage" their economies, they only succeeded in making matters worse. Price and wage controls and legal tender laws were passed, but it was like trying to hold back the tides. Rioting, corruption, lawlessness and a mindless mania for speculation and gambling engulfed the empire like a plague. With money so unreliable and debased, speculation in commodities became far more attractive than producing them.[6]

The long-term consequences for the Roman Empire were devastating. Although Rome up until the second century AD may not be characterized as a full-fledged free market capitalist economy, because it still had plenty of government restraints on economic activity, with the aureus it nonetheless established what was then the largest market in human history with the largest and most productive division of labor the world had ever known.[7] Citizens of Rome and the major cities obtained their basic necessities by trade with the far-flung corners of the empire, and this helps explain the growth in prosperity, and the devastating collapse the empire suffered when this division of labor fell apart. As taxes increased and inflation made price controls unworkable, the urbanites of the cities started fleeing to empty plots of land where they could at least have a chance of living in self-sufficiency, where their lack of income spared them having to pay taxes. The intricate civilizational edifice of the Roman Empire and the large division of labor across Europe and the Mediterranean began to crumble, and its descendants became self-sufficient peasants scattered in isolation and would soon turn into serfs living under feudal lords.

---

[6]Lips, Ferdinand. *Gold Wars: The Battle Against Sound Money as Seen from a Swiss Perspective*. New York, Foundation for the Advancement of Monetary Education, 2001.
[7]Mises, Ludwig von. *Human Action: The Scholar's Edition*. Auburn, AL, Ludwig von Mises Institute, 1998.

Byzantium and the Bezant

The emperor Diocletian has forever had his name associated with fiscal and monetary chicanery, and the Empire reached a nadir under his rule. A year after he abdicated, however, Constantine the Great took over the reins of the empire and reversed its fortunes by adopting economically responsible polices and reforms. Constantine, who was the first Christian emperor, committed to maintaining the solidus at 4.5 grams of gold without clipping or debasement and started minting it in large quantities in 312 AD. He moved east and established Constantinople at the meeting point of Asia and Europe, birthing the Eastern Roman Empire, which took the solidus as its coin. While Rome continued its economic, social, and cultural deterioration, finally collapsing in 476 AD, Byzantium survived for 1,123 years while the solidus became the longest-serving sound currency in human history.

The legacy of Constantine in maintaining the integrity of the solidus made it the world's most recognizable and widely accepted currency, and it came to be known as the *bezant*. While Rome burned under bankrupt emperors who could no longer afford to pay their soldiers as their currencies collapsed, Constantinople thrived and prospered for many more centuries with fiscal and monetary responsibility. While the Vandals and the Visigoths ran rampage in Rome, Constantinople remained prosperous and free from invasion for centuries. As with Rome, the fall of Constantinople happened only after its rulers had started devaluing the currency, a process that historians believe began in the reign of Constantine IX Monomachos (1042–1055).[8] Along with monetary decline came the fiscal, military, cultural, and spiritual decline of the Empire, as it trudged on with increasing crises until it was overtaken by the Ottomans in 1453.

Even after it was debased and its empire fell, the bezant lived on by inspiring another form of sound money that continues to circulate widely to this day in spite of not being the official currency of any nation anymore, and that is the Islamic dinar. As Islam rose during the golden age of Byzantium, the bezant and coins similar to it in weight and size

---

[8]Luscombe, David, and Jonathan Riley-Smith. *The New Cambridge Medieval History: Volume 4, C.1024–1198.* Cambridge University Press, 2008, p. 255.

were circulating in the regions to which Islam had spread. The Umayyad Caliph Abdul-Malik ibn Marwan defined the weight and value of the Islamic dinar and imprinted it with the Islamic *shahada* creed in 697 AD. The Umayyad dynasty fell, and after it several other Islamic states, and yet the dinar continues to be held and to circulate widely in Islamic regions in the original weight and size specifications of the bezant, and is used in dowries, gifts, and various religious and traditional customs to this day. Unlike the Romans and the Byzantines, Arab and Muslim civilizations' collapse was not linked to the collapse of their money as they maintained the integrity of their currencies for centuries. The solidus, first minted by Diocletian in AD 301, has changed its name to the bezant and the Islamic dinar, but it continues to circulate today. Seventeen centuries of people the world over have used this coin for transactions, emphasizing the salability of gold across time.

The Renaissance

After the economic and military collapse of the Roman Empire, feudalism emerged as the prime mode of organizing society. The destruction of sound money was pivotal in turning the former citizens of the Roman Empire into serfs under the mercy of their local feudal lords. Gold was concentrated in the hands of the feudal lords, and the main forms of money available for the peasantry of Europe at the time were copper and bronze coins, whose supply was easy to inflate as industrial production of these metals continued to become easier with the advance of metallurgy, making them terrible stores of value, as well as silver coins that were usually debased, cheated, and nonstandardized across the continent, giving them poor salability across space and limiting the scope of trade across the continent.

Taxation and inflation had destroyed the wealth and savings of the people of Europe. New generations of Europeans came to the world with no accumulated wealth passed on from their elders, and the absence of a widely accepted sound monetary standard severely restricted the scope for trade, closing societies off from one another and enhancing parochialism as once-prosperous and civilized trading societies fell into the Dark Ages of serfdom, diseases, closed-mindedness, and religious persecution.

While it is widely recognized that the rise of the city-states dragged Europe out of the Dark Ages and into the Renaissance, the role of sound money in this rise is less recognized. It was in the city-states that humans could live with the freedom to work, produce, trade, and flourish, and that was to a large extent the result of these city-states adopting a sound monetary standard. It all began in Florence in 1252, when the city minted the florin, the first major European sound coinage since Julius Caesar's aureus. Florence's rise made it the commercial center of Europe, with its florin becoming the prime European medium of exchange, allowing its banks to flourish across the entire continent. Venice was the first to follow Florence's example with its minting of the ducat, of the same specifications as the florin, in 1270, and by the end of the fourteenth century more than 150 European cities and states had minted coins of the same specifications as the florin, allowing their citizens the dignity and freedom to accumulate wealth and trade with a sound money that was highly salable across time and space, and divided into small coins, allowing for easy divisibility. With the economic liberation of the European peasantry came the political, scientific, intellectual, and cultural flourishing of the Italian city-states, which later spread across the European continent. Whether in Rome, Constantinople, Florence, or Venice, history shows that a sound monetary standard is a necessary prerequisite for human flourishing, without which society stands on the precipice of barbarism and destruction.

Although the period following the introduction of the florin witnessed an improvement in the soundness of money, with more and more Europeans able to adopt gold and silver for saving and trade, and the extent of markets expanding across Europe and the world, the situation was far from perfect. There were still many periods during which various sovereigns would debase their people's currency to finance war or lavish expenditure. Given that they were used physically, silver and gold complemented each other: gold's high stock-to-flow ratio meant it was ideal as a long-term store of value and a means of large payments, but silver's lower value per unit of weight made it easily divisible into quantities suitable for smaller transactions and for being held for shorter durations. While this arrangement had benefits, it had one major drawback: the fluctuating rate of exchange between gold and silver created trade and calculation problems. Attempts to fix the price of the two currencies relative to one another were continuously self-defeating, but gold's monetary edge was to win out.

As sovereigns set an exchange rate between the two commodities, they would change holders' incentives to hold or spend them. This inconvenient bimetallism continued for centuries across Europe and the world, but as with the move from salt, cattle, and seashells to metals, the inexorable advance of technology was to provide a solution to it.

Two particular technological advancements would move Europe and the world away from physical coins and in turn help bring about the demise of silver's monetary role: the telegraph, first deployed commercially in 1837, and the growing network of trains, allowing transportation across Europe. With these two innovations, it became increasingly feasible for banks to communicate with each other, sending payments efficiently across space when needed and debiting accounts instead of having to send physical payments. This led to the increased use of bills, checks, and paper receipts as monetary media instead of physical gold and silver coins.

More nations began to switch to a monetary standard of paper fully backed by, and instantly redeemable into, precious metals held in vaults. Some nations would choose gold, and others would choose silver, in a fateful decision that was to have enormous consequences. Britain was the first to adopt a modern gold standard in 1717, under the direction of physicist Isaac Newton, who was the warden of the Royal Mint, and the gold standard would play a great role in Britain advancing its trade across its empire worldwide. Britain would remain under a gold standard until 1914, although it would suspend it during the Napoleonic wars from 1797 to 1821. The economic supremacy of Britain was intricately linked to its being on a superior monetary standard, and other European countries began to follow it. The end of the Napoleonic wars heralded the beginning of the golden age of Europe, as, one by one, the major European nations began adopting the gold standard. The more nations officially adopted the gold standard, the more marketable gold became and the larger the incentive became for other nations to join.

Further, instead of individuals having to carry gold and silver coins for large and small transactions, respectively, they could now store their wealth in gold in banks while using paper receipts, bills, and checks to make payments of any size. The holders of paper receipts could just use them to make payment themselves; bills were discounted by banks and used for clearance and checks could be cashed from the banks that issued them. This solved the problem of gold's salability across scales, making gold the best monetary medium—for as long as the banks hoarding people's gold would not increase the supply of papers they issued as receipts.

With these media being backed by physical gold in the vaults and allowing payment in whichever quantity or size, there was no longer a real need for silver's role in small payments. The death knell for silver's monetary role was the end of the Franco–Prussian war, when Germany extracted an indemnity of £200 million in gold from France and used it to switch to a gold standard. With Germany now joining Britain, France, Holland, Switzerland, Belgium, and others on a gold standard, the monetary pendulum had swung decisively in favor of gold, leading to individuals and nations worldwide who used silver to witness a progressive loss of their purchasing power and a stronger incentive to shift to gold. India finally switched from silver to gold in 1898, while China and Hong Kong were the last economies in the world to abandon the silver standard in 1935.

For as long as gold and silver were used for payment directly, they both had a monetary role to play and their price relative to one another remained largely constant across time, at a ratio between twelve and fifteen ounces of silver per ounce of gold, in the same range as their relative scarcity in the crust of the earth and the relative difficulty and cost of extracting them. But as paper and financial instruments backed by these metals became more and more popular, there was no more justification for silver's monetary role, and individuals and nations shifted to holding gold, leading to a significant collapse in the price of silver, from which it would not recover. The average ratio between the two over the twentieth century was 47:1, and in 2017, it stood at 75:1. While gold still has a monetary role to play, as evidenced by central banks' hoarding of it, silver has arguably lost its monetary role. (See Figure 3.[9])

The demonetization of silver had a significantly negative effect on the nations that were using it as a monetary standard at the time. India witnessed a continuous devaluation of its rupee compared to gold-based

[9] *Source*: Officer, Lawrence H., and Samuel H. Williamson. *The Price of Gold, 1257–Present*. Measuring-Worth, 2017, *www.measuringworth.com/gold/*.

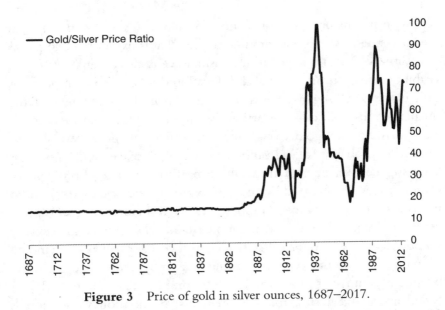

Figure 3 Price of gold in silver ounces, 1687–2017.

European countries, which led the British colonial government to increase taxes to finance its operation, leading to growing unrest and resentment of British colonialism. By the time India shifted the backing of its rupee to the gold-backed pound sterling in 1898, the silver backing its rupee had lost 56% of its value in the twenty-seven years since the end of the Franco-Prussian War. For China, which stayed on the silver standard until 1935, its silver (in various names and forms) lost 78% of its value over the period. It is the author's opinion that the history of China and India, and their failure to catch up to the West during the twentieth century, is inextricably linked to this massive destruction of wealth and capital brought about by the demonetization of the monetary metal these countries utilized. The demonetization of silver in effect left the Chinese and Indians in a situation similar to west Africans holding aggri beads as Europeans arrived: domestic hard money was easy money for foreigners, and was being driven out by foreign hard money, which allowed foreigners to control and own increasing quantities of the capital and resources of China and India during the period. This is a historical lesson of immense significance, and should be kept in mind by anyone who thinks his refusal of bitcoin means he doesn't have to deal with it. History shows it is not possible to insulate yourself from the consequences of others holding money that is harder than yours.

With gold in the hands of increasingly centralized banks, it gained salability across time, scales, and location, but lost its property as cash money, making payments in it subject to the agreement of the financial and political authorities issuing receipts, clearing checks, and hoarding the gold. Tragically, the only way gold was able to solve the problems of salability across scales, space, and time was by being centralized and thus falling prey to the major problem of sound money emphasized by the economists of the twentieth century: individual sovereignty over money and its resistance to government centralized control. We can thus understand why nineteenth-century sound money economists like Menger focused their understanding of money's soundness on its salability as a market good, whereas twentieth-century sound money economists, like Mises, Hayek, Rothbard, and Salerno, focused their analysis of money's soundness on its resistance to control by a sovereign. Because the Achilles heel of twentieth century money was its centralization in the hands of the government, we will see later how the money invented in the twenty-first century, bitcoin, was designed primarily to avoid centralized control.

La Belle Époque

The end of the Franco-Prussian War in 1871, and the consequent shift of all major European powers onto the same monetary standard, namely gold, led to a period of prosperity and flourishing that continues to appear more amazing with time and in retrospect. A case can be made for the nineteenth century—in particular, the second half of it—being the greatest period for human flourishing, innovation, and achievement that the world had ever witnessed, and the monetary role of gold was pivotal to it. With silver and other media of exchange increasingly demonetized, the majority of the planet used the same golden monetary standard, allowing the improvements in telecommunications and transportation to foster global capital accumulation and trade like never before.

Different currencies were simply different weights of physical gold, and the exchange rate between one nation's currency and the other

Table 1   Major European Economies' Periods Under the Gold Standard

Currency	Period Under Gold Standard	Years
French Franc	1814–1914	100 years
Dutch Guilder	1816–1914	98 years
Pound Sterling	1821–1914	93 years
Swiss Franc	1850–1936	86 years
Belgian Franc	1832–1914	82 years
Swedish Krona	1873–1931	58 years
German Mark	1875–1914	39 years
Italian Lira	1883–1914	31 years

was the simple conversion between different weight units, as straightforward as converting inches to centimeters. The British pound was defined as 7.3 grams of gold, while the French franc was 0.29 grams of gold and the Deutschmark 0.36 grams, meaning the exchange rate between them was necessarily fixed at 25.2 French francs and 20.4 Deutschmark per pound. In the same way metric and imperial units are just a way to measure the underlying length, national currencies were just a way to measure economic value as represented in the universal store of value, gold. Some countries' gold coins were fairly salable in other countries, as they were just gold. Each country's money supply was not a metric to be determined by central planning committees stocked with Ph.D. holders, but the natural working of the market system. People held as much money as they pleased and spent as much as they desired on local or foreign production, and the actual money supply was not even easily measurable.

The soundness of money was reflected in free trade across the world, but perhaps more importantly, was increasing savings rates across most advanced societies that were on the gold standard, allowing for capital accumulation to finance industrialization, urbanization, and the technological improvements that have shaped our modern life. (See Table 1.[10])

By 1900, around fifty nations were officially on the gold standard, including all industrialized nations, while the nations that were not on an official gold standard still had gold coins being used as the main medium

[10] *Source*: Lips, Ferdinand. *Gold Wars: The Battle Against Sound Money as Seen from a Swiss Perspective.* New York, Foundation for the Advancement of Monetary Education, 2001.

of exchange. Some of the most important technological, medical, economic, and artistic human achievements were invented during the era of the gold standard, which partly explains why it was known as *la belle époque*, or the beautiful era, across Europe. Britain witnessed the peak years of Pax Britannica, where the British Empire expanded worldwide and was not engaged in large military conflicts. In 1899, when American writer Nellie Bly set out on her record-breaking journey around the world in seventy-two days, she carried British gold coins and Bank of England notes with her.[11] It was possible to circumnavigate the globe and use one form of money everywhere Nellie went.

In the United States this era was called the Gilded Age, where economic growth boomed after the restoration of the gold standard in 1879 in the wake of the American Civil War. It was only interrupted by one episode of monetary insanity, which was effectively the last dying pang of silver as money, discussed in Chapter 6, when the Treasury tried to remonetize silver by mandating it as money. This caused a large increase in the money supply and a bank run by those seeking to sell Treasury notes and silver to gold. The result was the recession of 1893, after which U.S. economic growth resumed.

With the majority of the world on one sound monetary unit, there was never a period that witnessed as much capital accumulation, global trade, restraint on government, and transformation of living standards worldwide. Not only were the economies of the west far freer back then, the societies themselves were far freer. Governments had very few bureaucracies focused on micromanaging the lives of citizens. As Mises described it:

> The gold standard was the world standard of the age of capitalism, increasing welfare, liberty, and democracy, both political and economic. In the eyes of the free traders its main eminence was precisely the fact that it was an international standard as required by international trade and the transactions of the international money and capital markets. It was the medium of exchange by means of which Western industrialism and Western capital had borne Western civilization to the remotest parts of the earth's surface, everywhere destroying the fetters of old-aged prejudices and superstitions, sowing

[11]Bly, Nellie. *Around the World in Seventy-Two Days*. New York, Pictorial Weeklies, 1890.

the seeds of new life and new well-being, freeing minds and souls, and creating riches unheard of before. It accompanied the triumphal unprecedented progress of Western liberalism ready to unite all nations into a community of free nations peacefully cooperating with one another.

It is easy to understand why people viewed the gold standard as the symbol of this greatest and most beneficial of all historical changes.[12]

This world came crashing down in the catastrophic year 1914, which was not only the year of the outbreak of World War I, but the year that the world's major economies went off of the gold standard and replaced it with unsound government money. Only Switzerland and Sweden, who remained neutral during World War I, were to remain on a gold standard into the 1930s. The era of government-controlled money was to commence globally after that, with unmitigated disastrous consequences.

While the gold standard of the nineteenth century was arguably the closest thing that the world had ever seen to an ideal sound money, it nonetheless had its flaws. First, governments and banks were always creating media of exchange beyond the quantity of gold in their reserves. Second, many countries used not just gold in their reserves, but also currencies of other countries. Britain, as the global superpower at that time, had benefited from having its money used as a reserve currency all around the world, resulting in its reserves of gold being a tiny fraction of its outstanding money supply. With growing international trade relying on settlement of large quantities of money across the world, the Bank of England's banknotes became, in the minds of many at the time, "as good as gold." While gold was very hard money, the instruments used for settlements of payments between central banks, although nominally redeemable in gold, ended up in practice being easier to produce than gold.

These two flaws meant that the gold standard was always vulnerable to a run on gold in any country where circumstances might lead a large enough percentage of the population to demand redemption of their paper money in gold. The fatal flaw of the gold standard at the heart of these two problems was that settlement in physical gold is

---

[12]Mises, Ludwig von. *Human Action: The Scholar's Edition*. pp. 472–3.

cumbersome, expensive, and insecure, which meant it had to rely on centralizing physical gold reserves in a few locations—banks and central banks—leaving them vulnerable to being taken over by governments. As the number of payments and settlements conducted in physical gold became an infinitely smaller fraction of all payments, the banks and central banks holding the gold could create money unbacked by physical gold and use it for settlement. The network of settlement became valuable enough that its owners' credit was effectively monetized. As the ability to run a bank started to imply money creation, governments naturally gravitated to taking over the banking sector through central banking. The temptation was always too strong, and the virtually infinite financial wealth this secured could not only silence dissent, but also finance propagandists to promote such ideas. Gold offered no mechanism for restraining the sovereigns, and had to rely on trust in them not abusing the gold standard and the population remaining eternally vigilant against them doing so. This might have been feasible when the population was highly educated and knowledgeable about the dangers of unsound money, but with every passing generation displaying the intellectual complacence that tends to accompany wealth,[13] the siren song of con artists and court-jester economists would prove increasingly irresistible for more of the population, leaving only a minority of knowledgeable economists and historians fighting an uphill battle to convince people that wealth can't be generated by tampering with the money supply, that allowing a sovereign the control of the money can only lead to them increasing their control of everyone's life, and that civilized human living itself rests on the integrity of money providing a solid foundation for trade and capital accumulation.

Gold being centralized made it vulnerable to having its monetary role usurped by its enemies, and gold simply had too many enemies, as Mises himself well understood:

> The nationalists are fighting the gold standard because they want to sever their countries from the world market and to establish national autarky as far as possible. Interventionist governments and pressure groups are fighting the gold standard because they consider it the

---

[13] Glubb, John. *The Fate of Empires and Search for Survival*. Edinburgh, Scotland, William Blackwood and Sons, 1978.

most serious obstacle to their endeavours to manipulate prices and wage rates. But the most fanatical attacks against gold are made by those intent upon credit expansion. With them credit expansion is the panacea for all economic ills.[14]

The gold standard removes the determination of cash–induced changes in purchasing power from the political arena. Its general acceptance requires the acknowledgement of the truth that one cannot make all people richer by printing money. The abhorrence of the gold standard is inspired by the superstition that omnipotent governments can create wealth out of little scraps of paper [. . .] The governments were eager to destroy it, because they were committed to the fallacies that credit expansion is an appropriate means of lowering the rate of interest and of "improving" the balance of trade [. . .] People fight the gold standard because they want to substitute national autarky for free trade, war for peace, totalitarian government omnipotence for liberty.[15]

The twentieth century began with governments bringing their citizens' gold under their control through the invention of the modern central bank on the gold standard. As World War I started, the centralization of these reserves allowed these governments to expand the money supply beyond their gold reserves, reducing the value of their currency. Yet central banks continued to confiscate and accumulate more gold until the 1960s, where the move toward a U.S. dollar global standard began to shape up. Although gold was supposedly demonetized fully in 1971, central banks continued to hold significant gold reserves, and only disposed of them slowly, before returning to buying gold in the last decade. Even as central banks repeatedly declared the end of gold's monetary role, their actions in maintaining their gold reserves ring truer. From a monetary competition perspective, keeping gold reserves is a perfectly rational decision. Keeping reserves in foreign governments' easy money only will cause the value of the country's currency to devalue along with the reserve currencies, while the seigniorage accrues to the issuer of the reserve currency, not the nation's central bank. Further, should central banks sell all their gold holdings (estimated at around 20% of global gold stockpiles), the most likely impact is that

---

[14] Mises, Ludwig von. *Human Action: The Scholar's Edition.* p. 473.
[15] Ibid., p. 474.

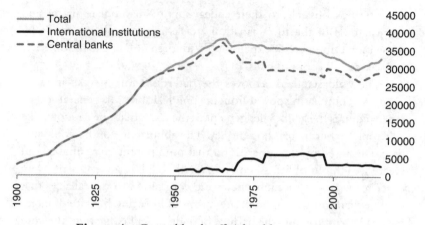

Figure 4   Central bank official gold reserves, tons.

gold, being highly prized for its industrial and aesthetic uses, would be bought up very quickly with little depreciation of its price and the central banks would be left without any gold reserves. The monetary competition between easy government money and hard gold will likely result in one winner in the long-run. Even in a world of government money, governments have not been able to decree gold's monetary role away, as their actions speak louder than their words. (See Figure 4.[16])

---

[16] *Source*: World Gold Council. *Reserve Statistics*, www.gold.org/goldhub/data/monthly-central-bank-statistics.

Chapter 4

Government Money

World War I saw the end of the era of monetary media being the choice decided by the free market, and the beginning of the era of government money. While gold continues to underpin the global monetary system to this day, government edicts, decisions, and monetary policy shape the monetary reality of the world more than any aspect of individual choice.

The common name for government money is *fiat money*, from the Latin word for decree, order, or authorization. Two important facts must be understood about government money from the outset. First, there is a very large difference between government money redeemable in gold, and irredeemable government money, even if both are run by the government. Under a gold standard, money is gold, and government just assumes a responsibility of minting standard units of the metal or printing paper backed by the gold. The government has no control over the supply of gold in the economy, and people are able to redeem their paper in physical gold at any time, and use other shapes and forms of gold, such as bullion bars and foreign coins, in their dealings with one another. With irredeemable government money, on the other hand, the government's debt and/or paper is used as money, and the government is able to increase its supply as it sees fit. Should anybody use other forms of money for exchange, or should they attempt to create more of the government's money, they run the risk of punishment.

The second and often overlooked fact, is that, contrary to what the name might imply, no fiat money has come into circulation solely through government fiat; they were all originally redeemable in gold or silver, or currencies that were redeemable in gold or silver. Only through redeemability into salable forms of money did government paper money gain its salability. Government may issue decrees mandating people use their paper for payments, but no government has imposed this salability on papers without these papers having first been redeemable in gold and silver. Until this day, all government central banks maintain reserves to back up the value of their national currency. The majority of countries maintain some gold in their reserves, and those countries which do not have gold reserves maintain reserves in the form of other countries' fiat currencies, which are in turn backed by gold reserves. No pure fiat currency exists in circulation without any form of backing. Contrary to the most egregiously erroneous and central tenet of the state theory of money, it was not government that decreed gold as money; rather, it is only by holding gold that governments could get their money to be accepted at all.

The oldest recorded example of fiat money was *jiaozi*, a paper currency issued by the Song dynasty in China in the tenth century. Initially, *jiaozi* was a receipt for gold or silver, but then government controlled its issuance and suspended redeemability, increasing the amount of currency printed until it collapsed. The Yuan dynasty also issued fiat currency in 1260, named *chao*, and exceeded the supply far beyond the metal backing, with predictably disastrous consequences. As the value of the money collapsed, the people fell into abject poverty, with many peasants resorting to selling their children into debt slavery.

Government money, then, is similar to primitive forms of money discussed in Chapter 2, and commodities other than gold, in that it is liable to having its supply increased quickly compared to its stock, leading to a quick loss of salability, destruction of purchasing power, and impoverishment of its holders. In this respect it differs from gold, whose supply cannot be increased due to the fundamental chemical properties of the metal discussed above. That the government demands payment in its money for its taxes may guarantee a longer life for that money, but only if the government is able to prevent the quick expansion of the supply can it protect its value from depreciating quickly. When comparing different national currencies, we find that the major and most widely used national currencies have a lower annual increase in their supply than the less salable minor currencies.

Monetary Nationalism and the End of the Free World

The many enemies of sound money whom Mises named in the quote referenced at the end of the last chapter were to have their victory over the gold standard with the beginning of a small war in Central Europe in 1914, which snowballed into the first global war in human history. Certainly, when the war started nobody had envisioned it lasting as long, and producing as many casualties, as it did. British newspapers, for example, heralded it as the August Bank Holiday War, expecting it to be a simple triumphant summer excursion for their troops. There was a sense that this would be a limited conflict. And, after decades of relative peace across Europe, a new generation of Europeans had not grown to appreciate the likely consequences of launching war. Today, historians still fail to offer a convincing strategic or geopolitical explanation for why a conflict between the Austro-Hungarian Empire and Serbian separatists was to trigger a global war that claimed the lives of millions and drastically reshaped most of the world's borders.

In retrospect, the major difference between World War I and the previous limited wars was neither geopolitical nor strategic, but rather, it was monetary. When governments were on a gold standard, they had direct control of large vaults of gold while their people were dealing with paper receipts of this gold. The ease with which a government could issue more paper currency was too tempting in the heat of the conflict, and far easier than demanding taxation from the citizens. Within a few weeks of the war starting, all major belligerents had suspended gold convertibility, effectively going off the gold standard and putting their population on a fiat standard, wherein the money they used was government–issued paper that was not redeemable for gold.

With the simple suspension of gold redeemability, governments' war efforts were no longer limited to the money that they had in their own treasuries, but extended virtually to the entire wealth of the population. For as long as the government could print more money and have that money accepted by its citizens and foreigners, it could keep financing the war. Previously, under a monetary system where gold as money was in the hands of the people, government only had its own treasuries to sustain its war effort, along with any taxation or bond issues to finance the war. This made conflict limited, and lay at the heart of the relatively long periods of peace experienced around the world before the twentieth century.

Had European nations remained on the gold standard, or had the people of Europe held their own gold in their own hands, forcing government to resort to taxation instead of inflation, history might have been different. It is likely that World War I would have been settled militarily within a few months of conflict, as one of the allied factions started running out of financing and faced difficulties in extracting wealth from a population that was not willing to part with its wealth to defend their regime's survival. But with the suspension of the gold standard, running out of financing was not enough to end the war; a sovereign had to run out of its people's accumulated wealth expropriated through inflation.

European countries devaluing their currency allowed the bloody stalemate to continue for four years, with no resolution or advancement. The senselessness of it all was not lost on the populations of these countries, and the soldiers on the front line risking their lives for no apparent reason but the unbounded vanity and ambition of monarchs who were usually related and intermarried. In the most vivid personification of the absolute senselessness of this war, on Christmas Eve 1914, French, English, and German soldiers stopped following orders to fight, laid down their arms, and crossed the battle lines to mingle and socialize with one another. Many of the German soldiers had worked in England and could speak English, and most soldiers had a fondness for football, and so many impromptu games were organized between the teams.[1]

---

[1] Brown, Malcolm, and Shirley Seaton. *Christmas Truce: The Western Front, December 1914*. London, PanMacmillan, 2014.

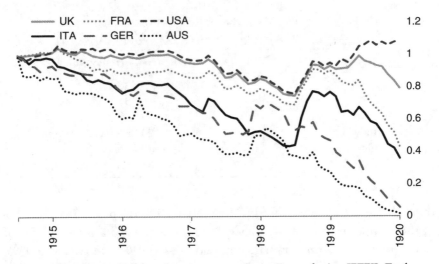

Figure 5   Major national exchange rates vs. Swiss Franc during WWI. Exchange rate in June 1914 = 1.

The astounding fact exposed by this truce is that these soldiers had nothing against each other, had nothing to gain from fighting this war, and could see no reason to continue it. A far better outlet for their nations' rivalry would be in football, a universally popular game where tribal and national affiliations can be played out peacefully.

The war was to continue for four more years with barely any progress, until the United States was to intervene in 1917 and swing the war in favor of one party at the expense of the other by bringing in a large amount of resources with which their enemies could no longer keep up. While all governments were funding their war machines with inflation, Germany and the Austro-Hungarian Empire began to witness serious decline in the value of their currency in 1918, making their defeat inevitable. Comparing the belligerents' currencies' exchange rates to the Swiss Franc, which was still on the gold standard at the time, provides a useful measure of the devaluation each currency experienced, as is shown in Figure 5.[2]

After the dust settled, the currencies of all major European powers had declined in real value. The losing powers, Germany and Austria, had

[2] *Source*: Hall, George. "Exchange Rates and Casualties During the First World War." *Journal of Monetary Economics*, Elsevier, vol. 51(8), Nov. 2004, pp. 1711–42.

Table 2 Change in Value of National Currency Against the
Swiss Franc During World War I (Jun 1914–Nov 1918)

Nation	Change in Currency Value
USA	−4.49%
UK	−6.63%
France	−9.40%
Italy	−23.25%
Germany	−49.17%
Austria	−68.81%

their average currency value in November 1918 drop to 51% and 31%
of their value in June 1914. Italy's currency witnessed a drop to 77% of
its original value while France's dropped only to 91%, the U.K.'s to 93%,
and the U.S. currency only to 96% of its original value.[3] (See Table 2.[4])

The geographic changes brought about by the war were hardly
worth the carnage, as most nations gained or lost marginal lands and no
victor could claim to have captured large territories worth the sacrifice.
The Austro-Hungarian Empire was broken up into smaller nations,
but these remained ruled by their own people, and not the winners of
the war. The major adjustment of the war was the removal of many
European monarchies and their replacement with republican regimes.
Whether such a transition was for the better pales in comparison to the
destruction and devastation that the war had inflicted on the citizens of
these countries.

With redemption of gold from central banks, and movement of gold
internationally suspended or severely restricted in the major economies,
governments could maintain the façade of the currency's value remaining
at its prewar peg to gold, even as prices were rising. As the war ended, the
international monetary system revolving around the gold standard was
no longer functional. All countries had gone off gold and had to face the

---

[3] I have wondered if the proximity of Germany and Austria to Switzerland, and the close relations
between these populations, may have led to more Germans and Austrians exchanging their currencies
for the Swiss Franc, which hastened the fall of these currencies, stretching the economic resources of
the governments, and playing a decisive role in the outcome of World War I. I have never come across
any research on this question, but if you do, dear reader, please do get in touch.

[4] *Source:* Hall, George. "Exchange Rates and Casualties During the First World War." *Journal of Monetary
Economics*, Elsevier, vol. 51(8), Nov. 2004, pp. 1711–42.

major dilemma of whether they should get back onto a gold standard, and if so, how to revalue their currencies compared to gold. A fair market valuation of their existing stock of currency to their stock of gold would be a hugely unpopular admission of the depreciation that the currency underwent. A return to the old rates of exchange would cause citizens to demand holding gold rather than the ubiquitous paper receipts, and lead to the flight of gold outside the country to where it was fairly valued.

This dilemma took money away from the market and turned it into a politically controlled economic decision. Instead of market participants freely choosing the most salable good as a medium of exchange, the value, supply, and interest rate for money now became centrally planned by national governments, a monetary system which Hayek named Monetary Nationalism, in a brilliant short book of the same name:

> By Monetary Nationalism I mean the doctrine that a country's share in the world's supply of money should not be left to be determined by the same principles and the same mechanism as those which determine the relative amounts of money in its different regions or localities. A truly International Monetary System would be one where the whole world possessed a homogeneous currency such as obtains within separate countries and where its flow between regions was left to be determined by the results of the action of all individuals.[5]

Never again would gold return to being the world's homogeneous currency, with central banks' monopoly position and restrictions on gold ownership forcing people to use national government moneys. The introduction of bitcoin, as a currency native to the Internet superseding national borders and outside the realm of governmental control, offers an intriguing possibility for the emergence of a new international monetary system, to be analyzed in Chapter 9.

The Interwar Era

Whereas under the international gold standard money flowed freely between nations in return for goods, and the exchange rate between

---

[5]Hayek, Friedrich. *Monetary Nationalism and International Stability*. London, Longmans, Green and Company, 1937.

different currencies was merely the conversion between different weights of gold, under monetary nationalism the money supply of each country, and the exchange rate between them, was to be determined in international agreements and meetings. Germany suffered from hyperinflation after the Treaty of Versailles had imposed large reparations on it and it sought to repay them using inflation. Britain had major problems with the flow of gold from its shores to France and the United States as it attempted to maintain a gold standard but with a rate that overvalued the British pound and undervalued gold.

The first major treaty of the century of monetary nationalism was the 1922 Treaty of Genoa. Under the terms of this treaty, the U.S. dollar and the British pound were to be considered reserve currencies similar to gold in their position in other countries' reserves. With this move, the U.K. had hoped to alleviate its problems with the overvalued sterling by having other countries purchase large quantities of it to place in their reserves. The world's major powers signaled their departure from the solidity of the gold standard toward inflationism as a solution to economic problems. The insanity of this arrangement was that these governments wanted to inflate while also maintaining the price of their currency stable in terms of gold at prewar levels. Safety was sought in numbers: if everyone devalued their currencies, there would be nowhere for capital to hide. But this did not and could not work and gold continued to flow out of Britain to the United States and France.

The drain of gold from Britain is a little-known story with enormous consequences. Liaquat Ahamed's *Lords of Finance* focuses on this episode, and does a good job of discussing the individuals involved and the drama taking place, but adopts the reigning Keynesian understanding of the issue, putting the blame for the entire episode on the gold standard. In spite of his extensive research, Ahamed fails to comprehend that the problem was not the gold standard, but that post–World War I governments had wanted to return to the gold standard at the pre–World War I rates. Had they admitted to their people the magnitude of the devaluation that took place to fight the war, and re-pegged their currencies to gold at new rates, there would have probably been a recessionary crash, after which the economy would have recovered on a sound monetary basis.

A better treatment of this episode, and its horrific aftermath, can be found in Murray Rothbard's *America's Great Depression*. As Britain's gold reserves were leaving its shores to places where they were better valued, the chief of the Bank of England, Sir Montagu Norman, leaned heavily on his French, German, and American counterparts to increase the money supply in their countries, devaluing their paper currencies in the hope that it would stem the flow of gold away from England. While the French and German bankers were not cooperative, Benjamin Strong, chairman of the New York Federal Reserve, was, and he engaged in inflationary monetary policy throughout the 1920s. This may have succeeded in reducing the outflow of gold from Britain up to a point, but the most important implication of it was that it created a larger bubble in the housing and stock markets in the United States. The U.S. Fed's inflationary policy ended by the end of 1928, at which point the U.S. economy was ripe for the inevitable collapse that follows from the suspension of inflationism. What followed was the 1929 stock market crash, and the reaction of the U.S. government turned that into the longest depression in modern recorded history.

The common story about the Great Depression posits that President Hoover chose to remain inactive in the face of the downturn, due to a misplaced faith in the ability of free markets to bring about recovery, and adherence to the gold standard. Only when he was replaced by Franklin Delano Roosevelt, who moved to an activist governmental role and suspended the gold standard, did the U.S. recovery ensue. This, to put it mildly, is nonsense. Hoover not only increased government spending on public work projects to fight the Depression, but he also leaned on the Federal Reserve to expand credit, and made the focus of his policy the insane quest to keep wages high in the face of declining wage rates. Further, price controls were instituted to keep prices of products, particularly agricultural, at high levels, similar to what was viewed as the fair and correct state that preceded the depression. The United States and all major global economies began to implement protective trade policies that made matters far worse across the world economy.[6]

---

[6] A thorough accounting of Hoover's interventionist policies can be found in Murray Rothbard's *America's Great Depression*.

It is a little-known fact, carefully airbrushed from the history books, that in the 1932 U.S. general election, Hoover ran on a highly interventionist platform while Franklin Delano Roosevelt ran on a platform of fiscal and monetary responsibility. Americans had actually voted against Hoover's policies, but when FDR got into power, he found it more convenient to play along with the interests that had influenced Hoover, and as a result, the interventionist policies of Hoover were amplified into what came to be known as the New Deal. It's important to realize there was nothing unique or new about the New Deal. It was a magnification of the heavily interventionist policies which Hoover had instituted.

A precursory understanding of economics will make it clear that price controls are always counterproductive, resulting in surpluses and shortages. The problems faced by the American economy in the 1930s were inextricably linked to the fixing of wages and prices. Wages were set too high, resulting in a very high unemployment rate, reaching 25% at certain points, while price controls had created shortages and surpluses of various goods. Some agricultural products were even burned in order to maintain their high prices, leading to the insane situation where people were going hungry, desperate for work, while producers couldn't hire them as they couldn't afford their wages, and the producers who could produce some crops had to burn some of them to keep the price high. All of this was done to maintain prices at the pre-1929 boom levels while holding onto the delusion that the dollar had still maintained its value compared to gold. The inflation of the 1920s had caused large asset bubbles to form in the housing and stock markets, causing an artificial rise in wages and prices. After the bubble burst, market prices sought readjustment via a drop in the value of the dollar compared to gold, and a drop in real wages and prices. The pigheadedness of deluded central planners who wanted to prevent all three from taking place paralyzed the economy: the dollar, wages, and prices were overvalued, leading to people seeking to drop their dollars for gold, as well as massive unemployment and failure of production.

None of this, of course, would be possible with sound money, and only through inflating the money supply did these problems occur. And even after the inflation, the effects would have been far less disastrous had they revalued the dollar to gold at a market-determined price and let wages and prices adjust freely. Instead of learning that lesson, the government economists of the era decided that the fault was not in inflationism, but rather, in the gold standard which restricted government's inflationism. In order to remove the golden fetters to inflationism, President Roosevelt issued an executive order banning the private ownership of gold, forcing Americans to sell their gold to the U.S. Treasury at a rate of $20.67 per ounce. With the population deprived of sound money, and forced to deal with dollars, Roosevelt then revalued the dollar on the international market from $20.67 per ounce to $35 per ounce, a 41% devaluation of the dollar in real terms (gold). This was the inevitable reality of years of inflationism which started in 1914 with the creation of the Federal Reserve and the financing of America's entry into World War II.

It was the abandonment of sound money and its replacement with government-issued fiat which turned the world's leading economies into centrally planned and government-directed failures. As governments controlled money, they controlled most economic, political, cultural, and educational activity. Having never studied economics or researched it professionally, Keynes captured the zeitgeist of omnipotent government to come up with the definitive track that gave governments what they wanted to hear. Gone were all the foundations of economic knowledge acquired over centuries of scholarship around the world, to be replaced with the new faith with the ever-so-convenient conclusions that suited high time-preference politicians and totalitarian governments: the state of the economy is determined by the lever of aggregate spending, and any rise in unemployment or slowdown in production had no underlying causes in the structure of production or in the distortion of markets by central planners; rather it was all a shortage of spending, and the remedy is the debauching of the currency and the increase of government spending. Saving reduces spending and because spending is all that matters, government must do all it can to deter its citizens from saving. Imports drive workers out of work, so spending increases must go on domestic goods. Governments loved this message, and Keynes himself knew that. His book was translated into German in 1937, at the height of the Nazi era, and in the introduction to the German edition Keynes wrote:

> The theory of aggregate production, which is the point of the following book, nevertheless can be much easier adapted to the conditions

of a totalitarian state than the theory of production and distribution of a given production put forth under conditions of free competition and a large degree of laissez-faire.[7]

The Keynesian deluge, from which the world is yet to recover, had begun. Universities lost their independence and became part and parcel of the government's ruling apparatus. Academic economics stopped being an intellectual discipline focused on understanding human choices under scarcity to improve their conditions. Instead it became an arm of the government, meant to direct policymakers toward the best policies for managing economic activities. The notion that government management of the economy is necessary became the unquestioned starting point of all modern economic education, as can be gleaned from looking at any modern economics textbook, where government plays the same role that God plays in religious scriptures: an omnipresent, omniscient, omnipotent force that merely needs to identify problems to satisfactorily address them. Government is immune to the concept of opportunity costs, and rarely are the negative results of government intervention in economic activity even considered, and if they are, it is only to justify even more government intervention. The classical liberal tradition that viewed economic freedom as the foundation of economic prosperity was quietly brushed aside as government propagandists masquerading as economists presented the Great Depression, caused and exacerbated by government controls, as the refutation of free markets. Classical liberals were the enemies of the political regimes of the 1930s; murdered and chased away from Russia, Italy, Germany, and Austria, they were fortunate to only be academically persecuted in the United States and the U.K., where these giants struggled to find employment while middling bureaucrats and failed statisticians filled every university economics department with their scientism and fake certainty.

Today government-approved economics curricula still blame the gold standard for the Great Depression. The same gold standard which produced more than four decades of virtually uninterrupted global growth and prosperity between 1870 and 1914 suddenly stopped working in the 1930s because it wouldn't allow governments to

---

[7] Quoted in Henry Hazlitt, *The Failure of the New Economics*. p. 277.

expand their money supply to fight the depression, whose causes these economists cannot explain beyond meaningless Keynesian allusions to animal spirits. And none of these economists seem to notice that if the problem was indeed the gold standard, then its suspension should have caused the beginning of recovery. Instead, it took more than a decade after its suspension for growth to resume. The conclusion obvious to anyone with a basic understanding of money and economics is that the cause of the Great Crash of 1929 was the diversion away from the gold standard in the post-WWI years, and that the deepening of the Depression was caused by government control and socialization of the economy in the Hoover and FDR years. Neither the suspension of the gold standard nor the wartime spending did anything to alleviate the Great Depression.

As the major economies of the world went off the gold standard, global trade was soon to be shipwrecked on the shores of oscillating fiat money. With no standard of value to allow an international price mechanism to exist, and with governments increasingly captured by statist and isolationist impulses, currency manipulation emerged as a tool of trade policy, with countries seeking to devalue their currencies in order to give their exporters an advantage. More trade barriers were erected, and economic nationalism became the ethos of that era, with predictably disastrous consequences. The nations that had prospered together 40 years earlier, trading under one universal gold standard, now had large monetary and trade barriers between them, loud populist leaders who blamed all their failures on other nations, and a rising tide of hateful nationalism that was soon to fulfill Otto Mallery's prophecy: "If soldiers are not to cross international boundaries, goods must do so. Unless the Shackles can be dropped from trade, bombs will be dropped from the sky."[8]

World War II and Bretton Woods

From the sky the bombs did drop, along with countless heretofore unimaginable forms of murder and horror. The war machines that

---

[8]Mallery, Otto. *Economic Union and Durable Peace*. New York, Harper and Brothers, 1943, p. 10.

the government-directed economies built were far more advanced than any the world had ever seen, thanks to the popularity of the most dangerous and absurd of all Keynesian fallacies, the notion that government spending on military effort would aid economic recovery. All spending is spending, in the naive economics of Keynesians, and so it matters not if that spending comes from individuals feeding their families or governments murdering foreigners: it all counts in aggregate demand and it all reduces unemployment! As an increasing number of people went hungry during the depression, all major governments spent generously on arming themselves, and the result was a return to the senseless destruction of three decades earlier.

For Keynesian economists, the war was what caused economic recovery, and if one looked at life merely through the lens of statistical aggregates collected by government bureaucrats, such a ridiculous notion is tenable. With government war expenditure and conscription on the rise, aggregate expenditure soared while unemployment plum- meted, so all countries involved in World War II had recovered because of their participation in the war. Anybody not afflicted with Keynesian economics, however, can realize that life during World War II, even in countries that did not witness war on their soil, like the United States, cannot by any stretch of the imagination be characterized as "economic recovery." On top of the death and destruction, the dedication of so much of the capital and labor resources of the belligerent countries to the war effort meant severe shortages of output at home, resulting in rationing and price controls. In the United States, construction of new housing and repair of existing housing were banned.[9] More obviously, one cannot possibly argue that soldiers fighting and dying at warfronts, who constituted a large percentage of the populations of belligerent nations, enjoyed any form of economic recovery, no matter how much aggregate expenditure went into making the weapons they were carrying.

But one of the most devastating blows to Keynesian theories of the aggregate demand as the determinant of the state of the economy came in the aftermath of World War II, particularly in the United States.

---

[9]Higgs, Robert. *World War II and the Triumph of Keynesianism*. Independent Institute, 2001, www.independent.org/publications/article.asp?id=317.

A confluence of factors had conspired to reduce government spending drastically, leading to Keynesian economists of the era predicting doom and gloom to follow the war: the end of military hostilities reduced government military spending dramatically. The death of the populist and powerful FDR and his replacement by the meeker and less iconic Truman, coming up against a Congress controlled by Republicans, created political deadlock that prevented the renewal of the statutes of the New Deal. All of these factors together, when analyzed by Keynesian economists, would point to impending disaster, as Paul Samuelson, the man who literally wrote the textbooks for economic education in the postwar era, wrote in 1943:

> The final conclusion to be drawn from our experience at the end of the last war is inescapable—were the war to end suddenly within the next 6 months, were we again planlessly to wind up our war effort in the greatest haste, to demobilize our armed forces, to liquidate price controls, to shift from astronomical deficits to even the large deficits of the thirties—then there would be ushered in the greatest period of unemployment and industrial dislocation which any economy has ever faced.[10]

The end of World War II and the dismantling of the New Deal meant the U.S. government cut its spending by an astonishing 75% between 1944 and 1948, and it also removed most price controls for good measure. And yet, the U.S. economy witnessed an extraordinary boom during these years. The roughly ten million men who were mobilized for the war came back home and were almost seamlessly absorbed into the labor force, as economic production boomed, flying in the face of all Keynesian predictions and utterly obliterating the ridiculous notion that the level of spending is what determines output in the economy. As soon as governmental central planning had abated for the first time since the 1929 crash, and as soon as prices were allowed to adjust freely, they served their role as the coordinating mechanism for economic activity, matching sellers and buyers, incentivizing the production of goods demanded by consumers and compensating workers for their effort. The

[10]Samuelson, Paul. "Full Employment After the War." *Postwar Economic Problems*, edited by Seymour Harris, McGraw-Hill, 1943, pp. 27–53.

situation was far from perfect, though, as the world remained off the gold standard, leading to ever-present distortions of the money supply which would continue to dog the world economy with crisis after crisis.

It is well-known that history is written by the victors, but in the era of government money, victors get to decide on the monetary systems, too. The United States summoned representatives of its allies to Bretton Woods in New Hampshire to discuss formulating a new global trading system. History has not been very kind to the architects of this system. Britain's representative was none other than John Maynard Keynes, whose economic teachings were to be wrecked on the shores of reality in the decades following the war, while America's representative, Harry Dexter White, would later be uncovered as a Communist who was in contact with the Soviet regime for many years.[11] In the battle for centrally planned global monetary orders, White was to emerge victorious with a plan that even made Keynes's look not entirely unhinged. The United States was to be the center of the global monetary system, with its dollars being used as a global reserve currency by other central banks, whose currencies would be convertible to dollars at fixed exchange rates, while the dollar itself would be convertible to gold at a fixed exchange rate. To facilitate this system, the United States would take gold from other countries' central banks.

---

[11] After being investigated and testifying in front of Congress, White suffered two heart attacks and died from an overdose of medication, which may have been suicide. A good treatment of this episode can be found in Benn Steil's *The Battle of Bretton Woods*, which pushes the view that White was a Soviet spy. An alternative reading of the situation can produce a more nuanced perspective, though hardly more flattering. The links between American progressives and Russian Communists precede the 1917 Russian putsch, and included significant U.S. funding to the Bolsheviks to depose the Russian monarchy, as thoroughly detailed by British–American historian Antony Sutton. Wilsonian American progressives, who were behind the League of Nations and later the United Nations, had sought a global, democratic, progressive, technocratic, managerial world government, and sought cooperation with global forces that would be supportive of this goal, and to depose reactionary monarchies that would not cooperate with this world order. Hence, American interests played a leading role in promoting the Bolsheviks and helping them take power, particularly through Leon Trotsky, who was in New York during the revolution, channeling funding and arms to his comrades in Russia. Whereas Trotsky was an internationalist socialist who would have cooperated with American interests, he was not to gain power in Russia, and instead Stalin was to succeed Lenin, and head in a more parochial direction, prioritizing socialism at home over global cooperation. From then on, American progressives maintained contact with Russian interests, attempting to sway Russia back into cooperation with American progressive interests, but to no avail. We can thus better understand White not as a Communist spy, but as an American progressive who sought cooperation with Russian Bolsheviks for the grand project of the postwar economic order the American progressives sought.

Whereas the American people were still prohibited from owning gold, the U.S. government promised to redeem dollars in gold to other countries' central banks at a fixed rate, opening what was known as the gold exchange window. In theory, the global monetary system was still based on gold, and if the U.S. government had maintained convertibility to gold by not inflating the dollar supply beyond their gold reserves while other countries had not inflated their money supply beyond their dollar reserves, the monetary system would have effectively been close to the gold standard of the pre–World War I era. They did not, of course, and in practice, the exchange rates were anything but fixed and provisions were made for allowing governments to alter these rates to address a "fundamental disequilibrium."[12]

In order to manage this global system of hopefully fixed exchange rates, and address any potential fundamental disequilibrium, the Bretton Woods conference established the International Monetary Fund, which acted as a global coordination body between central banks with the express aim of achieving stability of exchange rates and financial flows. In essence, Bretton Woods attempted to achieve through central planning what the international gold standard of the nineteenth century had achieved spontaneously. Under the classical gold standard the monetary unit was gold while capital and goods flowed freely between countries, spontaneously adjusting flows without any need for central control or direction, and never resulting in balance of payment crises: whatever amount of money or goods moved across borders did so at the discretion of its owners and no macroeconomic problems could emerge.

In the Bretton Woods system, however, governments were dominated by Keynesian economists who viewed activist fiscal and monetary policy as a natural and important part of government policy. The constant monetary and fiscal management would naturally lead to the fluctuation of the value of national currencies, resulting in imbalances in trade and capital flows. When a country's currency is devalued, its products become cheaper to foreigners, leading to more goods leaving the country, while holders of the currency seek to purchase foreign currencies to

---

[12] *Proceedings and Documents of the United Nations Monetary and Financial Conference.* vol. 1, Bretton Woods, NH, US Department of State, 1944.

protect themselves from devaluation. As devaluation is usually accompanied by artificially low interest rates, capital seeks exit from the country to go where it can be better rewarded, exacerbating the devaluation of the currency. On the other hand, countries which maintained their currency better than others would thus witness an influx of capital whenever their neighbors devalued, leading to their currency appreciating further. Devaluation would sow the seeds of more devaluation, whereas currency appreciation would lead to more appreciation, creating a problematic dynamic for the two governments. No such problems could exist with the gold standard, where the value of the currency in both countries was constant, because it was gold, and movements of goods and capital would not affect the value of the currency.

The automatic adjustment mechanisms of the gold standard had always provided a constant measuring rod against which all economic activity was measured, but the floating currencies gave the world economy imbalances. The International Monetary Fund's role was to perform an impossible balancing act between all the world's governments to attempt to find some form of stability or "equilibrium" in this mess, keeping exchange rates within some arbitrary range of predetermined values while trade and capital flows were moving and altering them. But without a stable unit of account for the global economy, this was a task as hopeless as attempting to build a house with an elastic measuring tape whose own length varied every time it was used.

Along with the establishment of the World Bank and IMF in Bretton Woods, the United States and its allies wanted to establish another international financial institution to specialize in arranging trade policy. The initial attempt to establish an International Trade Organization failed after the U.S. Congress refused to ratify the treaty, but a replacement was sought in the General Agreement on Trade and Tariffs, commencing in 1948. GATT was meant to help the IMF in the impossible task of balancing budgets and trade to ensure financial stability—in other words, centrally planning global trade and fiscal and monetary policy to remain in balance, as if such a thing were possible.

An important, but often overlooked, aspect of the Bretton Woods system was that most of the member countries had moved large amounts of their gold reserves to the United States and received dollars in exchange, at a rate of $35 per ounce. The rationale was that the U.S.

dollar would be the global currency for trade and central banks would trade through it and settle their accounts in it, obviating the need for the physical movement of gold. In essence, this system was akin to the entire world economy being run as one country on a gold standard, with the U.S. Federal Reserve acting as the world's central bank and all the world's central banks as regional banks, the main difference being that the monetary discipline of the gold standard was almost entirely lost in this world where there were no effective controls on all central banks in expanding the money supply, because no citizens could redeem their government money for gold. Only governments could redeem their dollars in gold from the United States, but that was to prove far more complicated than expected. Today, each ounce of gold for which foreign central banks received $35 is worth in excess of $1,200.

Monetary expansionism became the new global norm, and the tenuous link that the system had to gold proved powerless to stop the debauching of global currencies and the constant balance of payment crises affecting most countries. The United States, however, was put in a remarkable position, similar to, though massively exceeding in scope, the Roman Empire's pillaging and inflating the money supply used by most of the Old World. With its currency distributed all over the world, and central banks having to hold it as a reserve to trade with one another, the U.S. government could accrue significant seigniorage from expanding the supply of dollars, and also had no reason to worry about running a balance of payment deficit. French economist Jacques Reuff coined the phrase "deficit without tears" to describe the new economic reality that the United States inhabited, where it could purchase whatever it wanted from the world and finance it through debt monetized by inflating the currency that the entire world used.

The relative fiscal restraint of the first few years after World War II soon gave way to the politically irresistible temptation of buying free lunches through inflation, particularly to the warfare and welfare states. The military industry that prospered during World War II grew into what President Eisenhower called the Military–Industrial Complex—an enormous conglomerate of industries that was powerful enough to demand ever more funding from the government, and drive U.S. foreign policy toward an endless series of expensive conflicts with no rational end goal or clear objective. The doctrine of violent militant

Keynesianism claimed this spending would be good for the economy, which made the millions of lives it destroyed easier to stomach for the American electorate.

This war machine was also made more palatable for the American people because it came from the same politicians who intensified government welfare in various shapes and forms. From The Great Society to affordable housing, education, and healthcare, fiat money allowed the American electorate to ignore the laws of economics and believe that a free lunch, or at least a perpetually discounted one, was somehow possible. In the absence of gold convertibility and with the ability to disperse the costs of inflation on the rest of the world, the only winning political formula consisted of increasing government spending financed by inflation, and every single presidential term in the postwar era witnessed a growth in government expenditure and the national debt and a loss of the purchasing power of the dollar. In the presence of fiat money to finance government, political differences between parties disappear as politics no longer contains trade-offs and every candidate can champion every cause.

Government Money's Track Record

The tenuous link of gold exchangeability was an annoying detail for the U.S. government's inflationism, and it manifested in two symptoms: first, the global gold market was always seeking to reflect the reality of inflationism through a higher gold price. This was addressed through the establishment of the London Gold Pool, which sought to drop the price of gold by offloading some of the gold reserves that governments held onto the market. This worked only temporarily, but in 1968, the U.S. dollar had to start getting revalued compared to gold to acknowledge the years of inflation it had suffered. The second problem was that some countries started trying to repatriate their gold reserves from the United States as they started to recognize the diminishing purchasing power of their paper money. French president Charles de Gaulle even sent a French military carrier to New York to get his nation's gold back, but when the Germans attempted to repatriate their gold, the United States had decided it had had enough. Gold reserves were running low, and on August 15, 1971, President Richard Nixon announced the end of dollar convertibility to gold, thus letting the gold price float in the market freely. In effect, the United States had defaulted on its commitment to redeem its dollars in gold. The fixed exchange rates between the world's currencies, which the IMF was tasked with maintaining, had now been let loose to be determined by the movement of goods and capital across borders and in ever-more-sophisticated foreign exchange markets.

Freed from the final constraints of the pretense of gold redemption, the U.S. government expanded its monetary policy in unprecedented scale, causing a large drop in the purchasing power of the dollar, and a rise in prices across the board. Everyone and everything was blamed for the rise in prices by the U.S. government and its economists, except for the one actual source of the price rises, the increase in the supply of the U.S. dollar. Most other currencies fared even worse, as they were the victim of inflation of the U.S. dollars backing them, as well as the inflation by the central banks issuing them.

This move by President Nixon completed the process begun with World War I, transforming the world economy from a global gold standard to a standard based on several government-issued currencies. For a world that was growing increasingly globalized along with advancements in transportation and telecommunications, freely fluctuating exchange rates constituted what Hoppe termed "a system of partial barter."[13] Buying things from people who lived on the other side of imaginary lines in the sand now required utilizing more than one medium of exchange and reignited the age-old problem of lack of coincidence of wants. The seller does not want the currency held by the buyer, and so the buyer must purchase another currency first, and incur conversion costs. As advances in transportation and telecommunications continue to increase global economic integration, the cost of these inefficiencies just keeps getting bigger. The market for foreign exchange, at $5 trillion of daily volume, exists purely as a result of this inefficiency of the absence of a single global homogeneous international currency.

While most governments produce their own currencies, the U.S. government was the one that produced the prime reserve currency with

---

[13] Hoppe, Hans-Hermann. "How Is Fiat Money Possible?" *Review of Austrian Economics*, vol. 7, no. 2, 1994.

which other governments backed theirs. This was the first time in human history that the entire planet had run on government money, and while such an idea is considered normal and unquestionable in most academic circles, it is well worth examining the soundness of this predominant form of money.

It is theoretically possible to create an artificially scarce asset to endow it with a monetary role. Governments around the world did this after abandoning the gold standard, as did bitcoin's creator, with contrasting results. After the link between fiat money and gold was severed, paper monies have had a higher growth in their supply rate than gold, and as a result have seen a collapse in their value compared to gold. The total U.S. M2 measure of the money supply in 1971 was around $600 billion, while today it is in excess of $12 trillion, growing at an average annual rate of 6.7%. Correspondingly, in 1971, 1 ounce of gold was worth $35, and today it is worth more than $1,200.

Looking at the track record of government money paints a mixed picture about the stock-to-flow ratio of different currencies across time. The relatively stable and strong currencies of the developed countries have usually had growth rates in the single digits, but with a much higher variance, including contractions of the supply during deflationary recessions.[14] Developing country currencies have at many times experienced supply growth rates closer to those of consumable commodities, leading to disastrous hyperinflation and the destruction of the wealth of holders. The World Bank provides data on broad money growth for 167 countries for the period between 1960 and 2015. The data for the annual average for all countries is plotted in Figure 6. While the data is not complete for all countries and all years, the average growth of money supply is 32.16% per year per country.

The 32.16% figure does not include several hyperinflationary years during which a currency is completely destroyed and replaced by a new one, and so the results of this analysis cannot definitively tell us which currencies fared worst, as some of the most significant data cannot be

---

[14]This is an important but often underappreciated feature of government money. Because banks create money when they issue loans, the repayment of loans or the bankruptcy of the borrower leads to a reduction in the money supply. Money can have its supply increase or decrease depending on a variety of government and central bank decisions.

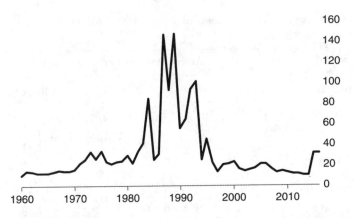

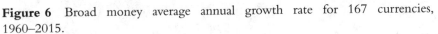

Figure 6 Broad money average annual growth rate for 167 currencies, 1960–2015.

Table 3 The Ten Countries with Highest Average Annual Broad Money Supply Growth, 1960–2015

Country	Average
Nicaragua	480.24
Congo, Dem. Rep.	410.92
Angola	293.79
Brazil	266.57
Peru	198.00
Bolivia	184.28
Argentina	148.17
Ukraine	133.84
Azerbaijan	109.25
Armenia	100.67

compared. But a look at the countries that have had the highest average increase of the money supply will show a list of countries that had several highly publicized episodes of inflationary struggle throughout the period covered. Table 3[15] shows the ten countries with the highest annual average increase in the money supply.

During hyperinflationary periods, people in developing countries sell their national currency and buy durable items, commodities, gold,

---

[15] *Source*: World Bank. www.worldbank.org/en/home.

Table 4 Average Annual Percent Increase in Broad Money Supply for the Ten Largest Global Currencies

Country/Region	Annual Money Supply Growth Rate	
	1960–2015	1990–2015
United States	7.42	5.45
Euro Area (19 countries)		5.55
Japan	10.27	1.91
United Kingdom	11.30	7.28
Australia	10.67	9.11
Canada	11.92	10.41
Switzerland	6.50	4.88
China	21.82	20.56
Sweden	7.94	6.00
New Zealand	12.30	6.78

and foreign currencies. International reserve currencies, such as the dollar, euro, yen, and Swiss franc, are available in most of the world, even if in black markets, and meet a significantly high portion of the global demand for a store of value. The reason for that becomes apparent when one examines the rates of growth of their supply, which have been relatively low over time. Seeing as they constitute the main store-of-value options available for most people around the world, it is worth examining their supply growth rates separately from the less stable currencies. The current ten largest currencies in the foreign exchange markets are listed in Table 4, along with their annual broad money supply increase for the periods between 1960–2015 and 1990–2015.[16] The average for the ten most internationally liquid currencies is 11.13% for the period 1960–2015, and only 7.79% for the period between 1990 and 2015. This shows that the currencies that are most accepted worldwide, and have the highest salability globally, have a higher stock-to-flow ratio than the other currencies, as this book's analysis would predict.

The period of the 1970s and 1980s, which contained the beginning of the floating national currencies era, was one in which most countries experienced high inflation. Things got better after 1990, and

---

[16] *Source*: Organization for Economic Co-operation and Development. stats.oecd.org/. World Bank. www.worldbank.org/en/home.

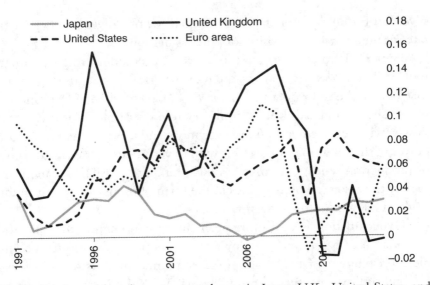

Figure 7 Annual broad money growth rate in Japan, U.K., United States, and Euro area.

average supply growth rates dropped. OECD data shows that for OECD countries over the period between 1990 and 2015, annual broad money supply growth rate averaged 7.17%.

We can see that the world's major national currencies generally have their supply grow at predictably low rates. Developed economies have had slower increases in the supply of their currencies than developing economies, which have witnessed faster price rises and several hyperinflationary episodes in recent history. The advanced economies have had their broad money grow at rates usually between 2% and 8%, averaging around 5%, and rarely climbing into double digits or dropping into negative territory. Developing countries have far more erratic growth rates, which fluctuate into the double digits, sometimes triple digits, and sometimes even quadruple digits, while occasionally dropping into negative territory, reflecting the higher financial instability in these countries and currencies. (See Figure 7.[17])

Growth at 5% per year may not sound like much, but it will double the money supply of a country in only 15 years. This was the reason

---

[17] *Source*: Organization for Economic Co-operation and Development. stats.oecd.org/

silver lost out in the monetary race to gold, whose lower supply growth rate meant a far slower erosion of purchasing power.

Hyperinflation is a form of economic disaster unique to government money. There was never an example of hyperinflation with economies that operated a gold or silver standard, and even when artifact money like seashells and beads lost its monetary role over time, it usually lost it slowly, with replacements taking over more and more of the purchasing power of the outgoing money. But with government money, whose cost of production tends to zero, it has become quite possible for an entire society to witness all of its savings in the form of money disappear in the space of a few months or even weeks.

Hyperinflation is a far more pernicious phenomenon than just the loss of a lot of economic value by a lot of people; it constitutes a complete breakdown of the structure of economic production of a society built up over centuries and millennia. With the collapse of money, it becomes impossible to trade, produce, or engage in anything other than scraping for the bare essentials of life. As the structures of production and trade that societies have developed over centuries break down due to the inability of consumers, producers, and workers to pay one another, the goods which humans take for granted begin to disappear. Capital is destroyed and sold off to finance consumption. First go the luxury goods, but soon follow the basic essentials of survival, until humans are brought back to a barbaric state wherein they need to fend for themselves and struggle to secure the most basic needs of survival. As the individual's quality of life degenerates markedly, despair begins to turn to anger, scapegoats are sought, and the most demagogic and opportunistic politicians take advantage of this situation, stoking people's anger to gain power. The most vivid example of this is inflation of the Weimar Republic in the 1920s, which not only led to the destruction and breakdown of one of the world's most advanced and prosperous economies, but also fueled the rise of Adolf Hitler to power.

Even if the textbooks were correct about the benefits of government management of the money supply, the damage from one episode of hyperinflation anywhere in the world far outweighs them. And the century of government money had far more than one of these calamitous episodes.

As these lines are written, it is Venezuela's turn to go through this travesty and witness the ravages of the destruction of money, but this is a process that has occurred fifty-six times since the end of World War I, according to research by Steve Hanke and Charles Bushnell, who define hyperinflation as a 50% increase in the price level over a period of a month. Hanke and Bushnell have been able to verify fifty-seven episodes of hyperinflation in history,[18] only one of which occurred before the era of monetary nationalism, and that was the inflation in France in 1795, in the wake of the Mississippi Bubble, which was also produced through government money and engineered by the honorary father of modern government money, John Law.

The problem with government-provided money is that its hardness depends entirely on the ability of those in charge to not inflate its supply. Only political constraints provide hardness, and there are no physical, economic, or natural constraints on how much money government can produce. Cattle, silver, gold, and seashells all require serious effort to produce them and can never be generated in large quantities at the drop of a hat, but government money requires only the fiat of the government. The constantly increasing supply means a continuous devaluation of the currency, expropriating the wealth of the holders to benefit those who print the currency, and those who receive it earliest.[19] History has shown that governments will inevitably succumb to the temptation of inflating the money supply. Whether it's because of downright graft, "national emergency," or an infestation of inflationist schools of economics, government will always find a reason and a way to print more money, expanding government power while reducing the wealth of the currency holders. This is no different from copper producers mining more copper in response to monetary demand for copper; it rewards the producers of

---

[18] Hanke, Steve, and Charles Bushnell. "Venezuela Enters the Record Book: The 57th Entry in the Hanke-Krus World Hyperinflation Table." *Studies in Applied Economics*, no. 69, Dec. 2016.

[19] This is termed the Cantillon Effect, after the Irish-French economist Richard Cantillon, who explained it in the eighteenth century. According to Cantillon, the beneficiaries from the expansion of the money supply are the first recipients of the new money, who are able to spend it before it has caused prices to rise. Whoever receives it from them is then able to spend it facing a small increase in the price level. As the money is spent more, the price level rises, until the later recipients suffer a reduction in their real purchasing power. This is the best explanation for why inflation hurts the poorest and helps the richest in the modern economy. Those who benefit from it most are the ones with the best access to government credit, and the ones who are hurt the most are those on fixed incomes or minimum wages.

the monetary good, but punishes those who choose to put their savings in copper.

Should a currency credibly demonstrate its supply cannot be expanded, it would immediately gain value significantly. In 2003, when the United States invaded Iraq, aerial bombardment destroyed the Iraqi central bank and with it the capability of the Iraqi government to print new Iraqi dinars. This led to the dinar drastically appreciating overnight as Iraqis became more confident in the currency given that no central bank could print it anymore.[20] A similar story happened to Somali shillings after their central bank was destroyed.[21] Money is more desirable when demonstrably scarce than when liable to being debased.

A few reasons keep government money as the prime money of our time. First, governments mandate that taxes are paid in government money, which means individuals are highly likely to accept it, giving it an edge in its salability. Second, government control and regulation of the banking system means that banks can only open accounts and transact in government-sanctioned money, thus giving government money a much higher degree of salability than any other potential competitor. Third, legal tender laws make it illegal in many countries to use other forms of money for payment. Fourth, all government moneys are still backed by gold reserves, or backed by currencies backed by gold reserves. According to data from the World Gold Council, central banks currently have around 33,000 tons of gold in their reserves. Central bank gold reserves rose quickly in the early part of the twentieth century as many governments confiscated their people's and banks' gold and forced them to use their money. In the late 1960s, with the Bretton Woods system straining under the pressure of increased money supply, governments began to offload some of their gold reserves. But in 2008 that trend reversed and central banks returned to buying gold and the global supply has increased. It is ironic, and very telling, that in the era of government money, governments themselves own far more gold in their official reserves than they did under the international gold standard of 1871–1914. Gold has clearly not lost its monetary role; it

---

[20]Anderson, William. "Dollar or Dinar?" *Mises Daily Articles*, Mises Institute, 4 Mar. 2003, mises.org/library/dollar-or-dinar.

[21]Koning, J. P. "Orphaned Currency: Odd Case of Somali Shillings." *Moneyness: The Blog of J. P. Koning*, 1 Mar. 2013, jpkoning.blogspot.com/2013/03/orphaned-currency-odd-case-of-somali.html.

remains the only final extinguisher of debt, the one money whose value is not a liability of anyone else, and the prime global asset which carries no counterparty risk. Access to its monetary role, however, has been restricted to central banks, while individuals have been directed toward using government money.

Central banks' large reserves of gold can be used as an emergency supply to sell or lease on the gold market to prevent the price of gold from rising during periods of increased demand, to protect the monopoly role of government money. As Alan Greenspan once explained: "Central banks stand ready to lease gold in increasing quantities should the price rise."[22] (See Figure 4.[23])

As technology has progressed to allow for ever-more-sophisticated forms of money, including paper money that is easy to carry around, a new problem of salability has been introduced, and that is the ability of the seller to sell her good without the intervention of any third parties that might place restraints on the salability of that money. This is not an issue that exists with commodity moneys, whose market value is emergent from the market and cannot be dictated by third parties to the transaction: cattle, salt, gold, and silver all have a market and willing buyers. But with government-issued money with negligible value as a commodity, salability can be compromised by the governments that issued it, declaring it no longer suitable as legal tender. Indians who woke up on November 8, 2016, to hear that their government had suspended the legal tender status of 500 and 1,000 rupee notes can certainly relate. In the blink of an eye, what was highly salable money lost its value and had to be exchanged at banks with very long lines. And as more of the world heads toward reducing its reliance on cash, more of people's money is being placed in government-supervised banks, making it vulnerable to confiscation or capital controls. The fact that these procedures generally happen during times of economic crisis, when individuals need that money most, is a major impediment to the salability of government-issued money.

---

[22] *The Regulation of OTC Derivatives*. Testimony of Chairman Alan Greenspan before the Committee on Banking and Financial Services, US House of Representatives, 24 Jul. 1998.

[23] *Source*: World Gold Council. *Reserve Statistics*, www.gold.org/data/gold-reserves.

Government control of money has turned money from being the reward for producing value to the reward for obedience to government officials. It is impractical for anyone to develop wealth in government money without government acceptance. Government can confiscate money from the banking monopolies it controls, inflate the currency to devalue holders' wealth and reward it to the most loyal of its subjects, impose draconian taxes and punish those who avoid them, and even confiscate bills.

Whereas in Austrian economist Menger's time the criteria for determining what is the best money revolved around understanding salability and what the market would choose as money, in the twentieth century, government control of money has meant a new and very important criterion being added to salability, and that is the salability of money according to the will of its holder and not some other party. Combining these criteria together formulates a complete understanding of the term *sound money* as the money that is chosen by the market freely and the money completely under the control of the person who earned it legitimately on the free market and not any other third party.

While a staunch defender of the role of gold as money during his time, Ludwig von Mises understood that this monetary role was not something inherent or intrinsic to gold. As one of the deans of the Austrian tradition in economics, Mises well understood that value does not exist outside of human consciousness, and that metals and substances had nothing inherent to them that could assign to them a monetary role. For Mises, gold's monetary status was due to its fulfillment of the criteria for sound money as he understood them:

> [T]he sound money principle has two aspects. It is affirmative in approving the market's choice of a commonly used medium of exchange. It is negative in obstructing the government's propensity to meddle with the currency system.[24]

Sound money, then, according to Mises, is what the market freely chooses to be money, and what remains under the control of its owner,

---

[24]Mises, Ludwig von. *The Theory of Money and Credit*. 2nd ed., Irvington-on-Hudson, NY, Foundation for Economic Education, 1971, pp. 414–6.

safe from coercive meddling and intervention. For as long as the money was controlled by anyone other than the owner, whoever controlled it would always face too strong an incentive to pilfer the value of the money through inflation or confiscation, and to use it as a political tool to achieve their political goals at the expense of the holders. This, in effect, takes wealth away from people who produce it and gives it to people who specialize in the control of money without actually producing things valued by society, in the same way European traders could pilfer African society by flooding them with cheap beads as mentioned in Chapter 2. No society could prosper when such an avenue for riches remained open, at the cost of impoverishing those who seek productive avenues for wealth. A sound money, on the other hand, makes service valuable to others the only avenue open for prosperity to anyone, thus concentrating society's efforts on production, cooperation, capital accumulation, and trade.

The twentieth century was the century of unsound money and the omnipotent state, as a market choice in money was denied by government diktat, and government-issued paper money was forced on people with the threat of violence. As time passed, governments moved away from sound money ever more as their spending and deficits increased, their currencies continuously devalued, and an ever-larger share of national income was controlled by the government. With government increasing its meddling in all aspects of life, it increasingly controlled the educational system and used it to imprint in people's minds the fanciful notion that the rules of economics did not apply to governments, which would prosper the more they spent. The work of monetary cranks like John Maynard Keynes taught in modern universities the notion that government spending only has benefits, never costs. The government, after all, can always print money and so faces no real constraints on its spending, which it can use to achieve whichever goal the electorate sets for it.

For those who worship government power and take joy in totalitarian control, such as the many totalitarian and mass-murdering regimes of the twentieth century, this monetary arrangement was a godsend. But for those who valued human liberty, peace, and cooperation among humans, it was a depressing time with the prospects of economic reform receding ever more with time and the prospects of the political process ever returning us to monetary sanity becoming an increasingly fanciful dream. As Friedrich Hayek put it:

> I don't believe we shall ever have a good money again before we take the thing out of the hands of government, that is, we can't take it violently out of the hands of government, all we can do is by some sly roundabout way introduce something that they can't stop.[25]

Speaking in 1984, completely oblivious to the actual form of this "something they can't stop," Friedrich Hayek's prescience sounds outstanding today. Three decades after he uttered these words, and a whole century after governments destroyed the last vestige of sound money that was the gold standard, individuals worldwide have the chance to save and transact with a new form of money, chosen freely on the market and outside government control. In its infancy, bitcoin already appears to satisfy all the requirements of Menger, Mises, and Hayek: it is a highly salable free-market option that is resistant to government meddling.

---

[25] Hayek, Friedrich. "Monetary Policy, the Gold Standard, Deficits, Inflation, and John Maynard Keynes." Interview by James U. Blanchard III, University of Freiburg, Germany, *Libertarianism*, 1984, www.libertarianism.org/media/video-collection/interview-f-hayek.

Chapter 5

Money and Time Preference

S ound money is chosen freely on the market for its salability, because it holds its value across time, because it can transfer value effectively across space, and because it can be divided and grouped into small and large scales. It is money whose supply cannot be manipulated by a coercive authority that imposes its use on others. From the preceding discussion, and from the understanding of monetary economics afforded to us by Austrian economics, the importance of sound money can be explained for three broad reasons: first, it protects value across time, which gives people a bigger incentive to think of their future, and lowers their time preference. The lowering of the time preference is what initiates the process of human civilization and allows for humans to cooperate, prosper, and live in peace. Second, sound money allows for trade to be based on a stable unit of measurement, facilitating ever-larger markets, free from government control and coercion, and with free trade comes peace and prosperity. Further, a unit of account is essential for all forms of economic calculation and planning, and unsound money makes economic calculation unreliable and is the root cause of economic recessions and crises. Finally, sound money is an essential requirement for individual freedom from despotism and repression, as the ability of a coercive state to create money can give it undue power over its subjects, power which by its very nature will attract the least worthy, and most immoral, to take its reins.

Sound money is a prime factor in determining individual *time preference*, an enormously important and widely neglected aspect of individual decision making. Time preference refers to the ratio at which individuals value the present compared to the future. Because humans do not live eternally, death could come to us at any point in time, making the future uncertain. And because consumption is necessary for survival, people always value present consumption more than future consumption, as the lack of present consumption could make the future never arrive. In other words, time preference is positive for all humans; there is always a discount on the future compared to the present.

Further, because more goods can be produced with time and resources, rational individuals would always prefer to have a given quantity of resources in the present than in the future, as they could use them to produce more. For an individual to be willing to defer her receipt of a good by a year, she would have to be offered a larger quantity of the good. The increase necessary to tempt an individual to delay her receipt of the good is what determines her time preference. All rational individuals have a nonzero time preference, but the time preference varies from one individual to another.

Animals' time preference is far higher than humans', as they act to the satisfaction of their immediate instinctive impulses and have little conception of the future. A few animals are capable of building nests or homes that can last for the future, and these have a lower time preference than the animals that act to the satisfaction of their immediate needs such as hunger and aggression. Human beings' lower time preference allows us to curb our instinctive and animalistic impulses, think of what is better for our future, and act rationally rather than impulsively. Instead of spending all our time producing goods for immediate consumption, we can choose to spend time engaged in production of goods that will take longer to complete, if they are superior goods. As humans reduce their time preference, they develop the scope for carrying out tasks over longer time horizons, for satisfaction of ever-more remote needs, and they develop the mental capacity to create goods not for immediate consumption but for the production of future goods, in other words, to create *capital goods*.

Whereas animals and humans can both hunt, humans differentiated themselves from animals by spending time developing tools for hunting. Some animals may occasionally use a tool in hunting another animal, but they have no capacity for owning these tools and maintaining them for long-term use. Only through a lower time preference can a human decide to take time away from hunting and dedicate that time to building a spear or fishing rod that cannot be eaten itself, but can allow him to hunt more proficiently. This is the essence of *investment*: as humans delay immediate gratification, they invest their time and resources in the production of capital goods which will make production more sophisticated or technologically advanced and extend it over a longer time-horizon. The only reason that an individual would choose to delay his gratification to engage in risky production over a longer period of time is that these longer processes will generate more output and superior goods. In other words, *investment raises the productivity of the producer.*

Economist Hans-Hermann Hoppe explains that once time preference drops enough to allow for any savings and capital or durable consumer-goods formation at all, the tendency is for time preference to drop even further as a "process of civilization" is initiated.[1]

The fisherman who builds a fishing rod is able to catch more fish per hour than the fisherman hunting with his bare hands. But the only way to build the fishing rod is to dedicate an initial amount of time to work that does not produce edible fish, but instead produces a fishing rod. This is an uncertain process, for the fishing rod might not work and the fisherman will have wasted his time to no avail. Not only does investment require delaying gratification, it also always carries with it a risk of failure, which means the investment will only be undertaken with an expectation of a reward. The lower an individual's time preference, the more likely he is to engage in investment, to delay gratification, and

[1] Hoppe, Hans-Hermann. *Democracy: The God That Failed.* Rutgers, NJ, Transaction Publishers, 2001, p. 6.

to accumulate capital. The more capital is accumulated, the higher the productivity of labor, and the longer the time horizon of production.

To understand the difference more vividly, contrast two hypothetical individuals who start off with nothing but their bare hands, and differing time preferences: Harry has a higher time preference than Linda. Harry chooses to only spend his time catching fish with his hands, needing about eight hours a day to catch enough fish to feed himself for the day. Linda, on the other hand, having a lower time preference, spends only six hours catching fish, making do with a smaller amount of fish every day, and spends the other two hours working on building a fishing rod. After a week has passed, Linda has succeeded in building a working fishing rod. In the second week, she can catch in eight hours double the quantity of fish which Harry catches. Linda's investment in the fishing rod could allow her to work for only four hours a day and eat the same amount of fish Harry eats, but because she has a lower time preference, she will not rest on her laurels. She will instead spend four hours catching as many fish as Harry catches in eight hours, and then spend another four hours engaged in further capital accumulation, building herself a fishing boat, for instance. A month later, Linda has a fishing rod and a boat that allows her to go deeper into the sea, to catch fish that Harry had never even seen. Linda's productivity is not just higher per hour; her fish are different from, and superior to, the ones Harry catches. She now only needs one hour of fishing to secure her food for a day, and so she dedicates the rest of her time to even more capital accumulation, building better and bigger fishing rods, nets, and boats, which in turn increases her productivity further and improves the quality of her life.

Should Harry and his descendants continue to work and consume with the same time preference, they will continue to live the same life he lived, with the same level of consumption and productivity. Should Linda and her descendants continue with the same lower time preference, they will continuously improve their quality of life over time, increasing their stock of capital and engaging in labor with ever-higher levels of productivity, in processes that take far longer to complete. The real-life equivalents of the descendants of Linda would today be the owners of *Annelies Ilena*, the world's largest fishing trawler. This formidable machine took decades to conceive, design, and build before it was completed in the year 2000, and it will continue to operate for decades to offer the lower-time-preference investors in it a return on the capital they provided to the building process many decades ago. The process of producing fish for Linda's descendants has become so long and sophisticated it takes decades to complete, whereas Harry's descendants still complete their process in a few hours every day. The difference, of course, is that Linda's descendants have vastly higher productivity than Harry's, and that's what makes engaging in the longer process worthwhile.

An important demonstration of the importance of time preference comes from the famous Stanford marshmallow experiment,[2] conducted in the late 1960s. Psychologist Walter Mischel would leave children in a room with a piece of marshmallow or a cookie, and tell the kids they were free to have it if they wanted, but that he will come back in 15 minutes, and if the children had not eaten the candy, he would offer them a second piece as a reward. In other words, the children had the choice between the immediate gratification of a piece of candy, or delaying gratification and receiving two pieces of candy. This is a simple way of testing children's time preference: students with a lower time preference were the ones who could wait for the second piece of candy, whereas the students with the higher time preference could not. Mischel followed up with the children decades later and found significant correlation between having a low time preference as measured with the marshmallow test and good academic achievement, high SAT score, low body mass index, and lack of addiction to drugs.

As an economics professor, I make sure to teach the marshmallow experiment in every course I teach, as I believe it is the single most important lesson economics can teach to individuals, and am astounded that university curricula in economics have almost entirely ignored this lesson, to the point that many academic economists have no familiarity with the term *time preference* altogether or its significance.

While microeconomics has focused on transactions between individuals, and macroeconomics on the role of government in the economy, the reality is that the most important economic decisions to any individual's well-being are the ones they conduct in their trade-offs with their future self. Every day, an individual will conduct a few

---

[2]Mischel, Walter, Ebbe Ebbesen, and Antonette Raskoff Zeiss. "Cognitive and Attentional Mechanisms in Delay of Gratification." *Journal of Personality and Social Psychology*, vol. 21, no. 2, 1972, pp. 204–18.

economic transactions with other people, but they will partake in a far larger number of transactions with their future self. The examples of these trades are infinite: deciding to save money rather than spend it; deciding to invest in acquiring skills for future employment rather than seeking immediate employment with low pay; buying a functional and affordable car rather than getting into debt for an expensive car; working overtime rather than going out to party with friends; or, my favorite example to use in class: deciding to study the course material every week of the semester rather than cramming the night before the final exam.

In each of these examples, there is nobody forcing the decision on the individual, and the prime beneficiary or loser from the consequences of these choices is the individual himself. The main factor determining a man's choices in life is his time preference. While people's time preference and self-control will vary from one situation to the other, in general, a strong correlation can be found across all aspects of decision making. The sobering reality to keep in mind is that a man's lot in life will be largely determined by these trades between him and his future self. As much as he'd like to blame others for his failures, or credit others with his success, the infinite trades he took with himself are likely to be more significant than any outside circumstances or conditions. No matter how circumstances conspire against the man with a low time preference, he will probably find a way to keep prioritizing his future self until he achieves his objectives. And no matter how much fortune favors the man with a high time preference, he will find a way to continue sabotaging and shortchanging his future self. The many stories of people who have triumphed against all odds and unfavorable circumstances stand in stark contrast to the stories of people blessed with skills and talent that rewarded them handsomely, who nonetheless managed to waste all that talent and achieve no lasting good for themselves. Many professional athletes and entertainers, gifted with talents that earn them large sums of money, nevertheless die penniless as their high time preference gets the better of them. On the other hand, many ordinary people with no special talents work diligently and save and invest for a lifetime to achieve financial security and bequeath their children a life better than the one they inherited.

It is only through the lowering of time preference that individuals begin to appreciate investing in the long run and start prioritizing future outcomes. A society in which individuals bequeath their children more than what they received from their parents is a civilized society: it is a place where life is improving, and people live with a purpose of making the next generation's lives better. As society's capital levels continue to increase, productivity increases and, along with it, quality of life. The security of their basic needs assured, and the dangers of the environment averted, people turn their attention toward more profound aspects of life than material well-being and the drudgery of work. They cultivate families and social ties; undertake cultural, artistic, and literary projects; and seek to offer lasting contributions to their community and the world. Civilization is not about more capital accumulation per se; rather, it is about what capital accumulation allows humans to achieve, the flourishing and freedom to seek higher meaning in life when their base needs are met and most pressing dangers averted.

There are many factors that come into play in determining the time preference of individuals.[3] Security of people in their person and property is arguably one of the most important. Individuals who live in areas of conflict and crime will have a significant chance of losing their life and are thus likely to more highly discount the future, resulting in a higher time preference than those who live in peaceful societies. Security of property is another major factor influencing individuals' time preference: societies where governments or thieves are likely to expropriate individuals' property capriciously would have higher time preference, as such actions would drive individuals to prioritize spending their resources on immediate gratification rather than investing them in property which could be appropriated at any time. Tax rates will also adversely affect time preference: the higher the taxes, the less of their income that individuals are allowed to keep; this would lead to individuals working less at the margin and saving less for their future, because the burden of taxes is more likely to reduce savings than consumption, particularly for those with a low income, most of which is needed for basic survival.

The factor affecting time preference that is most relevant to our discussion, however, is the expected future value of money. In a free market

---

[3]The reader is referred to the first chapter of Hoppe's *Democracy: The God That Failed* for an excellent discussion of these factors. More foundational and technical discussions can be found in Chapter 6 of Murray Rothbard's *Man, Economy, and State*, Chapters 18 and 19 in Mises' *Human Action*, and Eugen von Böhm-Bawerk's *Capital and Interest*.

where people are free to choose their money, they will choose the form of money most likely to hold its value over time. The better the money is at holding its value, the more it incentivizes people to delay consumption and instead dedicate resources for production in the future, leading to capital accumulation and improvement of living standards, while also engendering in people a low time preference in other, non-economic aspects of their life. When economic decision making is geared toward the future, it is natural that all manner of decisions are geared toward the future as well. People become more peaceful and cooperative, understanding that cooperation is a far more rewarding long-term strategy than any short-term gains from conflict. People develop a strong sense of morality, prioritizing the moral choices that will cause the best long-term outcomes for them and their children. A person who thinks of the long run is less likely to cheat, lie, or steal, because the reward for such activities may be positive in the short run, but can be devastatingly negative in the long run.

The reduction in the purchasing power of money is similar to a form of taxation or expropriation, reducing the real value of one's money even while the nominal value is constant. In modern economies government-issued money is inextricably linked to artificially lower interest rates, which is a desirable goal for modern economists because it promotes borrowing and investing. But the effect of this manipulation of the price of capital is to artificially reduce the interest rate that accrues to savers and investors, as well as the one paid by borrowers. The natural implication of this process is to reduce savings and increase borrowing. At the margin, individuals will consume more of their income and borrow more against the future. This will not just have implications on their time preference in financial decisions; it will likely reflect on everything in their lives.

The move from money that holds its value or appreciates to money that loses its value is very significant in the long run: society saves less, accumulates less capital, and possibly begins to consume its capital; worker productivity stays constant or declines, resulting in the stagnation of real wages, even if nominal wages can be made to increase through the magical power of printing ever more depreciating pieces of paper money. As people start spending more and saving less, they become more present-oriented in all their decision making, resulting in moral failings and a likelihood to engage in conflict and destructive and self-destructive behavior.

This helps explain why civilizations prosper under a sound monetary system, but disintegrate when their monetary systems are debased, as was the case with the Romans, the Byzantines, and modern European societies. The contrast between the nineteenth and twentieth centuries can be understood in the context of the move away from sound money and all the attendant problems that creates.

Monetary Inflation

The simple reality, demonstrated throughout history, is that any person who finds a way to create the monetary medium will try to do it. The temptation to engage in this is too strong, but the creation of the monetary medium is not an activity that is productive to society, as any supply of money is sufficient for any economy of any size. The more that a monetary medium restrains this drive for its creation, the better it is as a medium of exchange and stable store of value. Unlike all other goods, money's functions as a medium of exchange, store of value, and unit of account are completely orthogonal to its quantity. What matters in money is its purchasing power, not its quantity, and as such, any quantity of money is enough to fulfil the monetary functions, as long as it is divisible and groupable enough to satisfy holders' transaction and storage needs. Any quantity of economic transactions could be supported by a money supply of any size as long as the units are divisible enough.

A theoretically ideal money would be one whose supply is fixed, meaning nobody could produce more of it. The only noncriminal way to acquire money in such a society would be to produce something of value to others and exchange it with them for money. As everyone seeks to acquire more money, everyone works more and produces more, leading to improving material well-being for everyone, which in turn allows people to accumulate more capital and increase their productivity. Such a money would also work perfectly well as a store of value, by preventing others from increasing the money supply; the wealth stored into it would not depreciate over time, incentivizing people to save and allowing them to think more of the future. With growing wealth and productivity and an increased ability to focus on the future, people begin to reduce their time preference and can focus on improving non-material aspects of their life, including spiritual, social, and cultural endeavors.

It had, however, proved impossible to come up with a form of money of which more cannot be created. Whatever gets chosen as a medium of exchange will appreciate in value and lead to more people trying to produce more of it. The best form of money in history was the one that would cause the new supply of money to be the least significant compared to the existing stockpiles, and thus make its creation not a good source of profit. Seeing as gold is indestructible, it is the one metal whose stockpiles have only been growing since the first human mined it. Seeing as this mining has been going on for thousands of years, and alchemy has yet to prove large-scale commercial viability, new mining supply continues to be a reliably tiny fraction of existing stockpiles.

This property is why gold has been synonymous with sound money: it is money whose supply is guaranteed, thanks to the ironclad rules of physics and chemistry, to never be significantly increased. Try as they might, humans have for centuries failed to produce a form of money more sound than gold, and that is why it has been the prime monetary instrument used by most human civilizations throughout history. Even as the world has transitioned to government money as a store of value, medium of exchange, and unit of account, governments themselves continue to hold a significant percentage of their reserves in gold, constituting a significant percentage of total gold supply.

Keynes complained about goldmining being a wasteful activity that consumed a lot of resources while adding nothing to real wealth. While his critique does contain a kernel of truth, in the sense that increasing the supply of the monetary medium does not increase the wealth of the society using it, he misses the point that gold's monetary role is a result of it being the metal likely to attract the *least* human and capital resources toward its mining and prospecting, compared to all others. Because the supply of gold can only be increased by very small quantities, even with price spikes, and as gold is very rare and difficult to find, mining monetary gold would be less profitable than mining any other metal assuming a monetary role, leading to the least amount of human time and resources going to mining it. Were any other metal used as the monetary medium, whenever society's time preference drops and more people purchase the metal for savings, raising its price, there would be a significant opportunity for profit in producing more of the metal. Because the metal is perishable, the new production will always be far larger (relative to gold) as a percentage of existing stockpiles, as in the copper example above, bringing the price down and devaluing the savings of the holders. In such a society, savings would be effectively stolen from savers to reward people who engage in mining metals at quantities far beyond their economic use. Little saving and useful production would take place in such a society, impoverishment would ensue from the obsession with producing monetary media, and the society would be ripe for being overtaken and conquered by more productive societies whose individuals have better things to do than produce more monetary media.

The reality of monetary competition constantly has disadvantaged individuals and societies that invest their savings in metals other than gold while rewarding those who invest their savings in gold, because it cannot be inflated easily and because it forces people to direct their energies away from producing a monetary good and toward producing more useful goods and services. This helps explain why Arab polymath Ibn Khaldun referred to gold prospecting and mining as the least respectable of professions, after kidnapping for ransom.[4] The folly of Keynes condemning gold as money because its mining is wasteful is that it is the *least* wasteful of all potential metals to use as money. But the folly is doubly compounded by Keynes's "solution" to this shortcoming of gold being to propose a fiat monetary standard which has ended up dedicating far more human time, labor, and resources toward the management of the issuance of the money supply and the profiting from it. Never in the history of gold as a monetary medium did it employ as many miners and workers as today's central banks and all the associated banks and businesses profiting from having close access to the monetary printing presses, as will be discussed in Chapter 7.

When new supply is insignificant compared to existing supply, the market value of a form of money is determined through people's willingness to hold money and their desire to spend it. Such factors will vary significantly with time for each individual, as individuals' personal circumstances go from periods where they prioritize holding a lot of

---

[4]Ibn Khaldun, Abd Alrahman. *Al-Muqaddima*. 1377.

money to periods of holding less. But in the aggregate, they will vary slightly for society as a whole, because money is the market good with the least diminishing *marginal utility*. One of the fundamental laws of economics is the law of diminishing marginal utility, which means that acquiring more of any good reduces the marginal utility of each extra unit. Money, which is held not for its own sake, but for the sake of being exchanged with other goods, will have its utility diminish slower than any other good, because it can always be exchanged for any other good. As an individual's holdings of houses, cars, TVs, apples, or diamonds increases, the marginal valuation they put on each extra unit decreases, leading to a decreasing desire to accumulate more of each. But more money is not like any of these goods, because as more of it is held, the holder can simply exchange the money for more of the next good they value the most. The marginal utility of money does in fact decline, as evidenced by the fact that an extra dollar of income means a lot more to a person whose daily income is $1 than one whose daily income is $1,000. But money's marginal utility declines far slower than any other good, because it declines along with the utility of wanting any good, not one particular good.

The slowly declining marginal utility of holding money means demand for money at the margin will not vary significantly. Combining this with an almost constant supply results in a relatively stable market value for money in terms of goods and services. This means money is unlikely to appreciate or depreciate significantly, making it a lousy long-term investment but a good store of value. An investment would be expected to have a significant appreciation potential, but also carry a significant risk of loss or depreciation. Investment is a reward for taking risk, but sound money, having the least risk, offers no reward.

In the aggregate, demand for money will likely vary only with variance in time preference. As people develop a lower time preference overall, more people are likely to want to hold money, causing a rise in its market value compared to other goods and services, further rewarding its holders. A society that develops a higher time preference, on the other hand, would tend to decrease its holdings of money, slightly dropping its market value at the margin. In either case, holding money would remain the least risky and rewarding asset overall, and that in essence is the root cause for demand for it.

This analysis helps explain the remarkable ability of gold to hold its value over years, decades, and centuries. Observing prices of agricultural commodities in the Roman empire in terms of grams of gold shows they bear remarkable similarity to prices today. Examining Diocletian's edict[5] of prices from 301 AD and converting gold prices to their modern-day U.S. dollar equivalent, we find that a pound of beef cost around $4.50, while a pint of beer cost around $2, a pint of wine around $13 for high quality wine and $9 for lower quality, and a pint of olive oil cost around $20. Comparisons of various data for salaries of certain professions shows similar patterns, but these individual data points, while indicative, cannot be taken as a definitive settlement of the question.

Roy Jastram has produced a systematic study of the purchasing power of gold over the longest consistent datasets available.[6] Observing English data from 1560 to 1976 to analyze the change in gold's purchasing power in terms of commodities, Jastram finds gold dropping in purchasing power during the first 140 years, but then remaining relatively stable from 1700 to 1914, when Britain went off the gold standard. For more than two centuries during which Britain primarily used gold as money, its purchasing power remained relatively constant, as did the price of wholesale commodities. After Britain effectively went off the gold standard in the wake of World War I, the purchasing power of gold increased, as did the index of wholesale prices. (See Figure 8.[7])

It's important to understand that for a monetary medium to remain perfectly constant in value is not even theoretically possible or determinable. Goods and services which money purchases will change over time as new technologies introduce new goods that replace old ones, and as the conditions of supply and demand of different goods will vary over time. One of the prime functions of the monetary unit is to serve as the unit of measure for economic goods, whose value is constantly changing. It is thus not possible to satisfactorily measure the price of a monetary good precisely, although over long time horizons, studies similar to Jastram's can be indicative of an overall trend for a medium of

---

[5]Kent, R. "The Edict of Diocletian Fixing Maximum Prices." *University of Pennsylvania Law Review*, vol. 69, 1920, p. 35.

[6]Jastram, Roy. *The Golden Constant: The English and American Experience 1560–2007*. Cheltenham, UK, Edward Elgar, 2009.

[7] *Source*: Jastram, *The Golden Constant*.

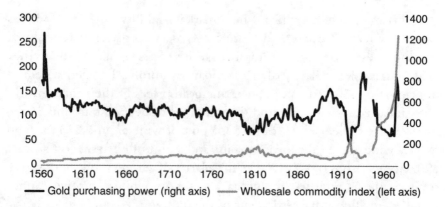

Figure 8 Purchasing power of gold and wholesale commodity index in England, 1560–1976.

exchange to hold its value, particularly when compared to other forms of money.

More recent data from the United States, focused on the last two centuries, which witnessed faster economic growth than the period covered in Jastram's data, shows that gold has even increased in value in terms of commodities, whose prices rose dramatically in terms of U.S. dollars. This is perfectly consistent with gold being the hardest money available. It is easier to keep increasing the supply of all commodities than gold, and so over time, all these other commodities will become relatively more abundant than gold, causing a rise in gold's purchasing power over time. As can be seen in Figure 9,[8] the U.S. dollar was also gaining value against commodities whenever it was tied to gold, but lost value significantly when its connection to gold was severed, as was the case during the U.S. Civil War and the printing of greenbacks, and in the period after the 1934 devaluation of the dollar and confiscation of citizens' gold.

The period between 1931 and 1971 was one in which money was nominally linked to gold, but only through various government arrangements that allowed for the exchange of gold for paper money under arcane conditions. This period witnessed instability in the value

---

[8] *Source*: Federal Reserve Economic Data. Historical Statistics of the United States, Series E 52-63 and E 23-3. fred.stlouisfed.org/.

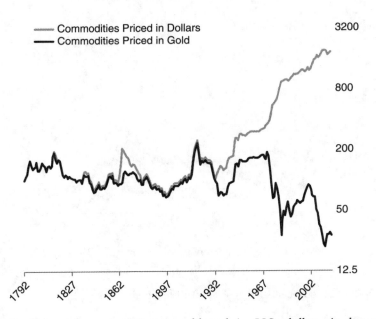

Figure 9 Price of commodities in gold and in U.S. dollars, in log scale, 1792–2016.

of both government money and gold along with the policy changes. For a comparison between gold and government money, it is more useful to look at the period from 1971 to the modern day, where free-floating national currencies have traded in markets with central banks tasked with guaranteeing their purchasing power. (See Figure 10.[9])

Even the best-performing and most stable government forms of money have witnessed their value decimated compared to gold, with their value currently running at around 2–3% of their value in 1971 when they were all delinked from gold. This does not represent a rise in the market value of gold, but rather a drop in the value of fiat currencies. When comparing prices of goods and services to the value of government money and gold, we find a significant rise in their prices as expressed in government money, but relative stability in their prices in gold. The price of a barrel of oil, for instance, which is one of the key commodities of modern industrial society, has been relatively

[9] *Source*: US Federal Reserve Statistics. fred.stlouisfed.org. Gold Price Data, World Gold Council. www.gold.org.

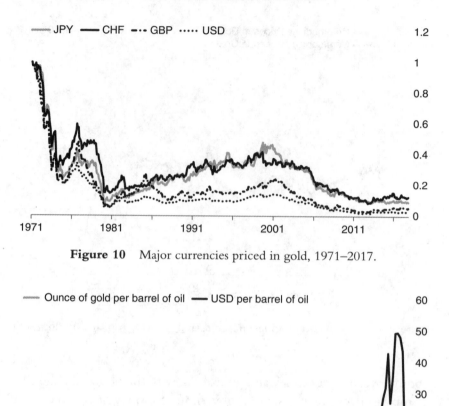

Figure 10   Major currencies priced in gold, 1971–2017.

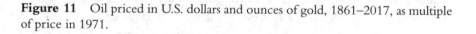

Figure 11   Oil priced in U.S. dollars and ounces of gold, 1861–2017, as multiple of price in 1971.

constant in terms of gold since 1971, while increasing by several orders of magnitude in terms of government money. (See Figure 11.[10])

Hard money, whose supply cannot be expanded easily, will likely be more stable in value than easy money because its supply is largely

---

[10] *Source*: BP Statistical Review & World Gold Council. www.gold.org.

inelastic while societal demand for money varies little over time as time preference varies. Easy money, on the other hand, because of the ability of its producers to vary its quantity drastically, will engender widely fluctuating demand from holders as the quantity varies and its reliability as a store of value falls and rises.

Relative stability of value is not just important to preserve the purchasing power of holders' savings, it is arguably more important for preserving the integrity of the monetary unit as a unit of account. When money is predictably stable in value due to the small variation in supply and demand, it can act as a reliable signal for changes in prices of other goods and services, as was the case with gold.

In the case of government money, on the other hand, the money supply increases through the expansion of the supply by the central bank and commercial banks, and contracts through deflationary recessions and bankruptcies, while the demand for money can vary even more unpredictably depending on people's expectations of the value of the money and the policies of the central bank. This highly volatile combination results in government money being unpredictable in value over the long term. Central banks' mission of ensuring price stability has them constantly managing the supply of money through their various tools to ensure price stability, making many major currencies appear less volatile in the short run compared to gold. But in the long run, the constant increase in the supply of government money compared to gold's steady and slow increase makes gold's value more predictable.

Sound money, chosen on a free market precisely for its likelihood to hold value over time, will naturally have a better stability than unsound money whose use is enforced through government coercion. Had government money been a superior unit of account and store of value, it would not need government legal tender laws to enforce it, nor would governments worldwide have had to confiscate large quantities of gold and continue to hold them in their central bank reserves. The fact that central banks continue to hold onto their gold, and have even started increasing their reserves, testifies to the confidence they have in their own currencies in the long term, and in the inescapable monetary role of gold as the value of paper currencies continues to plumb new depths.

Saving and Capital Accumulation

One of the key problems caused by a currency whose value is diminishing is that it negatively incentivizes saving for the future. Time preference is universally positive: given the choice between the same good today or in the future, any sane person would prefer to have it today. Only by increasing the return in the future will people consider delaying gratification. Sound money is money that gains in value slightly over time, meaning that holding onto it is likely to offer an increase in purchasing power. Unsound money, being controlled by central banks whose express mission is to keep inflation positive, will offer little incentive for holders to keep it, as they become more likely to spend it or to borrow it.

When it comes to investment, sound money creates an economic environment where any positive rate of return will be favorable to the investor, as the monetary unit is likely to hold onto its value, if not appreciate, thus strengthening the incentive to invest. With unsound money, on the other hand, only returns that are higher than the rate of depreciation of the currency will be positive in real terms, creating incentives for high-return but high-risk investment and spending. Further, as increases in the money supply effectively mean low interest rates, the incentive to save and invest is diminished while the incentive to borrow increases.

The track record of the 46-year experiment with unsound money bears out this conclusion. Savings rates have been declining across the developed countries, dropping to very low levels, while personal, municipal, and national debts have increased to levels which would have seemed unimaginable in the past. (See Figure 12.[11])

Only Switzerland, which remained on an official gold standard until 1936, and continued to back its currency with large reserves of gold until the early 1990s, has continued to have a high savings rate, standing as the last bastion of low-time-preference Western civilization with a savings rate in the double digits, as every other Western economy has plummeted into the single digits and even to negative saving rates in some cases. The average savings rate of the seven largest advanced

---

[11] *Source*: Organization for Economic Co-operation and Development. stats.oecd.org/.

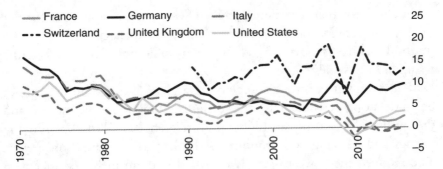

Figure 12 National savings rates in major economies, 1970–2016, %.

economies[12] was 12.66% in 1970, but has dropped to 3.39% in 2015, a fall of almost three-quarters.

While savings rates have plummeted across the western world, indebtedness continues to rise. The average household in the West is indebted by more than 100% of its annual income, while the total debt burden of the various levels of government and households exceeds GDP by multiples, with significant consequences. Such numbers have become normalized as Keynesian economists assure citizens that debt is good for growth and that saving would result in recessions. One of the most mendacious fantasies that pervades Keynesian economic thought is the idea that the national debt "does not matter, since we owe it to ourselves." Only a high-time-preference disciple of Keynes could fail to understand that this "ourselves" is not one homogeneous blob but is differentiated into several generations—namely, the current ones which consume recklessly at the expense of future ones. To make matters worse, this phrase is usually followed by emotional blackmail along the lines of "we would be short-changing ourselves if we didn't borrow to invest for our future."

Many pretend this is a miraculous modern discovery from Keynes's brilliant insight that spending is all that matters, and that by ensuring spending remains high, debts can continue to grow indefinitely and savings can be eliminated. In reality, there is nothing new in this policy, which was employed by the decadent emperors of Rome during its

---

[12]These are the United States, Japan, Germany, U.K., France, Italy, and Canada.

decline, except that it is being applied with government-issued paper money. Indeed, paper money allows it to be managed a little more smoothly, and less obviously, than the metallic coins of old. But the results are the same.

The twentieth century's binge on conspicuous consumption cannot be understood separately from the destruction of sound money and the outbreak of Keynesian high-time-preference thinking, in vilifying savings and deifying consumption as the key to economic prosperity. The reduced incentive to save is mirrored with an increased incentive to spend, and with interest rates regularly manipulated downwards and banks able to issue more credit than ever, lending stopped being restricted to investment, but has moved on to consumption. Credit cards and consumer loans allow individuals to borrow for the sake of consumption without even the pretense of performing investment in the future. It is an ironic sign of the depth of modern-day economic ignorance fomented by Keynesian economics that capitalism—an economic system based on *capital accumulation* from saving—is blamed for unleashing conspicuous consumption—the exact opposite of capital accumulation. Capitalism is what happens when people drop their time preference, defer immediate gratification, and invest in the future. Debt-fueled mass consumption is as much a normal part of capitalism as asphyxiation is a normal part of respiration.

This also helps explain one of the key Keynesian misunderstandings of economics, which considers that delaying current consumption by saving will put workers out of work and cause economic production to stall. Keynes viewed the level of spending at any point in time as being the most important determinant of the state of the economy because, having studied no economics, he had no understanding of capital theory and how employment does not only have to be in final goods, but can also be in the production of capital goods which will only produce final goods in the future. And having lived off of his family's considerable fortune without having to work real jobs, Keynes had no appreciation of saving or capital accumulation and their essential role in economic growth. Hence, Keynes would observe a recession concurrently with a fall in consumer spending and increase in saving, and assume the causality runs from increased savings to decreased consumption to recession. Had he had the temperament to study capital theory, he would have understood that the decreased consumption was a natural reaction to the business cycle, which was in turn caused by the expansion of the money supply, as will be discussed in Chapter 6. He would also have understood that the only cause of economic growth in the first place is delayed gratification, saving, and investment, which extend the length of the production cycle and increase the productivity of the methods of production, leading to better standards of living. He would have realized the only reason he was born into a rich family in a rich society was that his ancestors had spent centuries accumulating capital, deferring gratification and investing in the future. But, like the Roman emperors during the decay of the empire, he could never understand the work and sacrifice needed to build his affluence and believed instead that high consumption is the cause of prosperity rather than its consequence.

Debt is the opposite of saving. If saving creates the possibility of capital accumulation and civilizational advance, debt is what can reverse it, through the reduction in capital stocks across generations, reduced productivity, and a decline in living standards. Whether it is housing debt, Social Security obligations, or government debt that will require ever-higher taxes and debt monetization to refinance, the current generations may be the first in the western world since the demise of the Roman Empire (or, at least, the Industrial Revolution) to come into the world with less capital than their parents. Rather than witness their savings accumulate and raise the capital stock, this generation has to work to pay off the growing interest on its debt, working harder to fund entitlement programs they will barely get to enjoy while paying higher taxes and barely being able to save for their old age.

This move from sound money to depreciating money has led to several generations of accumulated wealth being squandered on conspicuous consumption within a generation or two, making indebtedness the new method for funding major expenses. Whereas 100 years ago most people would pay for their house, education, or marriage from their own labor or accumulated savings, such a notion seems ridiculous to people today. Even the wealthy will not live within their means and will instead use their wealth to allow them larger loans to finance large purchases. This sort of arrangement can last for a while, but its lasting cannot be mistaken for sustainability, as it is no more than the systematic consumption of the capital stock of society—the eating of the seed crop.

When money was nationalized, it was placed under the command of politicians who operate over short time-horizons of a few years, trying their best to get reelected. It was only natural that such a process would lead to short-term decision making where politicians abuse the currency to fund their reelection campaigns at the expense of future generations. As H. L. Mencken put it: "Every election is an advanced auction on stolen goods."[13] In a society where money is free and sound, individuals have to make decisions with their capital that affect their families in the long run. While it is likely that some would make irresponsible decisions that hurt their offspring, those who wanted to make responsible decisions had the choice to do so. With nationalized money, that became an increasingly harder choice to make, as central governmental control of money supply inevitably destroys incentives to save while increasing the incentive to borrow. No matter how prudent a person, his children will still witness their savings lose value and have to pay taxes to cover for the inflationary largesse of their government.

As the reduction in intergenerational inheritance has reduced the strength of the family as a unit, government's unlimited checkbook has increased its ability to direct and shape the lives of people, allowing it an increasingly important role to play in more aspects of individuals' lives. The family's ability to finance the individual has been eclipsed by the state's largesse, resulting in a declining incentives for maintaining a family.

In a traditional society, individuals are aware that they will need children to support them in the future, and so will spend their healthy young years starting a family and investing in giving their children the best life possible. But if long-term investment in general is disincentivized, if saving is likely to be counterproductive as money depreciates, this investment becomes less profitable. Further, as politicians sell people the lie that eternal welfare and retirement benefits are possible through the magic of the monetary printing press, the investment in a family becomes less and less valuable. Over time, the incentive to start a family

---

[13]Mencken, H. L. *A Carnival of Buncombe*, edited by Malcolm Moos, Baltimore, MD, Johns Hopkins Press, 1956, p. 325.

declines and more and more people end up leading single lives. More marriages are likely to break down as partners are less likely to put in the necessary emotional, moral, and financial investment to make them work, while marriages that do survive will likely produce fewer children. The well-known phenomenon of the modern breakdown of the family cannot be understood without recognizing the role of unsound money allowing the state to appropriate many of the essential roles that the family has played for millennia, and reducing the incentive of all members of a family to invest in long-term familial relations.

Substituting the family with government largesse has arguably been a losing trade for individuals who have partaken in it. Several studies show that life satisfaction depends to a large degree on establishing intimate long-term familial bonds with a partner and children.[14] Many studies also show that rates of depression and psychological diseases are rising over time as the family breaks down, particularly for women.[15] Cases of depression and psychological disorders very frequently have family breakdown as a leading cause.

It is no coincidence that the breakdown of the family has come about through the implementation of the economic teachings of a man who never had any interest in the long term. A son of a rich family that had accumulated significant capital over generations, Keynes was a libertine hedonist who wasted most of his adult life engaging in sexual relationships with children, including traveling around the Mediterranean to visit children's brothels.[16] Whereas Victorian Britain was a low-time-preference society with a strong sense of morality, low interpersonal conflict, and stable families, Keynes was part of a generation that rose against these traditions and viewed them as a repressive institution to be brought down. It is impossible to understand the economics

---

[14] Vaillant, George. *Triumphs of Experience: The Men of the Harvard Grant Study*. Cambridge, MA, Harvard University Press, 2012.

[15] Stevenson, Betsy, and Justin Wolfers. "The Paradox of Declining Female Happiness." *American Economic Journal: Economic Policy*, vol. 1, no. 2, 2009, pp. 190–225.

[16] See Michael Holroyd, *Lytton Strachey: The New Biography*, vol. I, p. 80, in which a letter sent by Keynes to his friend Lytton Strachey in the Bloomsbury set advised them to visit Tunis "where bed and boy were not expensive." See also David Felix, *Keynes: A Critical Life*, p. 112, which quotes a letter from Keynes in which he informs a friend, "I'm leaving for Egypt . . . I just learned that 'bed and boy' is prepared." In another letter, he recommended Strachey go to Tunis and Sicily "if you want to go to where the naked boys dance."

of Keynes without understanding the kind of morality he wanted to see in a society he increasingly believed he could shape according to his will.

Innovations: "Zero to One" versus "One to Many"

The impact of sound money on time preference and future orientation can be seen in more than just the level of savings, but also in the type of projects in which a society invests. Under a sound money regime, similar to what the world had in the late nineteenth century, individuals are far more likely to engage in long-term investments and to have large amounts of capital available to finance the sort of projects that will require a long time to pay off. As a result, some of the most important innovations in human history were born in the golden era at the end of the nineteenth century.

In their seminal work, *The History of Science and Technology*, Bunch and Hellemans compile a list of the 8,583 most important innovations and inventions in the history of science and technology. Physicist Jonathan Huebner[17] analyzed all these events along with the years in which they happened and global population at that year, and measured the rate of occurrence of these events per year per capita since the Dark Ages. Huebner found that while the total number of innovations rose in the twentieth century, the number of innovations per capita peaked in the nineteenth century.

A closer look at the innovations of the pre-1914 world lends support to Huebner's data. It is no exaggeration to say that our modern world was invented in the gold standard years preceding World War I. The twentieth century was the century that refined, improved, optimized, economized, and popularized the inventions of the nineteenth century. The wonders of the twentieth century's improvements make it easy to forget that the actual inventions—the transformative world-changing innovations—almost all came in the golden era.

In his popular book, *Zero to One*, Peter Thiel discusses the impact of the visionaries who create a new world by producing the first

---

[17] Huebner, Jonathan. "A Possible Declining Trend for Worldwide Innovation." *Technological Forecasting and Social Change*, vol. 72, no. 8, Elsevier, Oct. 2005, pp. 980–6.

successful example of a new technology. The move from having "zero to one" successful example of a technology, as he terms it, is the hardest and most significant step in an invention, whereas the move from "one to many" is a matter of scaling, marketing, and optimization. Those of us who are enamored with the concept of progress might find it hard to swallow the fact that the world of sound money pre-1914 was the world of zero to one, whereas the post-1914 world of government-produced money is the world of moving from one to many. There is nothing wrong with the move from one to many, but it certainly gives us plenty of food for thought to consider why we do not have many more zero-to-one transformations under our modern monetary system.

The majority of the technology we use in our modern life was invented in the nineteenth century, under the gold standard, financed with the ever-growing stock of capital accumulated by savers storing their wealth in a sound money and store of value which did not depreciate quickly. A summary of some of the most important innovations of the period is provided here:

- Hot and cold running water, indoor toilets, widespread indoor plumbing, waste-water treatment, central heating:

    These inventions, taken for granted today by anyone living in a civilized society, are the difference between life and death for most of us. They have been the main factor in the elimination of most infectious diseases across the globe, and allowed for the growth of urban areas without the ever-present scourge of diseases.

- Electricity, internal combustion engine, mass production:

    Our modern industrial society was built around the growth in utilization of hydrocarbon energy, without which none of the trappings of modern civilization would be possible. These foundational technologies of energy and industry were invented in the nineteenth century.

- Automobile, airplane, city subway, electric elevator:

    We have *la belle époque* to thank for our cities' streets not being littered with horse manure, and for our ability to travel around the world. The automobile was invented by Karl Benz in 1885, the airplane by the Wright brothers in 1906, the subway by Charles Pearson in 1843, and the electric elevator by Elisha Otis in 1852.

- Heart surgery; organ transplant; appendectomy; baby incubator; radiation therapy; anesthetics, aspirin, blood types and blood transfusions, vitamins, electrocardiograph, stethoscope:

  Surgery and modern medicine owe their most significant advances to *la belle époque* as well. The introduction of modern sanitation and reliable hydrocarbon energy allowed doctors to transform the way they cared for their patients after centuries of largely counterproductive measures.

- Petroleum-derived chemicals, stainless steel, nitrogen-based fertilizers:

  The industrial substances and materials which make our modern life possible derive from the transformative innovations of *la belle époque*, which allowed for mass industrialization, as well as mass agriculture. Plastics, and everything that comes from them, are a product of the utilization of petroleum-derived chemicals.

- Telephone, wireless telegraphy, voice recording, color photography, movies:

  While we like to think of our modern era as being the era of mass telecommunication, in reality, most of what we have achieved in the twentieth century was to improve on the innovations of the nineteenth. The first computer was the Babbage computer, designed in 1833 by Charles Babbage, but completed by his son Henry in 1888. It might be an exaggeration to say that the Internet and all it contains are bells and whistles added onto the invention of the telegraph in 1843, but it does contain a kernel of truth. It was the telegraph which fundamentally transformed human society by allowing for communication without the need for the physical transport of letters or messengers. That was telecommunication's zero-to-one moment, and everything that followed, for all its wonders, has been a one-to-many improvement.

Artistic Flourishing

The contributions of sound money to human flourishing are not restricted to scientific and technological advance; they can also be vividly seen in the art world. It is no coincidence that Florentine and

Venetian artists were the leaders of the Renaissance, as these were the two cities which led Europe in the adoption of sound money. The Baroque, Neoclassical, Romantic, Realistic, and post-Impressionistic schools were all financed by wealthy patrons holding sound money, with a very low time preference and the patience to wait for years, or even decades, for the completion of masterpieces meant to survive for centuries. The astonishing domes of Europe's churches, built and decorated over decades of inspired meticulous work by incomparable architects and artists like Filippo Brunelleschi and Michelangelo, were all financed with sound money by patrons with very low time preference. The only way to impress these patrons was to build artwork that would last long enough to immortalize their names as the owners of great collections and patrons of great artists. This is why Florence's Medicis are perhaps better remembered for their patronage of the arts than for their innovations in banking and finance, though the latter may be far more consequential.

Similarly, the musical works of Bach, Mozart, Beethoven, and the composers of the Renaissance, Classical, and Romantic eras put to shame today's animalistic noises recorded in batches of a few minutes, churned out by the ton by studios profiting from selling to man the titillation of his basest instincts. Whereas the music of the golden era spoke to man's soul and awakened him to think of higher callings than the mundane grind of daily life, today's musical noises speak to man's most base animalistic instincts, distracting him from the realities of life by inviting him to indulge in immediate sensory pleasures with no concern for long-term consequences or anything more profound. It was hard money that financed Bach's *Brandenburg Concertos* while easy money financed Miley Cyrus's twerks.

In times of sound money and low time preference, artists worked on perfecting their craft so they could produce valuable works in the long run. They spent years learning the intricate details and techniques of their work, perfecting it and excelling in developing it beyond the capabilities of others, to the astonishment of their patrons and the general public. Nobody stood a chance of being called an artist without years of hard work on developing their craft. Artists did not condescendingly lecture the public on what art is and why their lazy productions that took a day to make are profound. Bach never claimed to be a genius or spoke at length about how his music was better than that of others; he instead spent his life perfecting his craft. Michelangelo spent four years hanging from the ceiling of the Sistine Chapel working for most of the day with little food in order to paint his masterpiece. He even wrote a poem to describe the ordeal:[18]

> I've grown a goitre by dwelling in this den—
> As cats from stagnant streams in Lombardy,
> Or in what other land they hap to be—
> Which drives the belly close beneath the chin:
> My beard turns up to heaven; my nape falls in,
> Fixed on my spine: my breast-bone visibly
> Grows like a harp: a rich embroidery
> Bedews my face from brush-drops thick and thin.
> My loins into my paunch like levers grind:
> My buttock like a crupper bears my weight;
> My feet unguided wander to and fro;
> In front my skin grows loose and long; behind,
> By bending it becomes more taut and strait;
> Crosswise I strain me like a Syrian bow:
> Whence false and quaint, I know,
> Must be the fruit of squinting brain and eye;
> For ill can aim the gun that bends awry.
> Come then, Giovanni, try
> To succour my dead pictures and my fame;
> Since foul I fare and painting is my shame.

Only with such meticulous and dedicated effort over many decades did these geniuses succeed in producing these masterpieces, immortalizing their names as the masters of their craft. In the era of unsound money, no artist has the low time preference to work as hard or as long as Michelangelo or Bach to learn their craft properly or spend any significant amount of time perfecting it. A stroll through a modern art gallery shows artistic works whose production requires no more effort or talent than can be mustered by a bored 6-year-old. Modern artists have replaced

---

[18]Symonds, John Addington. *The Sonnets of Michael Angelo Buonarroti*. London, Smith Elder & Co., 1904.

craft and long hours of practice with pretentiousness, shock value, indignation, and existential angst as ways to cow audiences into appreciating their art, and often added some pretense to political ideals, usually of the puerile Marxist variety, to pretend-play profundity. To the extent that anything good can be said about modern "art," it is that it is clever, in the manner of a prank or practical joke. There is nothing beautiful or admirable about the output or the process of most modern art, because it was produced in a matter of hours by lazy talentless hacks who never bothered to practice their craft. Only cheap pretentiousness, obscenity, and shock value attract attention to the naked emperor of modern art, and only long pretentious diatribes shaming others for not understanding the work give it value.

As government money has replaced sound money, patrons with low time preference and refined tastes have been replaced by government bureaucrats with political agendas as crude as their artistic taste. Naturally, then, neither beauty nor longevity matters anymore, replaced with political prattling and the ability to impress bureaucrats who control the major funding sources to the large galleries and museums, which have become a government-protected monopoly on artistic taste and standards for artistic education. Free competition between artists and donors is now replaced with central planning by unaccountable bureaucrats, with predictably disastrous results. In free markets, the winners are always the ones who provide the goods deemed best by the public. When government is in charge of deciding winners and losers, the sort of people who have nothing better to do with their life than work as government bureaucrats are the arbiters of taste and beauty. Instead of art's success being determined by the people who have succeeded in attaining wealth through several generations of intelligence and low time preference, it is instead determined by the people with the opportunism to rise in the political and bureaucratic system best. A passing familiarity with this kind of people is enough to explain to anyone how we can end up with the monstrosities of today's art.

In their fiat-fueled ever-growing realm of control, almost all modern governments dedicate budgets to finance art and artists in various media. But as time has gone by, bizarre and barely believable stories have emerged about covert government meddling in arts for political agendas. While the Soviets funded and directed communist "art" to achieve political and propaganda goals, it has recently emerged that the CIA retorted by financing and promoting the work of abstract expressionist mattress and cardboard molesters such as Mark Rothko and Jackson Pollock to serve as an American counter.[19] Only with unsound money could we have reached this artistic calamity where the two largest economic, military, and political behemoths in the world were actively promoting and funding tasteless trash picked by people whose artistic tastes qualify them for careers in Washington and Moscow spy agencies and bureaucracies.

As the Medicis have been replaced with the artistic equivalents of DMV workers, the result is an art world teeming with visually repulsive garbage produced in a matter of minutes by lazy talentless hacks looking for a quick paycheck by scamming the world's aspirants to artistic class with concocted nonsensical stories about it symbolizing anything more than the utter depravity of the scoundrel pretending to be an artist who made it. Mark Rothko's "art" took mere hours to produce, but was sold to gullible collectors holding millions of today's unsound money, clearly solidifying modern art as the most lucrative get-rich-quick scam of our age. No talent, hard work, or effort is required on the part of a modern artist, just a straight face and a snobby attitude when recounting to the nouveau riche why the splatter of paint on a canvas is anything more than a hideous thoughtless splatter of paint, and how their inability to understand the work of art unexplained can be easily remedied with a fat check.

What is astounding is not just the preponderance of garbage like Rothko's in the modern art world; it is the conspicuous absence of great masterpieces that can compare with the great works of the past. One cannot help but notice that there aren't too many Sistine Chapels being constructed today anywhere; nor are there many masterpieces to compare with the great paintings of Leonardo, Rafael, Rembrandt, Carvaggio, or Vermeer. This is even more astonishing when one realizes that advances in technology and industrialization would make producing such artwork far easier to accomplish than it was in the golden era.

---

[19] Saunders, Frances Stonor. *The Cultural Cold War: The CIA and the World of Arts and Letters*. New York, The New Press, 2000.

The Sistine Chapel will leave its viewer in awe, and any further explanation of its content, method, and history will transform the awe into appreciation of the depth of thought, craft, and hard work that went into it. Before they became famous, even the most pretentious of art critics could have passed by a Rothko painting neglected on a sidewalk and not even noticed it, let alone bothered to pick it up and take it home. Only after a circle jerk of critics have spent endless hours pontificating to promote this work will the hangers-on and aspirant nouveau riche begin to pretend there is deeper meaning to it and spend modern unsound money on it.

Several stories have surfaced over the years of pranksters leaving random objects in modern art museums, only for modern art lovers to swarm around them in admiration, illustrating the utter vacuity of our era's artistic tastes. But there is perhaps no more fitting tribute to the value of modern art than the many janitors at art exhibits worldwide who, demonstrating admirable perceptiveness and dedication to their job, have repeatedly thrown expensive modern art installations into the dustbins to which they belong. Some of the most iconic "artists" of our era, such as Damien Hirst, Gustav Metzger, Tracey Emin, and Italian duo Sara Goldschmied and Eleonora Chiara, have received this critical appraisal by janitors more discerning than the insecure nouveau riche who spent millions of dollars on what the janitors threw away.

A case can be made for ignoring all this worthless scribbling as just a government-funded embarrassment to our era and looking beyond it for what is worthwhile. Nobody, after all, would judge a country like America by the behavior of its incompetent DMV employees napping on their shifts as they take out their frustrations on their hapless customers, and perhaps we shouldn't judge our era by the work of government workers spinning stories about piles of worthless cardboard as if they were artistic achievements. But even then, we find less and less that can hold a candle to the past. In *From Dawn to Decadence*, a devastating critique of modern "demotic" culture, Jacques Barzun concludes: "All that the 20C has contributed and created since is refinement by ANALYSIS or criticism by pastiche and parody." Barzun's work has resonated with many of this generation because it contains a large degree of depressing truth: once one overcomes one's inherent bias to believe in the inevitability of progress, there is no escaping the conclusion that ours is a generation that is inferior to its ancestors in culture and refinement, in the same way the Roman subjects of Diocletian, living off his inflationary spending and drunk on the barbaric spectacles of the Colosseum, could not hold a candle to the great Romans of Caesar's era, who had to earn their aureus coins with sober hard work.

Chapter 6

Capitalism's Information System

"The cause of waves of unemployment is not 'capitalism' but governments denying enterprise the right to produce good money."
—*Friedrich Hayek*[1]

Money's primary function as a medium of exchange is what allows economic actors to engage in economic planning and calculation. As economic production moves from the very primitive scale, it becomes harder for individuals to make production, consumption, and trade decisions without having a fixed frame of reference with which to compare the value of different objects to one another. This property, the unit of account, is the third function of money after being a medium of exchange and store of value. To understand the significance of this property to an economic system, we do

---

[1]Hayek, Friedrich. *Denationalisation of Money: The Argument Refined*. London, Institute of Economic Affairs, 1976.

105

what wise people always do when seeking to understand economic questions: turn to the work of dead Austrian economists.

"The Use of Knowledge in Society," by Friedrich Hayek, is arguably one of the most important economic papers to have ever been written. Unlike highly theoretical, inconsequential, and esoteric modern academic research that is read by nobody, the eleven pages of this paper continue to be read widely seventy years after its publication, and have had a lasting impact on the lives and businesses of many people worldwide, perhaps none as significant as its role in the founding of one of the most important websites on the Internet, and the largest single body of knowledge assembled in human history. Jimmy Wales, Wikipedia's founder, has stated that the idea for establishing Wikipedia came to him after he read this paper by Hayek and his explanation of knowledge.

Hayek explained that contrary to popular and elementary treatments of the topic, the economic problem is not merely the problem of allocating resources and products, but more accurately, the problem of allocating them using knowledge that is not given in its totality to any single individual or entity. Economic knowledge of the conditions of production, the relative availability and abundance of the factors of production, and the preferences of individuals, is not objective knowledge that can be fully known to a single entity. Rather, the knowledge of economic conditions is by its very nature *distributed* and situated with the people concerned by their individual decisions. Every human's mind is consumed in learning and understanding the economic information relevant to them. Highly intelligent and hardworking individuals will spend decades learning the economic realities of their industries in order to reach positions of authority over the production processes of one single good. It is inconceivable that all these individual decisions being carried out by everyone could be substituted by aggregating all that information into one individual's mind to perform the calculations for everyone. Nor is there a need for this insane quest to centralize all knowledge into one decision maker's hands.

In a free market economic system, prices are knowledge, and the signals that communicate information. Each individual decision maker is only able to carry out her decisions by examining the prices of the goods involved, which carry in them the distillation of all market conditions and realities into one actionable variable for that individual.

In turn, each individual's decisions will play a role in shaping the price. No central authority could ever internalize all the information that goes into forming a price or replace its function.

To understand Hayek's point, picture the scenario of an earthquake badly damaging the infrastructure of a country that is the world's major producer of a commodity, such as the 2010 earthquake in Chile, which is the world's largest producer of copper. As the earthquake hit a region with extensive copper mines, it caused damage to these mines and to the seaport from which they are exported. This meant a reduction in the supply of copper to the world markets and immediately resulted in a 6.2% rise in the price of copper.[2] Anybody in the world involved in the copper market will be affected by this, but they do not need to know anything about the earthquake, Chile, and the conditions of the market in order to decide how to act. The rise in the price itself contains all the relevant information they need. Immediately, all the firms demanding copper now have an incentive to demand a smaller quantity of it, delay purchases that weren't immediately necessary, and find substitutes. On the other hand, the rising price gives all firms that produce copper anywhere around the world an incentive to produce more of it, to capitalize on the price rise.

With the simple increase in the price, everyone involved in the copper industry around the world now has the incentive to act in a way that alleviates the negative consequences of the earthquake: other producers supply more while consumers demand less. As a result, the shortage caused by the earthquake is not as devastating as it could be, and the extra revenue from the rising prices can help the miners rebuild their infrastructure. Within a few days, the price was back to normal. As global markets have become more integrated and larger, such individual disruptions are becoming less impactful than ever, as market makers have the depth and liquidity to get around them quickly with the least disruption.

To understand the power of prices as a method of communicating knowledge, imagine that the day before the earthquake, the entirety of the global copper industry stopped being a market institution and was instead given over to be under the command of a specialized agency,

---

[2]Rooney, Ben. "Copper Strikes After Chile Quake." *CNN Money*, 1 Mar. 2010.

meaning production is allocated without any recourse to prices. How would such an agency react to the earthquake? Of all the many copper producers worldwide, how would they decide which producers should increase their production and by how much? In a price system, each firm's own management will look at the prices of copper and the prices of all inputs into its production and come up with an answer to the most efficient new level of production. Many professionals work for decades in a firm to arrive at these answers with the help of prices, and they know their own firm far more than the central planners, who cannot resort to prices. Further, how will the planners decide on which consumers of copper should reduce their consumption and by how much, when there are no prices allowing these consumers to reveal their preferences?

No matter how much objective data and knowledge the agency might collect, it can never know all the dispersed knowledge that bears on the decisions that each individual carries out, and that includes their own preferences and valuations of objects. Prices, then, are not simply a tool to allow capitalists to profit; they are the information system of economic production, communicating knowledge across the world and coordinating the complex processes of production. Any economic system that tries to dispense with prices will cause the complete breakdown of economic activity and bring a human society back to a primitive state.

Prices are the only mechanism that allows trade and specialization to occur in a market economy. Without resort to prices humans could not benefit from the division of labor and specialization beyond some very primitive small scale. Trade allows producers to increase their living standards through specialization in the goods in which they have a *comparative advantage*—goods which they can produce at a lower relative cost. Only with accurate prices expressed in a common medium of exchange is it possible for people to identify their comparative advantage and specialize in it. Specialization itself, guided by price signals, will lead to producers further improving their efficiency in the production of these goods through learning by doing, and more importantly, accumulating capital specific to it. In fact, even without inherent differences in the relative costs, specialization would allow each producer to accumulate capital relevant to their production and thus increase their marginal productivity in it, allowing them to decrease their marginal cost of production, and trade with those who accumulate capital to specialize in other goods.

Capital Market Socialism

While most understand the importance of the price system to the division of labor, few get the crucial role it plays in capital accumulation and allocation, for which we need to turn to the work of Mises. In his 1922 book, *Socialism*, Mises explained the quintessential reason why socialist systems must fail, and it was *not* the commonly held idea that socialism simply had an incentive problem (Why would anyone work if everyone got the same rewards regardless of effort?). Given that lack of application to one's job was usually punished with government murder or imprisonment, socialism arguably overcame the incentive problem successfully, regardless of how bloody the process. After a century in which around 100 million people worldwide were murdered by socialist regimes,[3] this punishment was clearly not theoretical, and the incentives to work were probably stronger than in a capitalist system. There must be more to socialist failure than just incentives, and Mises was the first to precisely explicate why socialism would fail even if it were to successfully overcome the incentive problem by creating "the new socialist man."

The fatal flaw of socialism that Mises exposed was that without a price mechanism emerging on a free market, socialism would fail at economic calculation, most crucially in the allocation of capital goods.[4] As discussed earlier, capital production involves progressively sophisticated methods of production, longer time horizons, and a larger number of intermediate goods not consumed for their own sake, but only produced so as to take part in the production of final consumer goods in the future. Sophisticated structures of production only emerge from an intricate web of individual calculations by producers of each capital and consumer good buying and selling inputs and outputs to one another.[5] The most productive allocation is determined only through the price mechanism allowing the most productive users of capital goods to bid highest

---

[3]Courtois, Stéphane, Nicolas Werth, Karel Bartosek, Andrzej Paczkowski, Jean-Louis Panné, and Jean-Louis Margolin. *The Black Book of Communism: Crimes, Terror, Repression*. Harvard University Press, 1997.

[4]Mises, Ludwig von. *Socialism: An Economic and Sociological Analysis*. Auburn, AL, Ludwig von Mises Institute, 1922.

[5]There is a lot wrong with Keynesian economics, but perhaps nothing is as ridiculous as the complete absence of any conception of how the structure of capital production functions.

for them. The supply and demand of capital goods emerges from the interaction of the producers and consumers and their iterative decisions.

In a socialist system, government owns and controls the means of production, making it at once the sole buyer and seller of all capital goods in the economy. That centralization stifles the functioning of an actual market, making sound decisions based on prices impossible. Without a market for capital where independent actors can bid for capital, there can be no price for capital overall or for individual capital goods. Without prices of capital goods reflecting their relative supply and demand, there is no rational way of determining the most productive uses of capital, nor is there a rational way of determining how much to produce of each capital good. In a world in which the government owns the steel factory, as well as all the factories that will utilize steel in the production of various consumer and capital goods, there can be no price emerging for steel, or for the goods it is used to produce, and hence, no possible way of knowing which uses of steel are the most important and valuable. How can the government determine whether its limited quantities of steel should be utilized in making cars or trains, given that it also owns the car and train factories and allocates by diktat to citizens how many cars and trains they can have? Without a price system for citizens to decide between trains and cars, there is no way of knowing what the optimal allocation is and no way of knowing where the steel would be most necessary. Asking citizens in surveys is a meaningless exercise, because people's choices are meaningless without a price to reflect the real opportunity cost involved in trade-offs between choices. A survey without prices would find that everyone would like their own Ferrari, but of course, when people have to pay, very few choose Ferraris. Central planners can never know the preferences of each individual nor allocate resources in the way that satisfies that individual's needs best.

Further, when the government owns all inputs into all the production processes of the economy, the absence of a price mechanism makes it virtually impossible to coordinate the production of various capital goods in the right quantities to allow all the factories to function. Scarcity is the starting point of all economics, and it is not possible to produce unlimited quantities of all inputs; trade-offs need to be made, so allocating capital, land, and labor to the production of steel must come at the expense of creating more copper. In a free market, as factories compete for the acquisition of copper and steel, they create scarcity and abundance in these markets and the prices allow copper and steel makers to compete for the resources that go into making them. A central planner is completely in the dark about this web of preferences and opportunity costs of trains, cars, copper, steel, labor, capital, and land. Without prices, there is no way to calculate how to allocate these resources to produce the optimal products, and the result is a complete breakdown in production.

And yet all of this is but one aspect of the calculation problem, pertaining merely to the production of existing goods in a static market. The problem is far more pronounced when one considers that nothing is static in human affairs, as humans are eternally seeking to improve their economic situation, to produce new goods, and find more and better ways of producing goods. The ever-present human impulse to tinker, improve, and innovate gives socialism its most intractable problem. Even if the central planning system succeeded in managing a static economy, it is powerless to accommodate change or to allow entrepreneurship. How can a socialist system make calculations for technologies and innovations that do not exist, and how can factors of production be allocated for them when there is yet no indication whether these products can even work?

> "Those who confuse entrepreneurship and management close their eyes to the economic problem.... The capitalist system is not a managerial system; it is an entrepreneurial system."
>
> —*Ludwig von Mises*[6]

The point of this exposition is not to argue against the socialist economic system, which no serious adult takes seriously in this day and age, after the catastrophic, bloody and comprehensive failure it has achieved in every society in which it has been tried over the last century. The point rather is to explicate clearly the difference between two ways of allocating capital and making production decisions: prices and planning. While most of the world's countries today do not have a central planning board responsible for the direct allocation of capital goods, it is nonetheless the case in every country in the world that there is a central planning board for the most important market of all, the market for capital. A free market is understood as one in which the buyers and

---

[6]Ludwig von Mises. *Human Action*, pp. 703–4.

sellers are free to transact on terms determined by them solely, and where entry and exit into the market are free: no third parties restrict sellers or buyers from entering the market, and no third parties stand to subsidize buyers and sellers who cannot transact in the market. No country in the world has a capital market that has these characteristics today.

The capital markets in a modern economy consist of the markets for loanable funds. As the structure of production becomes more complicated and long-term, individuals no longer invest their savings themselves, but lend them out, through various institutions, to businesses specialized in production. The interest rate is the price that the lender receives for lending their funds, and the price that the borrower pays to obtain them.

In a free market for loanable funds, the quantity of these funds supplied, like all supply curves, rises as the interest rate rises. In other words, the higher the interest rate, the more people are inclined to save and offer their savings to entrepreneurs and firms. The demand for loans, on the other hand, is negatively related to the interest rate, meaning that entrepreneurs and firms will want to borrow less when the interest rate rises.

The interest rate in a free market for capital is positive because people's positive time preference means that nobody would part with money unless he could receive more of it in the future. A society with a lot of individuals with low time preference is likely to have plenty of savings, bringing the interest rate down and providing for plenty of capital for firms to invest, generating significant economic growth for the future. As a society's time preference increases, people are less likely to save, interest rates would be high, and producers find less capital to borrow. Societies that live in peace and have secure property rights and a large degree of economic freedom are likely to have low time preference as they provide a strong incentive for individuals to discount their future less. Another Austrian economist, Eugen von Böhm-Bawerk, even argued that the interest rate in a nation reflected its cultural level: the higher a people's intelligence and moral strength, the more they save and the lower the rate of interest.

But this is not how a capital market functions in any modern economy today, thanks to the invention of the modern central bank and its incessant interventionist meddling in the most critical of markets.

Central banks determine the interest rate and the supply of loanable funds through a variety of monetary tools, operating through their control of the banking system.[7]

A fundamental fact to understand about the modern financial system is that banks create money whenever they engage in lending. In a fractional reserve banking system similar to the one present all over the world today, banks not only lend the savings of their customers, but also their demand deposits. In other words, the depositor can call on the money at any time while a large percentage of that money has been issued as a loan to a borrower. By giving the money to the borrower while keeping it available to the depositor, the bank effectively creates new money and that results in an increase in the money supply. This underlies the relationship between money supply and interest rates: when interest rates drop, there is an increase in lending, which leads to an increase in money creation and a rise in the money supply. On the other hand, a rise in interest rates causes a reduction in lending and contraction in the money supply, or at least a reduction in the rate of its growth.

Business Cycles and Financial Crises

Whereas in a free market for capital the supply of loanable funds is determined by the market participants who decide to lend based on the interest rate, in an economy with a central bank and fractional reserve banking, the supply of loanable funds is directed by a committee of economists under the influence of politicians, bankers, TV pundits, and sometimes, most spectacularly, military generals.

Any passing familiarity with economics will make the dangers of price controls clear and discernable. Should a government decide to set

---

[7]The main tools that central banks use are: setting the Federal Funds rate, setting the required reserve ratio, engaging in open market operations, and determining lending eligibility criteria. A detailed explanation of the mechanism of operation of these tools can be found in any preliminary macroeconomics textbook. To summarize: the central bank can engage in expansionary monetary policy by (1) reducing interest rates, which stimulates lending and increases money creation; (2) lowering the required reserve ratio, allowing banks to increase their lending, increasing money creation; (3) purchasing treasuries or financial assets, which also leads to money creation; and (4) relaxing lending eligibility criteria, allowing banks to increase lending and thus money creation. Contractionary monetary policy is conducted by reversing these steps, leading to a reduction of the money supply, or at least a reduction in the rate of growth in the money supply.

the price of apples and prevent it from moving, the outcome will be either a shortage or a surplus and large losses to society overall from overproduction or underproduction. In the capital markets, something similar happens, but the effects are far more devastating as they affect every sector of the economy, because capital is involved in the production of every economic good.

It is first important to understand the distinction between loanable funds and actual capital goods. In a free market economy with sound money, savers have to defer consumption in order to save. Money that is deposited in a bank as savings is money taken away from consumption by people who are delaying the gratification that consumption could give them in order to gain more gratification in the future. The exact amount of savings becomes the exact amount of loanable funds available for producers to borrow. The availability of capital goods is inextricably linked to the reduction of consumption: actual physical resources, labor, land, and capital goods will move from being employed in the provision of final consumption goods to the production of capital goods. The marginal worker is directed away from car sales and toward a job in the car factory; the proverbial corn seed will go into the ground instead of being eaten.

Scarcity is the fundamental starting point of all economics, and its most important implication is the notion that everything has an opportunity cost. In the capital market, the opportunity cost of capital is forgone consumption, and the opportunity cost of consumption is forgone capital investment. The interest rate is the price that regulates this relationship: as people demand more investments, the interest rate rises, incentivizing more savers to set aside more of their money for savings. As the interest rate drops, it incentivizes investors to engage in more investments, and to invest in more technologically advanced methods of production with a longer time horizon. A lower interest rate, then, allows for the engagement of methods of production that are longer and more productive: society moves from fishing with rods to fishing with oil-powered large boats.

As an economy advances and becomes increasingly sophisticated, the connection between physical capital and the loanable funds market does not change in reality, but it does get obfuscated in the minds of people. A modern economy with a central bank is built on ignoring this fundamental trade-off and assuming that banks can finance investment with new money without consumers having to forgo consumption. The link between savings and loanable funds is severed to the point where it is not even taught in the economics textbooks any more,[8] let alone the disastrous consequences of ignoring it.

As the central bank manages the money supply and interest rate, there will inevitably be a discrepancy between savings and loanable funds. Central banks are generally trying to spur economic growth and investment and to increase consumption, so they tend to increase the money supply and lower the interest rate, resulting in a larger quantity of loanable funds than savings. At these artificially low interest rates, businesses take on more debt to start projects than savers put aside to finance these investments. In other words, the value of consumption deferred is less than the value of the capital borrowed. Without enough consumption deferred, there will not be enough capital, land, and labor resources diverted away from consumption goods toward higher-order capital goods at the earliest stages of production. There is no free lunch, after all, and if consumers save less, there will have to be less capital available for investors. Creating new pieces of paper and digital entries to paper over the deficiency in savings does not magically increase society's physical capital stock; it only devalues the existing money supply and distorts prices.

This shortage of capital is not immediately apparent, because banks and the central bank can issue enough money for the borrowers—that is, after all, the main perk of using unsound money. In an economy with sound money, such manipulation of the price of capital would be impossible: as soon as the interest rate is set artificially low, the shortage in savings at banks is reflected in reduced capital available for borrowers, leading to a rise in the interest rate, which reduces demand for loans and raises the supply of savings until the two match.

Unsound money makes such manipulation possible, but only for a short while, of course, as reality cannot be deceived forever. The artificially low interest rates and the excess printed money deceive the

---

[8]It is always fun to teach my senior students about a hypothetical free market in capital, if only for watching the reaction on their faces when they compare the neat logic of how a free market in capital could work, versus the pseudoscientific Keynesian central planning theories they had the misfortune of learning in their monetary theory class.

producers into engaging in a production process requiring more capital resources than is actually available. The excess money, backed by no actual deferred consumption, initially makes more producers borrow, operating under the delusion that the money will allow them to buy all the capital goods necessary for their production process. As more and more producers are bidding for fewer capital goods and resources than they expect there to be, the natural outcome is a rise in the price of the capital goods during the production process. This is the point at which the manipulation is exposed, leading to the simultaneous collapse of several capital investments which suddenly become unprofitable at the new capital good prices; these projects are what Mises termed *malinvestments*—investments that would not have been undertaken without the distortions in the capital market and whose completion is not possible once the misallocations are exposed. The central bank's intervention in the capital market allows for more projects to be undertaken because of the distortion of prices that causes investors to miscalculate, but the central bank's intervention cannot increase the amount of actual capital available. So these extra projects are not completed and become an unnecessary waste of capital. The suspension of these projects at the same time causes a rise in unemployment across the economy. This economy-wide simultaneous failure of overextended businesses is what is referred to as a *recession*.

Only with an understanding of the capital structure and how interest rate manipulation destroys the incentive for capital accumulation can one understand the causes of recessions and the swings of the business cycle. The business cycle is the natural result of the manipulation of the interest rate distorting the market for capital by making investors imagine they can attain more capital than is available with the unsound money they have been given by the banks. Contrary to Keynesian animist mythology, business cycles are not mystic phenomena caused by flagging "animal spirits" whose cause is to be ignored as central bankers seek to try to engineer recovery.[9] Economic logic clearly shows how recessions are

---

[9]There is no shortage of alternatives to the Austrian capital theory as an explanation of recessions, yet all of these are largely just the rehashed arguments of monetary cranks from the early twentieth century. One does not even need to read modern rebuttals of the latest line of Keynesian and pop psychology theories. Reading Hayek's *Monetary Theory and the Trade Cycle*, from 1933, or Rothbard's *America's Great Depression*, from 1963, is sufficient.

the inevitable outcome of interest rate manipulation in the same way shortages are the inevitable outcome of price ceilings.

An analogy can be borrowed from Mises's work[10] (and embellished) to illustrate the point: imagine the capital stock of a society as building bricks, and the central bank as a contractor responsible for constructing them into houses. Each house requires 10,000 bricks to construct, and the developer is looking for a contractor who will be able to build 100 houses, requiring a total of 1 million. But a Keynesian contractor, eager to win the contract, realizes his chances of winning the contract will be enhanced if he can submit a tender promising to build 120 of the same house while only requiring 800,000 bricks. This is the equivalent of the interest rate manipulation: it reduces the supply of capital while increasing the demand for it. In reality, the 120 houses will require 1.2 million bricks, but there are only 800,000 available. The 800,000 bricks are sufficient to begin the construction of the 120 houses, but they are not sufficient to complete them. As the construction begins, the developer is very happy to see 20% more houses for 80% of the cost, thanks to the wonders of Keynesian engineering, which leads him to spend the 20% of the cost he saved on buying himself a new yacht. But the ruse cannot last as it will eventually become apparent that the houses cannot be completed and the construction must come to a halt. Not only has the contractor failed to deliver 120 houses, he will have failed to deliver any houses whatsoever, and instead, he's left the developer with 120 half-houses, effectively useless piles of bricks with no roofs. The contractor's ruse reduced the capital spent by the developer and resulted in the construction of fewer houses than would have been possible with accurate price signals. The developer would have had 100 houses if he went with an honest contractor. By going with a Keynesian contractor who distorts the numbers, the developer continues to waste his capital for as long as the capital is being allocated on a plan with no basis in reality. If the contractor realizes the mistake early on, the capital wasted on starting 120 houses might be very little, and a new contractor will be able to take the remaining bricks and use them to produce 90 houses. If the developer remains ignorant of the reality until the capital runs out, he

---

[10]Ludwig von Mises. *Human Action*, p. 560.

will only have 120 unfinished homes that are worthless as nobody will pay to live in a roofless house.

When the central bank manipulates the interest rate lower than the market clearing price by directing banks to create more money by lending, they are at once reducing the amount of savings available in society and increasing the quantity demanded by borrowers while also directing the borrowed capital toward projects which cannot be completed. Hence, the more unsound the form of money, and the easier it is for central banks to manipulate interest rates, the more severe the business cycles are. Monetary history testifies to how much more severe business cycles and recessions are when the money supply is manipulated than when it isn't.

While most people imagine that socialist societies are a thing of the past and that market systems rule capitalist economies, the reality is that a capitalist system cannot function without a free market in capital, where the price of capital emerges through the interaction of supply and demand and the decisions of capitalists are driven by accurate price signals. The central bank's meddling in the capital market is the root of all recessions and all the crises which most politicians, journalists, academics, and leftist activists like to blame on capitalism. Only through the central planning of the money supply can the price mechanism of the capital markets be corrupted to cause wide disruptions in the economy.

Whenever a government has started on the path of inflating the money supply, there is no escaping the negative consequences. If the central bank stops the inflation, interest rates rise, and a recession follows as many of the projects that were started are exposed as unprofitable and have to be abandoned, exposing the misallocation of resources and capital that took place. If the central bank were to continue its inflationary process indefinitely, it would just increase the scale of misallocations in the economy, wasting even more capital and making the inevitable recession even more painful. There is no escape from paying a hefty bill for the supposed free lunch that Keynesian cranks foisted upon us.

"We now have a tiger by the tail: how long can this inflation continue? If the tiger (of inflation) is freed he will eat us up; yet if he runs faster and faster while we desperately hold on, we are still finished! I'm glad I won't be here to see the final outcome."

—*Friedrich Hayek*[11]

Central bank planning of the money supply is neither desirable nor possible. It is rule by the most conceited, making the most important market in an economy under the command of the few people who are ignorant enough of the realities of market economies to believe they can centrally plan a market as large, abstract, and emergent as the capital market. Imagining that central banks can "prevent," "combat," or "manage" recessions is as fanciful and misguided as placing pyromaniacs and arsonists in charge of the fire brigade.

The relative stability of sound money, for which it is selected by the market, allows for the operation of a free market through price discovery and individual decision making. Unsound money, whose supply is centrally planned, cannot allow for the emergence of accurate price signals, because it is by its very nature controlled. Through centuries of price controls, central planners have tried to find the elusive best price to achieve the goals they wanted, to no avail.[12] The reason that price controls must fail is not that the central planners cannot pick the right price, but rather that by merely imposing a price—any price—they prevent the market process from allowing prices to coordinate consumption and production decisions among market participants, resulting in inevitable shortages or surpluses. Equivalently, central planning of credit markets must fail because it destroys markets' mechanisms for price-discovery providing market participants with the accurate signals and incentives to manage their consumption and production.

The form of failure that capital market central planning takes is the boom-and-bust cycle, as explained in Austrian business cycle theory. It is thus no wonder that this dysfunction is treated as a normal part of market economies, because, after all, in the minds of modern economists a central bank controlling interest rates is a normal part of a modern market economy. The track record of central banks in this area has been quite

---

[11] Hayek, Friedrich. *A Tiger by the Tail*. 3rd ed., compiled by Sudha Shenoy, Institute of Economic Affairs, and Ludwig von Mises Institute, 2009, p. 126.

[12] A highly recommended historical account of the disastrous and yet grimly hilarious consequences of price controls across history is *Forty Centuries of Price and Wage Controls: How Not to Fight Inflation*, by Robert Schuettinger and Eamonn Butler.

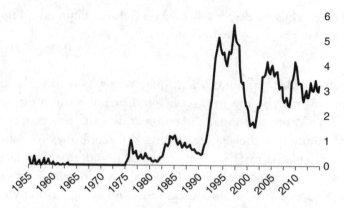

Figure 13   Unemployment rate in Switzerland, %.

abject, especially when compared to periods with no central planning and directing of the money supply. Established in 1914, the U.S. Federal Reserve was in charge of a sharp contraction in reserves in 1920–21, and then the sharp bust of 1929, whose fallout lasted until the end of 1945. From then on, economic depressions became a regular and painful part of the economy, recurring every few years and providing justification for growing government intervention to handle their fallout.

A good example of the benefits of sound money can be found look- ing at the fate of the Swiss economy, the last bastion of sound money, which had kept its currency pegged to gold until 1973. Before that time, involuntary unemployment in Switzerland practically didn't exist, as Austrian economists would expect from a free market in money. The severing of the franc's link to gold would then result in the rise of unem- ployment, and its remaining endemic to the Swiss economy. In 1992, Switzerland joined the IMF, adopted Keynesian dogma, and sold over half of their gold holdings, and as a result began to experience the plea- sures of Keynesian funny money, with unemployment rate rising to 5% within a few years, rarely ever dropping below 2%. (See Figure 13.[13])

When comparing depressions to periods of the gold standard, it must be remembered that the gold standard in Europe and the United States in the nineteenth century was far from a perfect form of sound money, as there were several flaws in it, most importantly, that banks

---

[13] *Source*: Federal Reserve Economic Data. Historical Statistics of the United States. fred.stlouisfed.org/.

and governments could often expand their supply of money and credit beyond the gold held in their reserves, causing booms and busts similar to those seen in the twentieth century, though to a much lesser degree.

With this background in mind, we can get a far clearer idea of modern monetary history than what is commonly taught in academic textbooks since the Keynesian deluge. The founding text of Monetarist thought is what is considered the definitive work of U.S. monetary history: *The Monetary History of the United States* by Milton Friedman and Anna Schwartz. A giant tome of 888 pages, the book is astounding in its ability to marshal endless facts, details, statistics, and analytical tools without once providing the unfortunate reader with an understanding of one key issue: the causes of financial crises and recessions.

The fundamental flaw of Friedman and Schwartz's book is typical of modern academic scholarship: it is an elaborate exercise in substituting rigor for logic. The book systematically and methodically avoids ever questioning the causes of the financial crises that have affected the U.S. economy over a century, and instead inundates the reader with impressively researched data, facts, trivia, and minutiae.

The central contention of the book is that recessions are the result of the government not responding quickly enough to a financial crisis, bank run, and deflationary collapse by increasing the money supply to re-inflate the banking sector. It is typical of the Milton Friedman brand of libertarianism in that it blames the government for an economic problem, but the flawed reasoning suggests even more government intervention as the solution. The glaring error in the book is that the authors never once discuss what causes these financial crises, bank runs, and deflationary collapses of the money supply. As we saw from the discussion of the Austrian business cycle theory, the only cause of an economy-wide recession is the inflation of the money supply in the first place. Relieved of the burden of understanding the cause, Friedman and Schwartz can then safely recommend the cause itself as the cure: governments need to step in to aggressively recapitalize the banking system and increase liquidity at the first sign of economic recession. You can begin to see why modern economists loathe understanding logical causality so much; it would debunk almost all their solutions.

Friedman and Schwartz begin their book in the year 1867, so that when analyzing the causes of the recession of 1873, they completely ignore the small matter of the U.S. government's printing of greenbacks to finance the Civil War, which was the ultimate cause of that recession. This is a pattern that will recur throughout the book.

Friedman and Schwartz barely discuss the causes of the 1893 recession, alluding to a drive for silver due to gold not being sufficient to cover the monetary needs of the economy, and then inundating the reader with trivia about the recession in that year. They fail to mention the Sherman Silver Purchase Act of 1890 approved by the U.S. Congress, which required the U.S. Treasury to buy large quantities of silver with a new issue of Treasury notes. Seeing as silver had been almost entirely demonetized worldwide at that point, people who held silver or Treasury notes sought to convert them to gold, leading to a drain on the Treasury's gold reserves. Effectively, the Treasury had engaged in a large misguided dose of monetary expansionism by increasing the money supply to try to pretend that silver was still money. All that did was devalue U.S. Treasury notes, creating a financial bubble which crashed as withdrawals of gold accelerated. Any history book of the period could make this clear to anyone with a cursory understanding of monetary theory, but Friedman and Schwartz impressively avoid any mention of this.

The book's treatment of the 1920 recession ignores the large dose of monetary expansion that had to happen to finance U.S. entry into World War I. Despite not mentioning it in their analysis, their data[14] tells you that there was a 115% increase in the money stock between June 1914 and May 1920. Only 26% of that increase was due to increases in gold holdings, meaning that the rest was driven by the government, banks, and the Federal Reserve. This was the central cause of the 1920 depression, but this, too, goes unmentioned.

Most curiously, however, is how they completely ignore the recovery from the depression of 1920–21, which was termed the "last natural recovery to full employment" by economist Benjamin Anderson, where taxes and government expenditures were reduced and wages were left to adjust freely, leading to a swift return to full employment in less than a year.[15] The 1920 depression saw one of the fastest contractions of output in American history (9% drop in a 10-month period from

[14]Friedman, Milton, and Anna Schwartz. *The Monetary History of the United States*. Princeton University Press, 1963, table 10, p. 206.

[15]Rothbard, Murray. *America's Great Depression*. 5th ed., Auburn, AL, Ludwig von Mises Institute, 2000, p. 186.

September 1920 to July 1921), and also the fastest recovery. In other depressions, with Keynesians and Monetarists injecting liquidity, increasing the money supply, and increasing government spending, the recovery was slower.

While everyone tries to learn the lesson of the Great Depression, mainstream economics textbooks never mention the 1920 depression, and never try to learn why it is that this depression was so quick to recover.[16] The president at the time, Warren Harding, had a strong commitment to free markets and refused to heed the call of interventionist economists. The malinvestments were liquidated, and the labor and capital employed in them was reallocated to new investments very quickly. Unemployment soon returned to normal levels precisely as a result of the absence of government intervention to deepen the distortions it had caused in the first place. This is the glaring opposite of everything Friedman and Schwartz recommend, and so it, too, does not even get a mention in their work.

The most famous chapter of the book (and the only one that anyone seems to have read) is Chapter 7, which focuses on the Great Depression. The chapter begins *after* the stock market crash of October 1929, while Chapter 6 ends in the year 1921. The entirety of the period from 1921 to October 1929, which would have to contain any cause of the Great Depression, is not deemed worthy of a single page of the 888 pages in the book.

Only briefly, Friedman and Schwartz mention that the price level had not risen too quickly during the 1920s, and thus conclude that the period was not inflationary and so the causes of the depression could not have been inflationary. But the 1920s witnessed very fast economic growth, which would lead to a drop in prices. There was also heavy monetary expansion, caused by the U.S. Federal Reserve attempting to help the Bank of England stem the flow of gold from its shores, which was in turn caused by the Bank of England inflating instead of letting wages adjust downward. The net effect of a rise in the money supply and fast economic growth was that the price level did not rise a lot, but that asset prices rose heavily—mainly housing and stocks; the increased money

---

[16] An excellent detailed treatment of this depression is found in James Grant's book, *The Forgotten Depression: 1921: The Crash that Cured Itself.*

supply had not translated to a rise in consumer good prices because it had mainly been directed by the Federal Reserve to stimulate the stock and housing markets. The money supply expanded by 68.1% over the period of 1921–29 while the gold stock only expanded by 15%.[17] It is this increase of the dollar stock, beyond the stock of gold, which is the root cause of the Great Depression.

An honorable mention has to go to the father of the Monetarists, Irving Fisher, who spent the 1920s engaged in the "scientific management of the price level." Fisher had imagined that as the United States was expanding the money supply, his extensive data collection and scientific management would allow him to control the growth in the money supply and asset prices to ensure that the price level remained stable. On October 16, 1929, Fisher proudly proclaimed in the *New York Times* that stocks had reached a "permanently high plateau."[18] The stock market was to crash starting October 24, 1929, and as the Depression deepened, it would not be until the mid-1950s, years after Fisher died, that the stock market would get back to the "permanently high plateau" Fisher had proclaimed in 1929. It is no wonder, then, that Milton Friedman would later proclaim Irving Fisher as the greatest economist America had produced.

The crash resulted from the monetary expansion of the 1920s, which generated a massive bubble of illusory wealth in the stock market. As soon as the expansion slowed down, the bubble was inevitably going to burst. Once it burst, this meant a deflationary spiral where all the illusory wealth of the bubble disappears. As wealth disappears, a run on banks is inevitable as banks struggle to meet their obligations. This exposes the problem of having a system of fractional reserve banking—it's a disaster waiting to happen. Given that, it would have been appropriate for the Fed to guarantee people's deposits—though not guarantee the losses of businesses and the stock market. Leaving the banks alone to suffer from this, allowing the liquidation to take place and prices to fall, is the only solution. It is true that this solution would have involved a painful recession—but that is exactly why the monetary expansion should not have happened in the first place! Attempting to avert the recession by

---

[17] Murray Rothbard, *America's Great Depression*.
[18] "Fisher Sees Stocks Permanently High," *New York Times*, October 16, 1929, p. 8.

pouring more liquidity into it will only exacerbate the distortions which caused the crisis in the first place.

The monetary expansion created illusory wealth that misallocated resources, and that wealth must disappear for the market to go back to functioning properly with a proper price mechanism. It was this illusory wealth that caused the collapse in the first place. Returning that illusory wealth to its original location is simply reassembling the house of cards again and preparing it for another, bigger and stronger fall.

Having summarily dismissed the era leading up to 1929 as having anything to do with the stock market crash, Friedman and Schwartz then conclude that it was merely the Fed's reaction to the crash which caused it to turn into a Great Depression. Had the Federal Reserve opened the monetary spigots to drench the banking system with liquidity, they argue, then the stock market losses would have been largely inconsequential to the wider economy and there would not have been a larger depression. The fact that the Fed was in fact expansionary in response to this crisis is ignored in the deluge of data. While the Federal Reserve did attempt to alleviate the liquidity shortages in the banking sector, it could not stem the collapse, not because of a shortage of resolve, but rather due to the economy-wide collapse of misallocated capital investments, and the heavily interventionist policies discussed in Chapter 4.

Three important questions remain unanswered in this gigantic work, exposing a glaring hole in its logic. First, why is there no comparison of the 1920 and 1929 depressions? The former didn't last long even though the Fed did not intervene in the way the authors recommend. Second, why is it that the United States had never suffered a financial crisis in the nineteenth century during the period when there was no central bank, except in the two instances when Congress had directed the Treasury to act like a central bank: during the Civil War with the printing of the greenbacks, and in 1890 after the monetization of silver? Third, and most tellingly, how did the United States manage one of its longest periods of sustained economic growth without any financial crises between 1873 and 1890 when there was no central bank at all, and the money supply was restricted, and the price level continued to drop? Friedman and Schwartz only mention this era in passing, remarking that the economy grew impressively "in spite" of the price level dropping, without caring to comment on how such a fact flies in the face of their price-level-drop phobia.

As Rothbard explained, there is nothing inherent about the workings of a market economy that will create a persistent problem of unemployment. The normal workings of a free market will witness many people lose or quit their jobs, and many businesses will go bankrupt or shut down for a wide variety of reasons, but these job losses will roughly cancel out with newly created jobs and businesses, leading to a negligibly small number of people being involuntarily unemployed at any point in time, as was the case during the years in which the gold standard was not abused in the nineteenth century, and as was the case with Switzerland pre-1992. Only when a central bank manipulates the money supply and interest rate does it become possible for large-scale failures across entire sectors of the economy to happen at the same time, causing waves of mass layoffs in entire industries, leaving a large number of workers jobless at the same time, with skills that are not easily transferrable to other fields.[19] As Hayek put it: "The cause of waves of unemployment is not 'capitalism' but governments denying enterprise the right to produce good money."[20]

Sound Basis for Trade

In the world of sound money, goods and capital flowed between different countries almost in the same way they flowed between different regions of the same country: according to the desires of their rightful owners as agreed upon in mutually beneficial exchange. Under Julius Caesar's aureus, or under the gold standard of the Bank of Amsterdam in the seventeenth century, or under the nineteenth century gold standard, physically moving a good from one location to the other was the most significant barrier to trade. Tariffs and trade barriers hardly existed, and if they did, they constituted little more than fees to pay for the management and maintenance of border crossing points and seaports.

---

[19]Rothbard, Murray. *Economic Depressions: Their Cause and Cure.* Auburn, AL, Ludwig von Mises Institute, 2009.

[20]Hayek, Friedrich. *Denationalization of Money: The Argument Refined.* London, Institute of Economic Affairs, 1976.

In the era of unsound money, such as in Europe's descent into feudalism or in the modern world's descent into monetary nationalism, trade stops being the prerogative of the transacting individuals and becomes a matter of national importance, requiring the oversight of the feudal lords or governments claiming sovereignty over the trading individuals. So ridiculously complete has this transformation of the nature of trade been that, in the twentieth century, the term *free trade* came to refer to trade carried out between two individuals across borders, according to terms agreed upon by their respective governments, not by the concerned individuals!

The abandonment of the gold standard in 1914 through the suspension and limitation of exchanging paper money for gold by most governments began the period Hayek named monetary nationalism. Money's value stopped being a fixed unit of gold, which was the commodity with the highest stock-to-flow ratio, and hence the lowest price elasticity of supply, keeping its value predictable and relatively constant. Instead, the value of money oscillated along with the vagaries of monetary and fiscal policy as well as international trade. Lower interest rates or increased money supply would drop the value of money, as would government spending financed by central bank lending to the government. While these two factors were nominally under the control of governments, who could at least delude themselves into thinking they could manage them to achieve stability, the third factor was a complex emergent outcome of the actions of all citizens and many foreigners. When a country's exports grew larger than its imports (a trade surplus), its currency would appreciate on the international exchange markets, whereas it would depreciate when its imports grew larger than exports (trade deficit). Policymakers, instead of taking this as a sign to stop tinkering with the value of money and allow people the freedom to use the least volatile commodity as money, took it as an invitation to micromanage the smallest details of global trade.

The value of money, supposed to be the unit of account with which all economic activity is measured and planned, went from being the value of the least volatile good on the market to being determined through the sum of three policy tools of the government—monetary, fiscal, and trade policy—and most unpredictably, through the reactions of individuals to these policy tools. Governments deciding to dictate the measure of value makes as much sense as governments attempting to dictate the measure of length based on the heights of individuals and buildings in their territories. One can only imagine the sort of confusion that would happen to all engineering projects were the length of the meter to oscillate daily with the pronouncements of a central measurements office.

Only the vanity of the insane can be affected by changing the unit with which they're measured. Making the meter shorter might make someone whose house's area is 200 square meters believe it is actually 400 square meters, but it would still be the same house. All that this redefinition of the meter has caused is ruin an engineer's ability to properly build or maintain a house. Similarly, devaluing a currency may make a country richer nominally, or increase the nominal value of its exports, but it does nothing to make the country more prosperous.

Modern economics has formulated "The Impossible Trinity" to express the plight of modern central bankers, which states: No government can successfully achieve all three goals of having a fixed foreign exchange rate, free capital flows, and an independent monetary policy. Should a government have a fixed exchange rate and free capital flows, it cannot have its own monetary policy, as altering the interest rate will cause capital to flow in or out to the point where the exchange rate becomes indefensible, and we all know how much modern economists appreciate having a monetary policy to "manage" the economy. Having an independent monetary policy and a fixed exchange rate can only be achieved by limiting capital flows, which was the situation prevalent in the period between 1946 and 1971. But even that was not sustainable as the flow of goods became the way in which exchange rates would try to redress the imbalance, with some countries exporting too much and others importing too much, leading to political negotiations to recalibrate the exchange rate. There can be no rational ground for determining the outcome of these negotiations in international organizations, as each country's government attempts to pursue its own special groups' interest and will do whatever it takes to do just that. After 1971, the world predominantly moved to having an independent monetary policy and free capital flows, but floating exchange rates between currencies.

This arrangement has the advantage of allowing Keynesian economists to play with their favorite tools for "managing" economies while also keeping international financial institutions and large capital owners happy. It is also a huge boon for large financial institutions which have generated a foreign exchange market worth trillions of dollars *a day*, where currencies and their futures are trading. But this arrangement is likely not to the benefit of almost everyone else, particularly for people who actually have productive enterprises that offer valuable goods to society.

In a highly globalized world where foreign exchange rates are dependent upon a plethora of domestic and international variables, running a productive business becomes challenging completely unnecessarily. A successful firm likely has inputs and outputs from its business come and go to multiple countries. Every single purchase and sale decision is dependent on the foreign exchange between the countries involved. In this world, a highly competitive firm could suffer high losses through nothing more than a shift in exchange rates, not even necessarily involving its own country. If the firm's major supplier's country witnesses a rise in the value of its currency, the firm's input costs could rise enough to destroy the firm's profitability. The same thing could happen if the currency of the main market to which it exports drops in value. Firms that have spent decades working on a competitive advantage could see it wiped out in 15 minutes of unpredictable foreign exchange volatility. This usually gets blamed on free trade, and economists and politicians likewise will use it as an excuse for implementing popular but destructive protectionist trade policies.

With free capital flows and free trade built on a shaky foundation of floating exchange rate quicksand, a much higher percentage of the country's businesses and professionals need to concern themselves with the movements of the currency. Every business needs to dedicate resources and manpower toward studying an issue of extreme importance over which they have no control. More and more people work in speculating on the actions of central banks, national governments, and currency movement. This elaborate apparatus of central planning and its attendant rituals tends to eventually get in the way of economic activity. Perhaps one of the most astonishing facts about the modern world economy is the size of the foreign exchange market compared to productive economic activity. The Bank of International Settlements[21] estimates the size of the foreign exchange market to be $5.1 trillion per day for April 2016, which would come out to around $1,860 trillion per year. The World Bank estimates the GDP of all the world's countries combined at around $75 trillion for the year 2016. This means that the foreign exchange market is around 25 times as large as all the economic production that takes place in the entire planet.[22] It's important to remember here that foreign exchange is not a productive process, which is why its volume isn't counted in GDP statistics; there is no economic value being created in transferring one currency to another; it is but a cost paid to overcome the large inconvenience of having different national currencies for different nations. What economist Hans-Hermann Hoppe has termed "a global system of partial barter"[23] across international borders is crippling the ability of global trade to benefit people, exacting a high amount of transaction costs to attempt to ameliorate its consequences. Not only is the world wasting large amounts of capital and labor attempting to overcome these barriers, businesses and individuals worldwide frequently incur significant losses through economic miscalculation caused by the quicksand of exchange rate volatility.

In a free market for money, individuals would choose the currencies they want to use, and the result would be that they would choose the currency with the reliably highest stock-to-flow ratio. This currency would oscillate the least with changes in demand and supply, and it would become a globally sought medium of exchange, allowing all economic calculation to be carried out with it, becoming a common unit of measure across time and space. The higher the salability of a good, the more suited it is for this role. The Roman aureus, Byzantine solidus, or the U.S. dollar were all examples of this to a limited extent, though

---

[21] *Triennial Central Bank Survey: Foreign Exchange Turnover in April 2016.* Basel, CH, Bank of International Settlements, 2016.

[22] For more on this see George Gilder, *The Scandal of Money: Why Wall Street Recovers but the Economy Never Does.* Washington, D.C., Regnery, 2016.

[23] Hoppe, Hans-Hermann. "How Is Fiat Money Possible?" *Review of Austrian Economics*, vol. 7, no. 2, 1994.

each had its drawbacks. The money that came closest to this was gold in the latter years of the international gold standard, although even then, some countries and societies remained on silver or other primitive forms of money.

It is an astonishing fact of modern life that an entrepreneur in the year 1900 could make global economic plans and calculations all denominated in any international currency, with no thought whatsoever given to exchange rate fluctuations. A century later, the equivalent entrepreneur trying to make an economic plan across borders faces an array of highly volatile exchange rates that might make him think he has walked into a Salvador Dali painting. Any sane analyst looking at this mess would conclude it would be best to just tie the value of money to gold again and be rid of this juggling act, thus solving the Impossible Trinity by eliminating the need for government-controlled monetary policy, and having free capital movement and free trade. This would at once create economic stability and free up a large amount of capital and resources to the production of valuable goods and services, rather than speculation on complex exchange rate oscillations.

Unfortunately, however, the people in charge of the current monetary system have a vested interest in it continuing, and have thus preferred to try to find ways to manage it, and to find ever-more-creative ways of vilifying and dismissing the gold standard. This is entirely understandable given their jobs depend on a government having access to a printing press to reward them.

The combination of floating exchange rates and Keynesian ideology has given our world the entirely modern phenomenon of currency wars: because Keynesian analysis says that increasing exports leads to an increase in GDP, and GDP is the holy grail of economic well-being, it thus follows, in the mind of Keynesians, that anything that boosts exports is good. Because a devalued currency makes exports cheaper, any country facing an economic slowdown can boost its GDP and employment by devaluing its currency and increasing its exports.

There are many things wrong with this worldview. Reducing the value of the currency does nothing to increase the competitiveness of the industries in real terms. Instead, it only creates a one-time discount on their outputs, thus offering them to foreigners at a lower price than locals, impoverishing locals and subsidizing foreigners. It also makes all the country's assets cheaper for foreigners, allowing them to come in and purchase land, capital, and resources in the country at a discount. In a liberal economic order, there is nothing wrong with foreigners buying local assets, but in a Keynesian economic order, foreigners are actively subsidized to come buy the country at a discount. Further, economic history shows that the most successful economies of the postwar era, such as Germany, Japan, and Switzerland, grew their exports significantly as their currency continued to appreciate. They did not need constant devaluation to make their exports grow; they developed a competitive advantage that made their products demanded globally, which in turn caused their currencies to appreciate compared to their trade partners, increasing the wealth of their population. It is counterproductive for the countries importing from them to think they can boost their exports by simply devaluing the currency. They would be destroying their people's wealth by simply allowing foreigners to purchase it at a discount. It is no coincidence that the countries that have seen their currencies devalue the most in the postwar period were also the ones that suffered economic stagnation and decline.

But even if all of these problems with devaluation as the route to prosperity were inaccurate, there is one simple reason why it cannot work, and that is: if it worked, and all countries tried it, all currencies would devalue and no single country would have an advantage over the others. This brings us to the current state of affairs in the global economy, where most governments attempt to devalue their currencies in order to boost their exports, and all complain about one another's "unfair" manipulation of their currencies. Effectively, each country is impoverishing its citizens in order to boost its exporters and raise GDP numbers, and complaining when other countries do the same. The economic ignorance is only matched by the mendacious hypocrisy of the politicians and economists parroting these lines. International economic summits are convened where world leaders try to negotiate each other's acceptable currency devaluation, making the value of the currency an issue of geopolitical importance.

None of this would be necessary if only the world were to be based on a sound global monetary system that serves as a global unit of account and measure of value, allowing producers and consumers worldwide to have an accurate assessment of their costs and revenues, separating economic profitability from government policy. Hard money, by taking the question of supply out of the hands of governments and their economist-propagandists, would force everyone to be productive to society instead of seeking to get rich through the fool's errand of monetary manipulation.

Chapter 7

Sound Money and Individual Freedom

"[G]overnments believe that ... when there is a choice between an unpopular tax and a very popular expenditure, there is a way out for them—the way toward inflation. This illustrates the problem of going away from the gold standard."

—*Ludwig von Mises*[1]

Under a sound monetary system, government had to function in a way that is unimaginable to generations reared on the twentieth-century news cycle: they had to be fiscally responsible. Without a central bank capable of increasing the money supply to pay off the government debt, government budgets had to obey the regular rules of financial responsibility which apply to every healthy normal

---

[1] Greaves, Bettina Bien. *Ludwig von Mises on Money and Inflation: A Synthesis of Several Lectures.* Auburn, AL, Ludwig von Mises Institute, 2010, p. 32.

entity, and which monetary nationalism has attempted to repeal and state education attempted to obfuscate.

For those of us alive today, raised on the propaganda of the omnipotent governments of the twentieth century, it is often hard to imagine a world in which individual freedom and responsibility supersede government authority. Yet such was the state of the world during the periods of greatest human progress and freedom: government was restrained to the scope of protection of national borders, private property, and individual freedoms, while leaving to individuals a very large magnitude of freedom to make their own choices and reap the benefits or bear the costs. We start by critically examining the question of whether the money supply needs to be managed by the government in the first place, before moving to consider the consequences of what happens when it is.

Should Government Manage the Money Supply?

The fundamental scam of modernity is the idea that government needs to manage the money supply. It is an unquestioned starting assumption of all mainstream economic schools of thought and political parties. There isn't a shred of real-world evidence to support this contention, and every attempt to manage the money supply has ended with economic disaster. Money supply management is the problem masquerading as its solution; the triumph of emotional hope over hard-headed reason; the root of all political free lunches sold to gullible voters. It functions like a highly addictive and destructive drug, such as crystal meth or sugar: it causes a beautiful high at the beginning, fooling its victims into feeling invincible, but as soon as the effect subsides, the come-down is devastating and has the victim begging for more. This is when the hard choice needs to be made: either suffer the withdrawal effects of ceasing the addiction, or take another hit, delay the reckoning by a day, and sustain severe long-term damage.

For Keynesian and Marxist economists, and other proponents of the state theory of money, money is whatever the state says is money, and therefore it is the prerogative of the state to do with it as it pleases, which is going to inevitably mean printing it to spend on achieving state objectives. The aim of economic research, then, is to decide how best to expand the money supply and to what ends. But the fact that gold has been used as money for thousands of years, from before nation states were ever invented, is itself enough refutation of this theory. The fact that central banks still hold large amounts of gold reserves and are still accumulating more of it testifies to gold's enduring monetary nature, in spite of no government mandating it. But whatever historical quibbles the proponents of the state theory of money may have with these facts, their theory has been obliterated before our very eyes over the last decade by the continued success and growth of bitcoin, which has achieved monetary status and gained value exceeding that of most state-backed currencies, purely due to its reliable salability in spite of no authority mandating its use as money.[2]

There are today two main government-approved mainstream schools of economic thought: Keynesians and Monetarists. While these two schools have widely disparate methodologies and analytical frameworks, and while they are engaged in bitter academic fights accusing each other of not caring about the poor, the children, the environment, inequality, or the buzzword *du jour*, they both agree on two unquestionable truths: first, the government has to expand the money supply. Second, both schools deserve more government funding to continue researching really important Big Questions which will lead them to find ever-more-creative ways of arriving at the first truth.

It's important to understand the different rationales for the two schools of thought in order to understand how they can both arrive at the same conclusion and be equally wrong. Keynes was a failed investor and statistician who never studied economics but was so well-connected with the ruling class in Britain that the embarrassing drivel he wrote in his most famous book, *The General Theory of Employment, Money, and Interest*, was immediately elevated into the status of founding truths of macroeconomics. His theory begins with the (completely unfounded and unwarranted) assumption that the most important metric in determining the state of the economy is the level of

---

[2]Matonis, John. "Bitcoin Obliterates 'The State Theory of Money.'" *Forbes*, 3 Apr. 2013, www.forbes.com/sites/jonmatonis/2013/04/03/bitcoin-obliterates-the-state-theory-of-money/#6b93e45f4b6d.

aggregate spending across society. When society collectively spends a lot, the spending incentivizes producers to create more products, thus employing more workers and reaching full-employment equilibrium. If spending rises too much, beyond the capacity of producers to keep up, it would lead to inflation and a rise in the overall price level. On the other hand, when society spends too little, producers reduce their production, firing workers and increasing unemployment, resulting in a recession.

Recessions, for Keynes, are caused by abrupt reductions in the aggregate level of spending. Keynes was not very good with grasping the concept of causality and logical explanations, so he never quite bothered to explain *why* it is that spending levels might suddenly drop, instead just coining another of his famous clumsy and utterly meaningless figures of speech to save him the hassle of an explanation. He blamed it on the flagging of "animal spirits." To this day, nobody knows exactly what these animal spirits are or why they might suddenly flag, but that of course has only meant that an entire cottage industry of state-funded economists have made a career out of attempting to explain them or finding real-world data that can correlate to them. This research has been very good for academic careers, but is of no value to anyone actually trying to understand business cycles. Put bluntly, pop psychology is no substitute for capital theory.[3]

Freed from the restraint of having to find a cause of the recession, Keynes can then happily recommend the solution he is selling. Whenever there is a recession, or a rise in the unemployment level, the cause is a drop in the aggregate level of spending and the solution is for the government to stimulate spending, which will in turn increase production and reduce unemployment. There are three ways of stimulating aggregate spending: increasing the money supply, increasing government spending, or reducing taxes. Reducing taxes is generally frowned upon by Keynesians. It is viewed as the least effective method, because people will not spend all the taxes they don't have to pay—some of that money will be saved, and Keynes absolutely detested saving. Saving would reduce spending, and reducing spending would be the worst

---

[3] And in capital theory, accept no substitutes for Austrian Capital Theory, as expounded by Böhm-Bawerk, Mises, Hayek, Rothbard, Huerta de Soto, Salerno, among others.

thing imaginable for an economy seeking recovery. It was government's role to impose high time preference on society by spending more or printing money. Seeing as it is hard to raise taxes during a recession, government spending would effectively translate to increasing the money supply. This, then, was the Keynesian Holy Grail: whenever the economy was not at full employment, an increase of the money supply would fix the problem. There is no point worrying about inflation, because as Keynes had "showed" (i.e., baselessly assumed) inflation only happens when spending is too high, and because unemployment is high, that means spending is too low. There may be consequences in the long run, but there was no point worrying about long-term consequences, because "in the long run, we are all dead,"[4] as Keynes's most famous defense of high-time-preference libertine irresponsibility famously stated.

The Keynesian view of the economy is, of course, at complete odds with reality. If Keynes's model had any truth to it, it would then necessarily follow that there can be no example of a society experiencing high inflation and high unemployment at the same time. But this has in fact happened many times, most notably in the United States in the 1970s, when, in spite of the assurances of Keynesian economists to the contrary, and in spite of the entire U.S. establishment, from President Nixon down to "free market economist" Milton Friedman, adopting the refrain, "We're all Keynesians now" as the government took it upon itself to eliminate unemployment with increased inflation, unemployment kept on rising as inflation soared, destroying the theory that there is a trade-off between these two. In any sane society, Keynes's ideas should have been removed from the economics textbooks and confined to the realm of academic comedy, but in a society where government controls academia to a very large degree, the textbooks continued to preach the Keynesian mantra that justified ever more money printing. Having the ability to

---

[4]Keynes, J. M. *A Tract on Monetary Reform*. London, Macmillan and Co., 1923, p. 80. It is worth remarking that modern-day Keynesians reject the interpretation of this quote as signifying Keynes's concern for the present at the expense of the future. Instead, Keynesians like Simon Taylor argue that this signifies Keynes's prioritizing of tackling unemployment immediately rather than worrying about the remote threat of inflation. This defense unfortunately serves only to expose Keynes's modern disciples to be as short-termist as he, and exactly as ignorant of the fundamental reality that it is precisely the inflationist policies that cause the unemployment in the first place. See Simon Taylor's "The True Meaning of 'In the Long Run We Are All Dead.'" www.simontaylorsblog.com/2013/05/05/the-true-meaning-of-in-the-long-runwe-are-all-dead/.

print money, literally and figuratively, increases the power of any government, and any government looks for anything that gives it more power.

The other main school of government-approved economic thought in our day and age is the Monetarist school, whose intellectual father is Milton Friedman. Monetarists are best understood as the battered wives of the Keynesians: they are there to provide a weak, watered-down strawman version of a free market argument to create the illusion of a climate of intellectual debate, and to be constantly and comprehensively rebutted to safely prevent the intellectually curious from thinking of free markets seriously. The percentage of economists who are actually Monetarists is minuscule compared to Keynesians, but they are given far too much space to express their ideas as if there are two equal sides. Monetarists largely agree with Keynesians on the basic assumptions of the Keynesian models, but find elaborate and sophisticated mathematical quibbles with some conclusions of the model, which exceptions always lead them to dare to suggest a slightly reduced role for government in the macroeconomy, which immediately gets them dismissed as heartless evil capitalist scum who do not care about the poor.

Monetarists generally oppose Keynesian efforts to spend money to eliminate unemployment, arguing that in the long run, the effect on unemployment will be eliminated while causing inflation. Instead, Monetarists prefer tax cuts to stimulate the economy, because they argue that the free market will better allocate resources than government spending. While this debate over tax cuts versus spending increases rages on, the reality is that both policies result in increased government deficits which can only be financed with monetized debt, effectively an increase in the money supply. However, the central tenet of Monetarist thought is for the pressing need for governments to prevent collapses in the money supply and/or drops in the price level, which they view as the root of all economic problems. A decline in the price level, or *deflation* as the Monetarists and Keynesians like to call it, would result in people hoarding their money, reducing their spending, causing increases in unemployment, causing a recession. Most worryingly for Monetarists, deflation is usually accompanied by collapses in the banking sector balance sheets, and because they, too, share an aversion for understanding cause and effect, it thus follows that central banks must do everything possible to ensure that deflation never happens. For the canonical treatment of why Monetarists are so scared of deflation, see a 2002 speech by former Chairman of the Federal Reserve Ben Bernanke entitled *Deflation: Making Sure "It" Doesn't Happen Here*.[5]

The sum total of the contribution of both these schools of thought is the consensus taught in undergraduate macroeconomics courses across the world: that the central bank should be in the business of expanding the money supply at a controlled pace, to encourage people to spend more and thus keep the unemployment level sufficiently low. Should a central bank contract the money supply, or fail to expand it adequately, then a deflationary spiral can take place, which would discourage people from spending their money and thus harm employment and cause an economic downturn.[6] Such is the nature of this debate that most mainstream economists and textbooks do not even consider the question of whether the money supply should be increased at all, assuming that its increase is a given and discussing how central banks need to manage this increase and dictate its rates. The creed of Keynes, which is universally popular today, is the creed of consumption and spending to satisfy immediate wants. By constantly expanding the money supply, central banks' monetary policy makes saving and investment less attractive and thus it encourages people to save and invest less while consuming more. The real impact of this is the widespread culture of conspicuous consumption, where people live their lives to buy ever-larger quantities of crap they do not need. When the alternative to spending money is witnessing your savings lose value over time, you might as well enjoy spending it before it loses its value. The financial decisions of people also reflect on all other aspects of their personality, engendering a high time preference in all aspects of life: depreciating currency causes less saving, more borrowing, more short-termism in economic production and in artistic and cultural endeavors, and perhaps most damagingly, the depletion of the soil of its nutrients, leading to ever-lower levels of nutrients in food.

In contrast to these two schools of thought stands the classical tradition of economics, which is the culmination of hundreds of years of scholarship from around the world. Commonly referred to today as

[5] *Deflation: Making Sure "It" Doesn't Happen Here*. Remarks by Governor Ben S. Bernanke before the National Economists Club, Washington, D.C., 21 Nov. 2002.
[6] McConnell, Campbell, Stanley Brue, and Sean Flynn. *Economics*. McGraw-Hill, 2009, p. 535.

the Austrian school, in honor of the last great generation of economists from Austria in its golden age pre–World War I, this school draws on the work of Classical Scottish, French, Spanish, Arab, and Ancient Greek economists in explicating its understanding of economics. Unlike Keynesian and Monetarist fixation on rigorous numerical analysis and mathematical sophistry, the Austrian school is focused on establishing an *understanding* of phenomena in a causal manner and logically deducing implications from demonstrably true axioms.

The Austrian theory of money posits that money emerges in a market as the most marketable commodity and most salable asset, the one asset whose holders can sell with the most ease, in favorable conditions.[7] An asset that holds its value is preferable to an asset that loses value, and savers who want to choose a medium of exchange will gravitate toward assets that hold value over time as monetary assets. Network effects mean that eventually only one, or a few, assets can emerge as media of exchange. For Mises, the absence of control by government is a necessary condition for the soundness of money, seeing as government will have the temptation to debase its money whenever it begins to accrue wealth as savers invest in it.

By placing a hard cap on the total supply of bitcoins, as discussed in Chapter 8, Nakamoto was clearly unpersuaded by the arguments of the standard macroeconomics textbook and more influenced by the Austrian school, which argues that the quantity of money itself is irrelevant, that any supply of money is sufficient to run an economy of any size, because the currency units are infinitely divisible, and because it is only the purchasing power of money in terms of real goods and services that matters, and not its numerical quantity. As Ludwig von Mises put it:[8]

> The services money renders are conditioned by the height of its purchasing power. Nobody wants to have in his cash holding a definite number of pieces of money or a definite weight of money; he wants to keep a cash holding of a definite amount of purchasing power. As the operation of the market tends to determine the final state of money's purchasing power at a height at which the supply of and the demand for money coincide, there can never be an excess or a deficiency of

---

[7] Menger, Carl. "On the Origins of Money." Trans. C. A. Foley. *Economic Journal*, vol. 2, 1892.
[8] Ludwig von Mises. *Human Action*. p. 421.

money. Each individual and all individuals together always enjoy fully the advantages which they can derive from indirect exchange and the use of money, no matter whether the total quantity of money is great or small ... the services which money renders can be neither improved nor impaired by changing the supply of money.... The quantity of money available in the whole economy is always sufficient to secure for everybody all that money does and can do.

Murray Rothbard concurs with Mises:[9]

A world of constant money supply would be one similar to that of much of the eighteenth and nineteenth centuries, marked by the successful flowering of the Industrial Revolution with increased capital investment increasing the supply of goods and with falling prices for those goods as well as falling costs of production.

According to the Austrian view, if the money supply is fixed, then economic growth will cause prices of real goods and services to drop, allowing people to purchase increasing quantities of goods and services with their money in the future. Such a world would indeed discourage immediate consumption as the Keynesians fear, but encourage saving and investment for the future where more consumption can happen. For a school of thought steeped in high time preference, it is understandable that Keynes could not understand that increased savings' impact on consumption in any present moment is more than outweighed by the increases in spending caused by the increased savings of the past. A society which constantly defers consumption will actually end up being a society that consumes more in the long run than a low savings society, since the low-time-preference society invests more, thus producing more income for its members. Even with a larger percentage of their income going to savings, the low-time-preference societies will end up having higher levels of consumption in the long run as well as a larger capital stock.

If society were a little girl in that marshmallow experiment, Keynesian economics seeks to alter the experiment so that waiting would punish the girl by giving her half a marshmallow instead of

---

[9]Rothbard, Murray. "The Austrian Theory of Money." *The Foundations of Modern Austrian Economics*, edited by Edwin Dolan, Kansas City, Sheed and Ward, 1976, pp. 160–84.

two, making the entire concept of self-control and low time preference appear counterproductive. Indulging immediate pleasures is the more likely course of action economically, and that will then reflect on culture and society at large. The Austrian school, on the other hand, by preaching sound money, recognizes the reality of the trade-off that nature provides humans, and that if the child waits, there will be more reward for her, making her happier in the long run, encouraging her to defer her gratification to increase it.

When the value of money appreciates, people are likely to be far more discerning with their consumption and to save far more of their income for the future. The culture of conspicuous consumption, of shopping as therapy, of always needing to replace cheap plastic crap with newer, flashier cheap plastic crap will not have a place in a society with a money which appreciates in value over time. Such a world would cause people to develop a lower time preference, as their monetary decisions will orient their actions toward the future, teaching them to value the future more and more. We can thus see how such a society would cause people not only to save and invest more, but also to be morally, artistically, and culturally oriented toward the long-term future.

A currency that appreciates in value incentivizes saving, as savings gain purchasing power over time. Hence, it encourages deferred consumption, resulting in lower time preference. A currency that depreciates in value, on the other hand, leaves citizens constantly searching for returns to beat inflation, returns that must come with a risk, and so leads to an increase in investment in risky projects and an increased risk tolerance among investors, leading to increased losses. Societies with money of stable value generally develop a low time preference, learning to save and think of the future, while societies with high inflation and depreciating economies will develop high time preference as people lose track of the importance of saving and concentrate on immediate enjoyment.

Further, an economy with an appreciating currency would witness investment only in projects that offer a positive real return over the rate of appreciation of money, meaning that only projects expected to increase society's capital stock will tend to get funded. By contrast, an economy with a depreciating currency incentivizes individuals to invest in projects that offer positive returns in terms of the depreciating currency, but negative real returns. The projects that beat inflation but do not offer positive real returns effectively reduce society's capital stock, but are nonetheless a rational alternative for investors because they reduce their capital slower than the depreciating currency. These investments are what Ludwig von Mises terms *malinvestments*—unprofitable projects and investments that only appear profitable during the period of inflation and artificially low interest rates, and whose unprofitability will be exposed as soon as inflation rates drop and interest rates rise, causing the bust part of the boom-and-bust cycle. As Mises puts it, "The boom squanders through malinvestment scarce factors of production and reduces the stock available through overconsumption; its alleged blessings are paid for by impoverishment."[10]

This exposition helps explain why Austrian school economists are more favorable to the use of gold as money while Keynesian mainstream economists support the government's issuance of elastic money that can be expanded at the government's behest. For Keynesians, the fact that the whole world's central banks run on fiat currencies is testament to the superiority of their ideas. For Austrians, on the other hand, the fact that governments have to resort to coercive measures of banning gold as money and enforcing payment in fiat currencies is at once testament to the inferiority of fiat money and its inability to succeed in a free market. It is also the root cause of all business cycles' booms and busts. While the Keynesian economists have no explanation for why recessions happen other than invoking "animal spirits," Austrian school economists have developed the only coherent theory that explains the cause of business cycles: the Austrian Theory of the Business Cycle.[11]

Unsound Money and Perpetual War

As discussed in Chapter 4 on the history of money, it was no coincidence that the era of central bank-controlled money was inaugurated with the first world war in human history. There are three fundamental reasons that drive the relationship between unsound money and war.

---

[10]Ludwig von Mises. *Human Action*. p. 575.
[11]Rothbard, Murray. *Economic Depressions: Their Cause and Cure*. Auburn, AL, Ludwig von Mises Institute, 2009.

First, unsound money is itself a barrier to trade between countries, because it distorts value between the countries and makes trade flows a political issue, creating animosity and enmity between governments and populations. Second, government having access to a printing press allows it to continue fighting until it completely destroys the value of its currency, and not just until it runs out of money. With sound money, the government's war effort was limited by the taxes it could collect. With unsound money, it is restrained by how much money it can create before the currency is destroyed, making it able to appropriate wealth far more easily. Third, individuals dealing with sound money develop a lower time preference, allowing them to think more of cooperation rather than conflict, as discussed in Chapter 5.

The larger the extent of the market with which individuals can trade, the more specialized they can be in their production, and the larger their gains from trade. The same amount of labor expended working in a primitive economy of 10 people would lead to a far lower material living standard than if it had been expended within a larger market of 1,000 or 1,000,000 people. The modern individual living in a free-trading society is able to work for a few hours a day in a highly specialized job, and with the money she makes she is able to purchase the goods she wants from whichever producers in the entire planet make them with the lowest cost and best quality. To fully appreciate the gains from trade that accrue to you, just imagine trying to live your life in self-sufficiency. Basic survival would become a very hard task for any of us, as our time is spent inefficiently and fruitlessly attempting to provide the very basics of survival to ourselves.

Money is the medium through which trade takes place, and the only tool through which trade can expand beyond the scope of small communities with close personal relationships. For the price mechanism to work, prices need to be denominated in a sound form of money across the community that trades with it. The larger the area using a common currency, the easier and the larger the scope of trade within the area. Trade between peoples creates peaceful coexistence by giving them a vested interest in each other's prosperity. When communities use different kinds of unsound money, trade becomes more complicated, as prices vary along with the variation in the value of the currencies, making the terms of trade unpredictable, and making it often counterproductive to plan economic activity across borders.

Being predisposed to focus on the future, individuals with a low time preference are less likely to engage in conflict than those with a present orientation. Conflict is by its very nature destructive, and in most cases, intelligent and future-oriented people understand that there are no winners in violent conflict, because the winners will likely suffer more losses than if they had just abstained from taking part in the conflict in the first place. Civilized societies function on the premise that people respect one another's wills, and if there are conflicts, they attempt a peaceful resolution. Should an amicable solution not be found, people are more likely to part ways and avoid each other than continue to agitate and remain in conflict. This helps explain why prosperous civilized societies generally do not witness much crime, violence, or conflict.

On a national level, nations using sound money are far more likely to stay peaceful, or to have limited conflict with one another, because sound money places real constraints on the ability of government to finance its military operations. In nineteenth-century Europe, kings who wanted to fight each other had to tax their populations in order to finance their militaries. In the long run, such a strategy could only be profitable for kings who would employ their military defensively, not offensively. Defensive military action always has a stronger advantage than offensive military nature, because the defender is fighting on its own soil, near its people and its supply lines. A monarch who focused the military on defensive action would find his citizens willing to pay taxes to defend themselves from foreign invaders. But a monarch who engaged in protracted foreign adventures to enrich himself would likely face resentment from his population and incur significant costs in fighting other armies on their home soil.

This can help explain why the twentieth century was the deadliest in recorded history. The 2005 United Nations Human Development Report[12] analyzed death from conflicts over the past five centuries, and found the twentieth century to be the deadliest. Even when major European nations went to war with one another in the gold standard era,

---

[12] *Human Development Report 2005: International Cooperation at a Crossroads: Aid, Trade and Security in an Unequal World.* United Nations Development Program, New York, 2005, hdr.undp.org/en/content/human-development-report-2005.

Table 5 Conflict Deaths in the Last Five Centuries

	Conflicts Steadily Cost More in Human Lives		
Period	Conflict-Related Deaths (millions)	World Population, Midcentury (millions)	Conflict-Related Deaths as Share of World Population (%)
16th century	1.6	493.3	0.32
17th century	6.1	579.1	1.05
18th century	7.0	757.4	0.92
19th century	19.4	1,172.9	1.65
20th century	109.7	2,519.5	4.35

the wars were usually brief and fought in battlefields between professional armies. A major war of the nineteenth century in Europe was the Franco-Prussian war of 1870–1871, which lasted for 9 months and killed around 150,000 people, roughly an average week's tally in World War II, financed by the easy government money of the twentieth century. With the gold standard restricting them to finance war from taxation, European governments had to have their expenses prepared before battle, spend them on preparing their military as effectively as possible, and attempt a decisive victory. As soon as the tide of the battle began to turn against one of the armies, it was a logistically and economically losing battle to try to increase taxes to rearm the military and turn the tide—better to try to negotiate a peace with as few losses as possible. The deadliest wars of the nineteenth century were the Napoleonic wars, which were carried out before the gold standard was formally adopted across the continent, after the French revolution's foolish experiments with inflation. (See Table 5.[13])

As it stands, a large number of firms in all advanced economies specialize in warfare as a business, and are thus reliant on perpetuating war to continue being in business. They live off government spending exclusively, and have their entire existence reliant on there being perpetual wars necessitating ever-larger arms spending. In the United

---

[13] *Source: Human Development Report 2005: International Cooperation at a Crossroads: Aid, Trade and Security in an Unequal World.* United Nations Development Program, New York, 2005, hdr.undp.org/en/content/human-development-report-2005.

States, whose defense spending is almost equal to that of the rest of the planet combined, these industries have a vested interest in keeping the U.S. government involved in some form of military adventure or other. This, more than any strategic, cultural, ideological, or security operations, explains why the United States has been involved in so many conflicts in parts of the world that cannot possibly have any bearing on the life of the average American. Only with unsound money can these firms grow to such enormous magnitude that they can influence the press, academia, and think tanks to continuously beat the drums of more war.

Limited versus Omnipotent Government

In his sweeping history of five centuries of Western civilization, *From Dawn to Decadence*, Jacques Barzun identifies the end of World War I as the crucial turning point to begin the decadence, decay, and demise of the West. It was after this war that the West suffered from what Barzun terms "The Great Switch," the replacement of liberalism by liberality, the impostor claiming its mantle but in reality being its exact opposite.[14]

> Liberalism triumphed on the principle that the best government is that which governs least; now for all the western nations political wisdom has recast this ideal of liberty into liberality. The shift has thrown the vocabulary into disorder.

Whereas liberalism held the role of government as allowing individuals to live in liberty and enjoy the benefits, and suffer the consequences, of their actions, liberality was the radical notion that it was government's role to allow individuals to indulge in all their desires while protecting them from the consequences. Socially, economically, and politically, the role of government was recast as the wish-granting genie, and the population merely had to vote for what it wanted to have fulfilled.

---

[14]Barzun, Jacques. *From Dawn to Decadence: 500 Years of Western Cultural Life*. HarperCollins, 2000, p. 688.

French historian Élie Halévy defined the Era of Tyrannies as having begun in 1914 with World War I, when the major powers of the world shifted toward economic and intellectual nationalization. They nationalized the means of production and shifted to syndicalist and corporatist modes of societal organization, all while suppressing ideas viewed as opposed to the national interest, as well as the promotion of nationalism in what he termed "the organization of enthusiasm."[15]

This classical liberal conception of government is only possible in a world with sound money, which acted as a natural restraint against government authoritarianism and overreach. As long as government had to tax its people to finance its operations, it had to restrict its operations to what its subjects deemed tolerable. Governments had to keep a balanced budget by always keeping consumption within the limits of earnings from taxation. In a society of sound money, government is reliant on the consent of its population to finance its operations. Every new proposal for government action will have to be paid for upfront in taxes or by the sale of long-term government bonds, giving the population an accurate measure of the true costs of this strategy, which they could easily compare to the benefits. A government seeking funding for legitimate national defense and infrastructure projects would have little trouble imposing taxes on, and selling bonds to, the population that saw the benefits before their eyes. But a government which raises taxes to fund a monarch's lavish lifestyle will engender mass resentment among his population, endangering the legitimacy of his rule and making it ever more precarious. The more onerous the taxation and impositions of the government, the more likely the population is to refuse to pay taxes, make tax collection costs rise significantly, or rise up against the government and replace it, whether by ballot or bullet.

Sound money, then, enforced a measure of honesty and transparency on governments, restricting their rule to within what was desirable and tolerable to the population. It allowed for society-wide honest accounting of costs and benefits of actions, as well as the economic responsibility necessary for any organization, individual, or living being to succeed in life: consumption must come after production.

---

[15]Halévy, Élie and May Wallas. "The Age of Tyrannies." *Economica*, New Series, vol. 8, no. 29, Feb. 1941, pp. 77–93.

Unsound money, on the other hand, allows governments to buy allegiance and popularity by spending on achieving popular objectives without having to present the bill to their people. Government simply increases the money supply to finance any harebrained scheme it concocts, and the true cost of such schemes is only felt by the population in years to come when the inflation of the money supply causes prices to rise, at which point the destruction of the value of the currency can be easily blamed on myriad factors, usually involving some nefarious plots by foreigners, bankers, local ethnic minorities, or previous or future governments. Unsound money is a particularly dangerous tool in the hands of modern democratic governments facing constant reelection pressure. Modern voters are unlikely to favor the candidates who are upfront about the costs and benefits of their schemes; they are far more likely to go with the scoundrels who promise a free lunch and blame the bill on their predecessors or some nefarious conspiracy. Democracy thus becomes a mass delusion of people attempting to override the rules of economics by voting themselves a free lunch and being manipulated into violent tantrums against scapegoats whenever the bill for the free lunch arrives via inflation and economic recessions.

Unsound money is at the heart of the modern delusion believed by most voters and those unfortunate enough to study modern macroeconomics at university level: that government actions have no opportunity costs, and that government can act with an omnipotent magic wand to create the reality it wants. Whether it's poverty reduction, morality enforcement, healthcare, education, infrastructure, reforming other countries' political and economic institutions, or overriding the rules of supply and demand for any emotionally important good, most modern citizens live in the delusional dreamland wherein none of these have actual costs, and all that is needed for these goals to be achieved is "political will," "strong leadership," and an absence of corruption. Unsound money has eradicated the notion of trade-offs and opportunity costs from the mind of individuals thinking of public affairs. It will shock the average citizen to have the startlingly obvious pointed out to them: all of these nice things you want cannot be summoned costlessly out of thin air by your favorite politician, or his opponent. They all need to be provided by real people—people who need to wake up in the morning and spend days and years toiling at giving you what you want, denying themselves the chance to work on other things they might prefer to produce. Though no politician has ever been elected by acknowledging this reality, the ballot box cannot overturn the fundamental scarcity of human time. Any time government decides to provide something, it does not increase economic output; it just means more central planning of economic output with predictable consequences.[16]

Unsound money was a boon to tyrants, repressive regimes, and illegitimate governments by allowing them to avoid the reality of costs and benefits by increasing the money supply to finance their undertakings first, and letting the population handle the consequences later as they witness their wealth and purchasing power evaporate. History is replete with examples of how governments that have the prerogative to create money out of thin air have almost always abused this privilege by turning it against their own people.

It is no coincidence that when recounting the most horrific tyrants of history, one finds that every single one of them operated a system of government-issued money which was constantly inflated to finance government operation. There is a very good reason that Vladimir Lenin, Joseph Stalin, Mao Ze Dong, Adolf Hitler, Maximilien Robespierre, Pol Pot, Benito Mussolini, Kim Jong Il, and many other notorious criminals all ruled in periods of unsound government-issued money which they could print at will to finance their genocidal and totalitarian megalomania. It is the same reason that the same societies which birthed these mass murderers did not produce anyone close to their level of criminality when living under sound monetary systems which required governments to tax before they spent. None of these monsters ever repealed sound money in order to fund their mass murder. The destruction of sound money had come before, hailed with wonderful feel-good stories involving children, education, worker liberation, and national pride. But once sound money was destroyed, it became very easy for these criminals to take over power and take command of all of their society's resources by increasing the supply of unsound money.

---

[16]Rothbard, Murray. "The End of Socialism and the Calculation Debate Revisited." *Review of Austrian Economics*, vol. 5, no. 2, 1991.

Unsound money makes government power potentially unlimited, with large consequences to every individual, forcing politics to the center stage of their life and redirecting much of society's energy and resources to the zero-sum game of who gets to rule and how. Sound money, on the other hand, makes the form of government a question with limited consequences. A democracy, republic, or monarchy are all restrained by sound money, allowing most individuals a large degree of freedom in their personal life.

Whether in the Soviet or capitalist economies, the notion of the government "running" or "managing" the economy to achieve economic goals is viewed as good and necessary. It is worth returning here to the views of John Maynard Keynes to understand the motivations of the economic system he proposes, with which humanity has had to contend for the past decades. In one of his lesser-known papers, *The End of Laissez-Faire*, Keynes offers his conception of what the role of government in a society should be. Keynes expresses his opposition of liberalism and individualism, which one would expect, but also presents the grounds of his opposition to socialism, stating:

> Nineteenth-century State Socialism sprang from Bentham, free competition, etc., and is in some respects a clearer, in some respects a more muddled, version of just the same philosophy as underlies nineteenth-century individualism. Both equally laid all their stress on freedom, the one negatively to avoid limitations on existing freedom, the other positively to destroy natural or acquired monopolies. They are different reactions to the same intellectual atmosphere.

Keynes's problem with socialism, then, is that its end goal was increasing individual freedom. For Keynes, the end goal should not be concerned with trivial issues like individual freedom, but for government to control aspects of the economy to his liking. He outlines three main arenas where he views government's role to be vital: first, "the deliberate control of the currency and of credit by a central institution," the belief that laid the groundwork for modern central banking. Second, and relatedly, Keynes believed it was the role of the government to decide on "the scale on which it is desirable that the community as a whole should save, the scale on which these savings should go abroad in the form of foreign investments, and whether the present organization of the investment market distributes savings along the most nationally productive channels. I do not think that these matters should be left entirely to the chances of private judgement and private profits, as they are at present." And finally, Keynes believed it was the role of the government to devise "a considered national policy about what size of population, whether larger or smaller than at present or the same, is most expedient. And having settled this policy, we must take steps to carry it into operation. The time may arrive a little later when the community as a whole must pay attention to the innate quality as well as to the mere numbers of its future members."[17]

In other words, the Keynesian conception of the state, from which came the modern central banking doctrines held widely by all central bankers, and which shape the vast majority of economic textbooks written worldwide, comes from a place of a man who wanted government direction of two important areas of life: first, the control of money, credit, saving, and investment decisions, which meant the totalitarian centralization of capital allocation and destruction of free individual enterprise, making individuals utterly dependent on government for their basic survival, and second, the control of population quantity and quality, which meant eugenics. And unlike socialists, Keynes did not seek this level of control over individuals in order to enhance their freedom in the long run, but rather to develop a grander vision of society as he sees fit. While socialists may have had the decency to at least pretend to want to enslave man for his own good, to free him in the future, Keynes wanted government enslavement for its own sake, as the ultimate end. This may help explain why Murray Rothbard said, "There is only one good thing about Marx, at least he was not a Keynesian."[18]

While such a conception might appeal to ivory-tower idealists who imagine it will only lead to positive outcomes, in reality this leads to the destruction of the market mechanisms necessary for economic production to take place. In such a system, money stops functioning as an information system for production, but rather as a government loyalty program.

---

[17] Keynes, J. M. "The End of Laissez-Faire." *Essays in Persuasion*, London, The Royal Economic Society, 1931, pp. 272–95.
[18] Rothbard, Murray. "A Conversation with Murray Rothbard." *Austrian Economics Newsletter*, vol. 11, no. 2, Auburn, AL, Mises Institute, Summer 1990.

The Bezzle

Chapter 3 explained how any commodity acquiring a monetary role would incentivize people to produce more of that commodity. A money which can be easily produced will lead to more economic resources and human time being dedicated toward its production. As money is acquired not for its own properties, but to be exchanged for other goods and services, its purchasing power is important, not its absolute quantity. There is therefore no societal benefit from any activity which increases the supply of money. This is why in a free market, whatever assumes a monetary role will have a reliably high stock-to-flow ratio: the new supply of the money is small compared to the overall existing supply. This ensures that the least possible amount of society's labor and capital resources is dedicated toward producing more monetary media, and is instead dedicated toward the production of useful goods and services whose absolute quantity, unlike that of money, matters. Gold became the leading global monetary standard because its new production was always a reliably tiny percentage of its existing supply, making goldmining a highly uncertain and unprofitable business, thus forcing more and more of the world's capital and labor to be directed toward the production of nonmonetary goods.

For John Maynard Keynes and Milton Friedman, one of the main attractions of moving away from the gold standard was the reduction in the costs of goldmining that would ensue from switching to government-issued paper money, whose cost of production is far lower than that of gold. They not only misunderstood that gold has very few resources going to its production compared to other goods whose supply can be inflated far more easily, they also severely underestimated the real costs to society from a form of money whose supply can be expanded at the will of a government susceptible to democratic and special-interest politics. The real cost is not in the direct cost of running the printing presses, but from all the economic activity forgone as productive resources chase after the new government-issued money rather than engage in economic production.

Inflationary credit creation can be understood as a society-wide example of what economist John Kenneth Galbraith[19] called "the

---

[19] Galbraith, John Kenneth. *The Great Crash, 1929*. Boston, Houghton Mifflin Harcourt, 1997, p. 133.

bezzle" in his book on the Great Depression. As credit expansion in the 1920s soared, corporations were awash with money, and it was very easy for people to embezzle that money in various ways. For as long as the credit keeps flowing, the victims are oblivious, and an illusion of increased wealth is created across society as both the victim and the robber think they have the money. Credit creation by central banks causes unsustainable booms by allowing the financing of unprofitable projects and allowing them to continue consuming resources on unproductive activities.

In a sound monetary system, any business that survives does so by offering value to society, by receiving a higher revenue for its products than the costs it incurs for its inputs. The business is productive because it transforms inputs of a certain market price into outputs with a higher market price. Any firm that produces outputs valued at less than its inputs would go out of business, its resources freed up to be used by other, more productive firms, in what economist Joseph Schumpeter termed *creative destruction*. There can be no profit in a free market without the real risk of loss, and everyone is forced to have skin in the game: failure is always a real possibility, and can be costly. Government-issued unsound money, however, can stall this process, keeping unproductive firms undead but not truly alive, the economic equivalent of zombies or vampires drawing on the resources of the alive and productive firms to produce things of less value than the resources needed to make them. It creates a new societal caste that exists according to rules different from those of everyone else, with no skin in the game. Facing no market test for their work, they are insulated from consequences to their actions. This new caste exists in every economic sector supported by government money.

It is not possible to estimate with any degree of accuracy what percentage of the economic activity in the modern world economy goes toward pursuing government-printed money rather than the production of goods and services useful to society, but it is possible to get an idea by looking at which firms and sectors survive because of succeeding in the test of the free market, and which are only alive thanks to government largesse—be it fiscal or monetary.

Fiscal support is the more straightforward of zombie-creation methods to detect. Any firms that receive direct government support, and the vast majority of firms that are alive thanks to selling their products to the public sector, are effectively zombies. Had these firms been productive to society, free individuals would have willingly parted with their money to pay for their products. That they cannot survive on voluntary payments shows that these firms are a burden and not a productive asset for society.

But the more pernicious method of creating zombies is not through direct government payments, but through access to low–interest-rate credit. As fiat money has slowly eroded society's ability to save, capital investments no longer come from savers' savings, but from government-created debt, which devalues existing money holdings. In a society with sound money, the more a person saves, the more he is able to accumulate capital and the more he can invest, meaning that capital owners tend to be those with lower time preference. But when capital comes from government credit creation, the allocators of capital are no longer the future-oriented, but members of various bureaucratic agencies.

In a free market with sound money, capital owners choose to allocate their capital to the investments they find most productive, and can utilize investment banks to manage this allocation process. The process rewards firms that serve customers successfully, and the investors who identify them, while punishing mistakes. In a fiat monetary system, however, the central bank is de facto responsible for the entirety of the credit allocation process. It controls and supervises the banks that allocate capital, sets the lending eligibility criteria, and attempts to quantify risks in a mathematical manner that ignores how real-world risks work. The test of the free market is suspended as central bank direction of credit can overrule the economic reality of profit and loss.

In the world of fiat money, having access to the central bank's monetary spigots is more important than serving customers. Firms that can get low-interest-rate credit to operate will have a persistent advantage over competitors that cannot. The criteria for success in the market becomes more and more related to being able to secure funding at lower interest rates than to providing services to society.

This simple phenomenon explains much of modern economic reality, such as the large number of industries that make money but produce nothing of value to anyone. Government agencies are the prime example, and the global notoriety they have earned for their employees' incompetence can only be understood as a function of the bezzle funding that finances them being completely detached from economic reality. Instead of the hard test of market success by serving citizens, government agencies test themselves and invariably conclude the answer to all their failings lies in more funding. No matter the level of incompetence, negligence, or failure, government agencies and employees rarely ever face real consequences. Even after the rationale for a government agency's existence has been removed, the agency will continue operating and find itself more duties and responsibility. Lebanon, for instance, continues to have a train authority decades after its trains were decommissioned and the tracks rusted into irrelevance.[20]

In a globalized world, the bezzle is not restricted to national governmental organizations, but has grown to include international governmental organizations, a globally renowned drain of time and effort of no conceivable benefit to anyone but those employed in them. Being located away from the taxpayers that fund them, these organizations face even less scrutiny than national governmental organizations, and as such function with even less accountability and a more relaxed approach toward budgets, deadlines, and work.

Academia is another good example, where students pay ever-more-exorbitant fees to enter universities only to be taught by professors who spend very little time and effort on the teaching and mentoring of students, focusing most their time on publishing unreadable research to get government grants and climb the corporate academic ladder. In a free market, academics would have to contribute value by teaching or writing things people actually read and benefit from. But the average academic paper is rarely ever read by anyone except the small circle of academics in each discipline who approve each other's grants and enforce the standards of groupthink and politically motivated conclusions masquerading as academic rigor.

The most popular and influential economics textbook in the postwar period was written by Nobel Laureate Paul Samuelson. We saw in

---

[20] For more on this topic, see James M. Buchanan and Gordon Tullock, *The Calculus of Consent: Logical Foundations of Constitutional Democracy*. Ann Arbor, University of Michigan Press, 1962.

Chapter 4 how Samuelson predicted that ending World War II would cause the biggest recession in world history, only for one of the biggest booms in U.S. history to ensue. But it gets better: Samuelson wrote the most popular economics textbook of the postwar era, *Economics: An Introductory Analysis*, which has sold millions of copies over six decades.[21] Levy and Peart[22] studied the different versions of Samuelson's textbook to find him repeatedly presenting the Soviet economic model as being more conducive to economic growth, predicting in the fourth edition in 1961 that the Soviet Union's economy would overtake that of the United States sometime between 1984 and 1997. These forecasts for Soviets overtaking the United States continued to be made with increasing confidence through seven editions of the textbook, until the eleventh edition in 1980, with varying estimates for when the overtaking would occur. In the thirteenth edition, published in 1989, which hit the desks of university students as the Soviet Union was beginning to unravel, Samuelson and his then-co-author William Nordhaus wrote, "The Soviet economy is proof that, contrary to what many skeptics had earlier believed, a socialist command economy can function and even thrive."[23] Nor was this confined to one textbook, as Levy and Peart show that such insights were common in the many editions of what is probably the second most popular economics textbook, McConnell's *Economics: Principles, Problems, and Policies*, as well as several other textbooks. Any student who learned economics in the postwar period in a university following an American curriculum (the majority of the world's students) learned that the Soviet model is a more efficient way of organizing economic activity. Even after the collapse and utter failure of the Soviet Union, the same textbooks continued to be taught in the same universities, with the newer editions removing the grandiose proclamations about Soviet success, without questioning the rest of their economic worldview and methodological tools. How is it that such patently failed textbooks continue to be taught, and how is the Keynesian worldview, so brutally

---

[21]Skousen, Mark. "The Perseverance of Paul Samuelson's Economics." *Journal of Economic Perspectives*, vol. 11, no. 2, 1997, pp. 137–52.
[22]Levy, David and Sandra Peart. "Soviet Growth and American Textbooks: An Endogenous Past." *Journal of Economic Behavior & Organization*, vol. 78, iss. 1–2, Apr. 2011, pp. 110–25.
[23]Skousen, Mark. "The Perseverance of Paul Samuelson's Economics."

assaulted beyond repair by reality over the past seven decades—from the boom after World War II, to the stagflation of the seventies, to the collapse of the Soviet Union—still taught in universities? The dean of today's Keynesian economists, Paul Krugman, has even written of how an alien invasion would be great for the economy as it would force government to spend and mobilize resources.[24]

In a free market economic system, no self-respecting university would want to teach its students things that are so patently wrong and absurd, as it strives to arm its students with the most useful knowledge. But in an academic system completely corrupted by government money, the curriculum is not determined through its accordance with reality, but through its accordance with the political agenda of the governments funding it. And governments, universally, love Keynesian economics today for the same reason they loved it in the 1930s: it offers them the sophistry and justification for acquiring ever more power and money.

This discussion can continue to include many other fields and disciplines in modern academia, where the same pattern repeats: funding coming from government agencies is monopolized by groups of like-minded scholars sharing fundamental biases. You do not get a job or funding in this system by producing important scholarship that is productive and useful to the real world, but by furthering the agenda of the funders. That the funding comes from one source only eliminates the possibility for a free marketplace of ideas. Academic debates concern ever-more-arcane minutiae, and all parties in these fraternal disputes can always agree that both parties need more funding to continue these important disagreements. The debates of academia are almost entirely irrelevant to the real world, and its journals' articles are almost never read by anyone except the people who write them for job promotion purposes, but the government bezzle indefinitely rolls on because there is no mechanism by which government funding can ever be reduced when it does not benefit anybody.

In a society with sound money, banking is a very important and productive job, where bankers perform two highly pivotal functions for economic prosperity: the safekeeping of assets as deposits, and the

---

[24]Krugman, Paul. "Secular Stagnation, Coalmines, Bubbles, and Larry Summers." *New York Times*, 16 Nov. 2003.

matching of maturity and risk tolerance between investors and investment opportunities. Bankers make their money by taking a cut from the profits if they succeed in their job, but make no profit if they fail. Only the successful bankers and banks stay in their job, as those that fail are weeded out. In a society of sound money, there are no liquidity concerns over the failure of a bank, as all banks hold all their deposits on hand, and have investments of matched maturity. In other words, there is no distinction between illiquidity and insolvency, and there is no systemic risk that could make any bank "too big to fail." A bank that fails is the problem of its shareholders and lenders, and nobody else.

Unsound money allows the possibility of mismatching maturity, of which fractional reserve banking is but a subset, and this leaves banks always liable to a liquidity crisis, or a bank run. Maturity mismatching, or fractional reserve banking as a special case of it, is always liable to a liquidity crisis if lenders and depositors were to demand their deposits at the same time. The only way to make maturity mismatching safe is with the presence of a lender of last resort standing ready to lend to banks in case of a bank run.[25] In a society with sound money, a central bank would have to tax everyone not involved in the bank in order to bail out the bank. In a society with unsound money, the central bank is simply able to create new money supply and use it to support the bank's liquidity. Unsound money thus creates a distinction between liquidity and solvency: a bank could be solvent in terms of the net present value of its assets but face a liquidity problem that prevents it from meeting its financial obligations within a certain period of time. But the lack of liquidity itself could trigger a bank run as depositors and lenders seek to get their deposits out of the bank. Worse, the lack of liquidity in one bank could lead to a lack of liquidity in other banks dealing with this bank, creating systemic risk problems. If the central bank credibly commits to providing liquidity in such cases, however, there will be no fear of a liquidity crisis, which in turn averts the scenario of a bank run and leaves the banking system safe.

Fractional reserve banking, or maturity mismatching more generally, is likely to continue to cause financial crises without a central bank

---

[25] For a formal modeling of this statement, see D.W. Diamond and P. H. Dybvig, "Bank Runs, Deposit Insurance, and Liquidity." *Journal of Political Economy*, vol. 91, no. 3, 1983, pp. 401–19.

using an elastic money supply to bail out these banks. But the presence of a central bank able to bail out the banks creates a major problem of moral hazard for these banks. They can now take excessive risks knowing that the central bank will be inclined to bail them out to avert a systemic crisis. From this we see how banking has evolved into a business that generates returns without risks to bankers and simultaneously creates risks without returns for everyone else.

Banking is an industry that seemingly only grows these days, and banks cannot go out of business. Due to the systemic risks involved in running a bank, any failure of a bank can be viewed as a liquidity problem and will very likely get the support of the central bank. No other ostensibly private industry enjoys such an exorbitant privilege, combining the highest rates of profitability in the private sector with the protection of the public sector. This combination has made bankers' work as creative and productive as that of public sector employees, but more rewarding than most other jobs. As a result, the financial industry just keeps growing as the U.S. economy becomes ever more "financialized." Since the repeal of the Glass-Steagall Act in 1999, the separation between deposit and investment banking has been removed, and so the deposit banks who had FDIC deposit guarantee can now also engage in investment financing, having the FDIC guarantee protect them from investment losses. An investor who has a loss guarantee has a free option, effectively, a license to print money. Making profitable investments allows them to accrue all the gains, whereas losses can be socialized. Anybody with such a guarantee can make large amounts of money by simply borrowing and investing his money. He gets to keep the profits, but will have his losses covered. It is no wonder that this has led to an ever-larger share of the capital and labor resources gravitating toward finance, as it's the closest thing the world has to a free lunch.

Economist Thomas Philippon[26] has produced detailed studies of the size of the financial sector as a percentage of GDP over the past 150 years. The ratio was less than 3% during the years preceding World War I, but was to shoot up afterwards, collapsing during the Great Depression, but growing seemingly in an unstoppable manner since the end of

---

[26] Philippon, Thomas, and Ariell Reshef. "An International Look at the Growth of Modern Finance." *Journal of Economic Perspectives*, vol. 27, no. 2, 2013, pp. 73–96.

World War II. Anecdotally, one can see this reflected in the high percentage of university students who are interested in pursuing careers in finance, rather than in engineering, medicine, or other more productive industries.

As telecommunications have advanced, one would expect that more and more of the financial industry's work can be automated and done mechanistically, leading to the industry shrinking in size over time. But in reality it continues to mushroom, not because of any fundamental demand, but because it is protected from losses by government and allowed to thrive.

The bezzle may be most pronounced in the financial industry, but it does not stop at the banking industry. It arguably constitutes a longstanding competitive advantage for firms of larger size over those of a smaller size. In a society in which capital investments are financed from savings, capital is owned by those with a lower time preference, and they allocate it based on their own estimation of the likelihoods of market success, receiving rewards for being correct and losses for being wrong. But with unsound money, savings are destroyed and capital is instead created from inflationary bank credit, and its allocation is decided by the central bank and its member banks. Instead of the allocation being decided by the most prudent members of society with the lowest time preference and best market foresight, it is decided by government bureaucrats whose incentive is to lend as much as possible, not to make profit, as they are significantly protected from the downside.

Centrally planning credit allocation is no different from any kind of central planning. It results in bureaucrats checking boxes and filling in paperwork to ensure they meet their bosses' requirements while the ostensible purpose of the work is lost. The insight of the banker and the diligence of examining the real value of investments is replaced with the box-ticking of meeting central bank lending requirements. A major advantage in securing centralized credit is scale, as it appears quantitatively less risky to lend to large-scale lenders. The larger the firm, the more predictable the formula for its success, the larger the collateral in case it fails, and the more secure bank bureaucrats feel when making loans according to central bank lending criteria. While many industries could benefit from economies of scale, centralized credit issuance accentuates the advantages of size above and beyond what would be the case in a free market. Any industry that can borrow more money than it knows what to do with is a good candidate, seeing as such a scenario cannot possibly materialize in a world of savings-financed capital.

The larger the firm, the easier it is for it to secure low-interest funding, giving it a large advantage over smaller independent producers. In a society where investment is financed from savings, a small mom-and-pop diner competes for customers and financing with a fast-food giant on an equal footing: customers and investors have a free choice in allocating their money between the two industries. The benefits of economies of scale are up against the benefits of the personal attention and relationship between cook and customer of the small diner, and the market test decides. But in a world where central banks allocate credit, the larger firm has an advantage in being able to secure funding at a low rate which its smaller competitors cannot get.[27] This helps explain why large-scale food producers proliferate so widely around the world, as their lower interest rates allow them higher margins. The triumph of bland, mass-produced junk food cannot be understood outside the great benefits that large scale affords to producers.

In a world in which almost all firms are financed through central bank credit expansion, there can be no simple way of discerning which industries are growing because of the injection of bezzle steroids, but there are some telltale symptoms. Any industry in which people complain about their asshole boss is likely part of the bezzle, because bosses can only really afford to be assholes in the economic fake reality of the bezzle. In a productive firm offering valuable service to society, success depends on pleasing customers. Workers are rewarded for how well they do that essential task, and bosses who mistreat their workers will either lose the workers to competitors or destroy their business

---

[27] The centralization of credit issuance can be viewed as a government intervention in the operation of Coase's Law, described by Coase in his essay: "The Nature of the Firm," *Economica*, vol. 4, no. 16 (1937): 386–405. According to Coase, the reason firms exist is that the individual contracting of tasks can be more expensive because it involves transaction costs, such as search and information, bargaining, contracting, and enforcement costs. A firm will thus grow for as long as it can benefit from doing activities in-house to overcome higher external contracting costs. In a world of depreciating currency and centrally allocated credit, achieving financing becomes one of the main cost advantages of growing in size. Large firms have more capital goods and collateral, which allows them lower funding terms. The incentive for every business is thus to grow beyond what consumers would prefer. In a free market for capital where firms had to rely much more on their revenues and securing credit on free markets, the output will favor the scale of production most suited to consumers' preferences.

quickly. In an unproductive firm that does not serve society and relies on bureaucratic largesse for its survival, there is no meaningful standard by which to reward or punish workers. The bezzle can appear seductive from outside, thanks to the generous regular paychecks and the lack of actual work involved, but if there's one lesson economics teaches us, it is that there is no such a thing as a free lunch. Money being handed out to unproductive people will attract a lot of people who want to do these jobs, driving up the cost of doing these jobs in time and dignity. Hiring, firing, promotion, and punishment all happen at the discretion of layer upon layer of bureaucrats. No work is valuable to the firm, everyone is dispensable, and the only way anyone maintains a job is by proving valuable to the layer above him. A job in these firms is a full-time game of office politics. Such jobs are only appealing to shallow materialistic people who enjoy having power over others, and years of being maltreated are endured for the paycheck and the hope of being able to inflict this maltreatment on others. It is no wonder that people who work these jobs are regularly depressed and in need of constant medication and psychotherapy to maintain basic functionality. No amount of bezzle money is worth the spiritual destruction that such an environment creates in people. While these organizations face no real accountability, the flipside of having no productivity is that it is quite possible for a newly elected official to come into office and completely defund them out of existence in a matter of weeks. This is a far more tragic fate for the workers in these organizations as they generally have no useful skills whatsoever that can be transferred to other avenues of work.

The only cure that can work for these pathologies is sound money, which will eradicate the notion of people working for the sake of ticking boxes and pleasing sadistic bosses, and make market discipline the only arbiter for anyone's income. If you find yourself toiling away in one of these industries, where the stress of your job centers purely on pleasing your boss rather than producing something of value, and are not happy with this reality, you may be relieved or frightened to realize the world doesn't have to be this way, and your job may not survive forever, as your government's printing press might not continue working forever. Read on, because the virtues of sound money may inspire a new world of opportunity for you.

Chapter 8

Digital Money

The global telecommunication revolution, starting with the production of the first fully programmable computer in the 1950s, has encroached on an increasing number of material aspects of life, providing engineering solutions to hitherto age-old problems. While banks and startup firms increasingly utilized computer and network technology for payments and recordkeeping, the innovations that succeeded did not provide a new form of money, and the innovations that tried to provide a new form of money all failed. Bitcoin represents the first truly digital solution to the problem of money, and in it we find a potential solution to the problems of salability, soundness, and sovereignty. Bitcoin has operated with practically no failure for the past 9 years, and if it continues to operate like this for the next 90, it will be a compelling solution to the problem of money, offering individuals sovereignty over money that is resistant to unexpected inflation while also being highly salable across space, scale, and time. Should bitcoin continue to operate as it already has, all the previous technologies humans have employed as money—shells, salt, cattle, precious metals, and government paper—may appear quaint anachronisms in our modern world—abacuses next to our modern computers.

We saw how the introduction of metallurgy produced solutions to the problem of money that were superior to beads, shellfish, and other artifacts, and how the emergence of regular coinage allowed gold and silver coins to emerge as superior forms of money to irregular lumps of metal. We further saw how gold-backed banking allowed gold to dominate as the global monetary standard and led to the demonetization of silver. From the necessity of centralizing gold arose government money backed by gold, which was more salable in scale, but with it came government expansion of the money supply and coercive control which eventually destroyed money's soundness and sovereignty. Every step of the way, technological advances and realities shaped the monetary standards that people employed, and the consequences to economies and society were enormous. Societies and individuals who chose a sound monetary standard, such as the Romans under Caesar, the Byzantines under Constantine, or Europeans under the gold standard, benefited immensely. Those who had unsound or technologically inferior money, such as Yap Islanders with the arrival of O'Keefe, West Africans using glass beads, or the Chinese on a silver standard in the nineteenth century, paid a heavy price.

Bitcoin represents a new technological solution to the money problem, born out of the digital age, utilizing several technological innovations that were developed over the past few decades and building on many attempts at producing digital money to deliver something which was almost unimaginable before it was invented. To understand why, we will focus on the monetary properties of bitcoin as well as the economic performance of the network since its inception. In the same way that a book on the gold standard would not discuss the chemical properties of gold, this chapter will not delve too much into the technical details of the operation of the bitcoin network, instead focusing on the monetary properties of the bitcoin currency.

Bitcoin as Digital Cash

To understand the significance of a technology for digital cash, it is instructive to look at the world before bitcoin was invented, when one could neatly divide payment methods into two distinct non-overlapping categories:

1. Cash payments, which are carried out in person between two parties. These payments have the convenience of being immediate and final, and require no trust on the part of either transacting party. There is no delay in the execution of the payment, and no third party can effectively intervene to stop such payments. Their main drawback is the need for the two parties to be physically present in the same place at the same time, a problem which becomes more and more pronounced as telecommunication makes it more likely for individuals to want to transact with persons who are not in their immediate vicinity.

2. Intermediated payments, which require a trusted third party, and comprise cheques, credit cards, debit cards, bank wire transfers, money transfer services, and more recent innovations such as PayPal. By definition, intermediated payment involves a third party handling the money transfer between the two transacting parties. The main advantages of intermediated payments are allowing payments without the two parties having to be at the same place at the same time, and allowing the payer to make payment without having to carry her money on her. Their main drawback is the trust that is required in execution of the transactions, the risk of the third party being compromised, and the costs and time required for the payment to be completed and cleared to allow the recipient to spend it.

Both forms of payment have their advantages and drawbacks, and most people resort to a combination of the two in their economic transactions. Before the invention of bitcoin, intermediated payments included (though were not limited to) all forms of digital payment. The nature of digital objects, since the inception of computers, is that they are not scarce. They can be reproduced endlessly, and as such it was impossible to make a currency out of them, because sending them will only duplicate them. Any form of electronic payment had to be carried out via an intermediary because of the danger of double-spending: there was no way of guaranteeing that the payer was being honest with his funds, and not using them more than once, unless there was a trusted third party overseeing the account and able to verify the integrity of the payments carried out. Cash transactions were confined to the physical realm of direct contact, while all digital forms of payments had to be supervised by a third party.

After years of innovative trial and error by many programmers, and through relying on a wide range of technologies, bitcoin was the first engineering solution that allowed for digital payments without having to rely on a trusted third-party intermediary. By being the first digital object that is verifiably scarce, bitcoin is the first example of *digital cash*.

There are several drawbacks to transacting through trusted third parties which make digital cash a valuable proposition for many. Third parties are by their very nature an added security weakness[1]—involving an extra party in your transaction inherently introduces risk, because it opens up new possibilities for theft or technical failure. Further, payment through intermediaries leaves the parties vulnerable to surveillance and bans by political authorities. In other words, when resorting to any form of digital payment, there was no alternative to trusting in a third party, and whichever political authorities rule over it, and being subject to the risk of the political authority stopping the payment under pretexts of security, terrorism, or money laundering. To make matters worse, intermediated payments always involve a risk of fraud, which raises transaction costs and delays final settlement of payments.

In other words, intermediated payments take away a significant share of the properties of money as a medium of exchange controlled by its owner, with high liquidity for him to sell whenever he wants. Of the most persistent characteristics of money historically are fungibility (any unit of money is equivalent to any other unit), and liquidity (ability of the owner to sell quickly at market price). People choose moneys that are fungible and liquid because they want sovereignty over their money. Sovereign money contains within it all the permission needed to spend it; the desire for others to hold it exceeds the ability of others to impose controls on it.

While intermediated payments compromise some of the desirable features of money, these shortcomings are not present in physical cash

---

[1] Szabo, Nick. "Trusted Third Parties Are Security Holes." *Satoshi Nakamoto Institute*, 2001, nakamotoinstitute.org/trusted-third-parties/.

transactions. But as more trade and employment takes place over long distances thanks to modern telecommunication, physical cash transactions become prohibitively impractical. The move toward digital payments was reducing the amount of sovereignty people have over their own money and leaving them subject to the whims of the third parties they had no choice but to trust. Further, the move from gold, which is money that nobody can print, toward fiat currencies whose supply is controlled by central banks further reduced people's sovereignty over their wealth and left them helpless in the face of the slow erosion of the value of their money as central banks inflated the money supply to fund government operation. It became increasingly impractical to accumulate capital and wealth without the permission of the government issuing that money.

Satoshi Nakamoto's motivation for bitcoin was to create a "purely peer-to-peer form of electronic cash" that would not require trust in third parties for transactions and whose supply cannot be altered by any other party. In other words, bitcoin would bring the desirable features of physical cash (lack of intermediaries, finality of transactions) to the digital realm and combine them with an ironclad monetary policy that cannot be manipulated to produce unexpected inflation to benefit an outside party at the expense of holders. Nakamoto succeeded in achieving this through the utilization of a few important though not widely understood technologies: a distributed peer-to-peer network with no single point of failure, hashing, digital signatures, and proof-of-work.[2]

Nakamoto removed the need for trust in a third party by building bitcoin on a foundation of very thorough and ironclad *proof* and *verification*. It is fair to say that the central operational feature of bitcoin is verification, and only because of that can bitcoin remove the need for trust completely.[3] Every transaction has to be recorded by every member of the network so that they all share one common ledger of balances and transactions. Whenever a member of the network transfers a sum to another member, all network members can verify the sender has a sufficient balance, and nodes compete to be the first to update

---

[2]A brief description of the first three of these technologies is provided in the Appendix to this chapter, while proof-of-work is discussed in more detail in this chapter and in Chapter 10.
[3]Graf, Konrad. "On the Origins of Bitcoin: Stages of Monetary Evolution." *Konrad S. Graf*, 2013, www .konradsgraf.com.

the ledger with a new block of transactions every ten minutes. In order for a node to commit a block of transactions to the ledger, it has to expend processing power on solving complicated mathematical problems that are hard to solve but whose correct solution is easy to verify. This is the proof-of-work (PoW) system, and only with a correct solution can a block be committed and verified by all network members. While these mathematical problems are unrelated to the bitcoin transactions, they are indispensable to the operation of the system as they force the verifying nodes to expend processing power which would be wasted if they included fraudulent transactions. Once a node solves the proof-of-work correctly and announces the transactions, other nodes on the network vote for its validity, and once a majority has voted to approve the block, nodes begin committing transactions to a new block to be appended to the previous one and solving the new proof-of-work for it. Crucially, the node that commits a valid block of transactions to the network receives a *block reward* consisting of brand-new bitcoins added to the supply along with all the transaction fees paid by the people who are transacting.

The process is what is referred to as *mining*, analogous to the mining of precious metals, and is why nodes that solve proof-of-work are known as miners. This block reward compensates the miners for the resources they committed to proof-of-work. Whereas in a modern central bank the new money created goes to finance lending and government spending, in bitcoin the new money goes only to those who spend resources on updating the ledger. Nakamoto programmed bitcoin to produce a new block roughly every ten minutes, and for each block to contain a reward of 50 coins in the first four years of bitcoin's operation, to be halved afterwards to 25 coins, and further halved every four years.

The quantity of bitcoins created is preprogrammed and cannot be altered no matter how much effort and energy is expended on proof-of-work. This is achieved through a process called difficulty adjustment, which is perhaps the most ingenious aspect of bitcoin's design. As more people choose to hold bitcoin, this drives up the market value of bitcoin and makes mining new coins more profitable, which drives more miners to expend more resources on solving proof-of-work problems. More miners means more processing power, which results in the solutions to the proof-of-work being arrived at faster, thus increasing the rate of issuance of new bitcoins. But as the processing power rises, bitcoin will raise the difficulty of the mathematical problems needed to unlock the mining rewards to ensure blocks will continue to take around ten minutes to be produced.

Difficulty adjustment is the most reliable technology for making hard money and preventing the stock-to-flow ratio from declining, and it makes bitcoin fundamentally different from every other money. Whereas the rise in value of any money leads to more resources dedicated to its production and thus an increase in its supply, as bitcoin's value rises, more effort to produce bitcoins does not lead to the production of more bitcoins. Instead, it just leads to an increase in the processing power necessary to commit valid transactions to the bitcoin network, which only serves to make the network more secure and difficult to compromise. Bitcoin is the hardest money ever invented: growth in its value cannot possibly increase its supply; it can only make the network more secure and immune to attack.

For every other money, as its value rises, those who can produce it will start producing more of it. Whether it is Rai stones, seashells, silver, gold, copper, or government money, everyone will have an incentive to try to produce more. The harder it was to produce new quantities of the money in response to price rises, the more likely it was to be adopted widely and used, and the more a society would prosper because it would mean individuals' efforts at producing wealth will go toward serving one another, not producing money, an activity with no added value to society because any supply of money is enough to run any economy. Gold became the prime money of every civilized society precisely because it was the hardest to produce, but bitcoin's difficulty adjustment makes it even harder to produce. A massive increase in the price of gold will, in the long run, lead to larger quantities being produced, but no matter how high the price of bitcoins rises, the supply stays the same and the safety of the network only increases.

The security of bitcoin lies in the asymmetry between the cost of solving the proof-of-work necessary to commit a transaction to the ledger and the cost of verifying its validity. It costs ever-increasing quantities of electricity and processing power to record transactions, but the cost of verifying the validity of the transactions is close to zero and will remain at that level no matter how much bitcoin grows. To try to commit fraudulent transactions to the bitcoin ledger is to deliberately waste resources on solving the proof-of-work only to watch nodes reject it at almost no cost, thereby withholding the block reward from the miner.

As time goes by, it becomes increasingly difficult to alter the record, as the energy needed is larger than the energy already expended, which only grows with time. This highly complex iterative process has grown to require vast quantities of processing power and electricity but produces a ledger of ownership and transactions that is beyond dispute, without having to rely on the trustworthiness of any single third party. Bitcoin is built on 100% verification and 0% trust.[4]

Bitcoin's shared ledger can be likened to the Rai stones of Yap Island discussed in Chapter 2, in that the money does not actually move for transactions to take place. Whereas in Yap the islanders would meet to announce the transfer of the ownership of a stone from one person to the other, and the entire town would know who owned which stone, in bitcoin members of the network would broadcast their transaction to all network members, who would verify that the sender has the balance necessary for the transaction, and credit it to the recipient. To the extent that the digital coins exist, they are simply entries on a ledger, and a verified transaction changes the ownership of the coins on the ledger from the sender to the recipient. Ownership of the coins is assigned through public addresses, not by name of the holder, and access to the coins owned by an address is secured through the ownership of the private key, a string of characters analogous to a password.[5]

Whereas the Rai stones' physical heft makes their divisibility highly impractical, bitcoin faces no such problem. Bitcoin's supply is made up of a maximum of 21,000,000 coins, each of which is divisible into

---

[4] I do not intend to drag this book and the reader into metaphysical questions, but it did occur to me once that the bitcoin ledger of transactions might just be the only objective set of facts in the world. You could argue (as many philosophers do) that every fact is subjective and its truthfulness is based on the person stating or hearing it, but the bitcoin ledger of transactions is created through converting electricity and processing power to truth without having to rely on the word of anyone.

[5] The only way to own bitcoins is to have control of the private keys. Should someone manage to gain access to your private keys, they have your bitcoins. Theft of private keys is like theft of physical dollars or gold; it is final and irreversible. There is no authority you can call to rescind the theft. This is an unavoidable part of bitcoin being cash and an important point that potential investors in bitcoin need to understand full well before putting any sum of money into bitcoin. Securing the private keys is not a simple task, and not being able to secure them is very risky.

100,000,000 satoshis, making it highly salable across scales. Whereas the Yapese stones were only practical for a few transactions in a small island with a small population who knew each other very well, bitcoin has far superior salability across space, because the digital ledger is accessible by anyone worldwide with an Internet connection.

What keeps bitcoin nodes honest, individually, is that if they were dishonest, they would be discovered immediately, making dishonesty exactly as effective as doing nothing but involving a higher cost. Collectively, what prevents a majority from colluding to be dishonest is that if they were to succeed in compromising the integrity of the ledger of transactions, the entire value proposition of bitcoin would be destroyed and the bitcoin tokens' value would collapse to nothing. Collusion costs a lot, but it would itself lead to its loot becoming worthless. In other words, bitcoin relies on economic incentives, making fraud far costlier than its rewards.

No single entity is relied upon for maintaining the ledger and no single individual can alter the record on it without the consent of a majority of network members. What determines the validity of the trans-action is not the word of a single authority, but the software running the individual nodes on the network.

Ralph Merkle, inventor of the Merkle tree data structure, which is utilized by bitcoin to record transactions, had a remarkable way of describing bitcoin:

> Bitcoin is the first example of a new form of life. It lives and breathes on the internet. It lives because it can pay people to keep it alive. It lives because it performs a useful service that people will pay it to perform. It lives because anyone, anywhere, can run a copy of its code. It lives because all the running copies are constantly talking to each other. It lives because if any one copy is corrupted it is discarded, quickly and without any fuss or muss. It lives because it is radically transparent: anyone can see its code and see exactly what it does.
>
> It can't be changed. It can't be argued with. It can't be tampered with. It can't be corrupted. It can't be stopped. It can't even be interrupted.
>
> If nuclear war destroyed half of our planet, it would continue to live, uncorrupted. It would continue to offer its services. It would continue to pay people to keep it alive.

The only way to shut it down is to kill every server that hosts it. Which is hard, because a lot of servers host it, in a lot of countries, and a lot of people want to use it.

Realistically, the only way to kill it is to make the service it offers so useless and obsolete that no one wants to use it. So obsolete that no one wants to pay for it. No one wants to host it. Then it will have no money to pay anyone. Then it will starve to death.

But as long as there are people who want to use it, it's very hard to kill, or corrupt, or stop, or interrupt.[6]

Bitcoin is a technology that survives for the very same reason the wheel, knife, phone, or any technology survives: it offers its users benefits from using it. Users, miners, and node operators are all rewarded economically from interacting with bitcoin, and that is what keeps it going. It's worth adding that all the parties that make bitcoin work are individually dispensable to its operation. Nobody is essential to bitcoin, and if anybody wants to alter bitcoin, bitcoin is perfectly capable of continuing to operate as it is without whatever input anyone has on this. This will help us understand the immutable nature of bitcoin in Chapter 10, and why attempts at making serious changes to the bitcoin code will almost inevitably lead to the creation of a knockoff version of bitcoin, but one that cannot possibly recreate the economic balance of incentives that keeps bitcoin operational and immutable.

Bitcoin can also be understood as a spontaneously emergent and autonomous firm which provides a new form of money and a new payments network. There is no management or corporate structure to this firm, as all decisions are automated and preprogrammed. Volunteer coders in an open source project can present changes and improvements to the code, but it is up to users to choose to adopt them or not. The value proposition of this firm is that its money supply is completely inelastic in response to increased demand and price; instead, increased demand just leads to a safer network due to the mining difficulty adjustment. Miners invest electricity and processing power in the mining infrastructure that protects the network because they are rewarded for it. Bitcoin users pay transaction fees and buy the

---

[6]Merkle, Ralph. "DAOs, Democracy and Governance." *Cryonics*, vol. 37, no. 4, Jul.–Aug. 2016, Alcor, pp. 28–40,www.alcor.org.

coins from the miners because they want to utilize digital cash and benefit from the appreciation over time, and in the process they finance the miners' investment in operating the network. The investment in PoW mining hardware makes the network more secure and can be understood as the firm's capital. The more the demand for the network grows, the more valuable the miners' rewards and transaction fees become, which necessitates more processing power to generate new coins, increasing the company's capital, making the network more secure and the coins harder to produce. It is an economic arrangement that has been productive and lucrative to everyone involved, which in turn leads to the network continuing to grow at an astonishing pace.

With this technological design, Nakamoto was able to invent *digital scarcity*. Bitcoin is the first example of a digital good that is scarce and cannot be reproduced infinitely. While it is trivial to send a digital object from one location to another in a digital network, as is done with email, text messaging, or file downloads, it is more accurate to describe these processes as *copying* rather than *sending*, because the digital objects remain with the sender and can be reproduced infinitely. Bitcoin is the first example of a digital good whose transfer stops it from being owned by the sender.

Beyond digital scarcity, bitcoin is also the first example of *absolute scarcity*, the only liquid commodity (digital or physical) with a set fixed quantity that cannot conceivably be increased. Until the invention of bitcoin, scarcity was always relative, never absolute. It is a common misconception to imagine that any physical good is finite, or absolutely scarce, because the limit on the quantity we can produce of any good is never its prevalence in the planet, but the effort and time dedicated to producing it. With its absolute scarcity bitcoin is highly salable across time. This is a critical point which will be explicated further in Chapter 9 on bitcoin's role as a store of value.

Supply, Value, and Transactions

It had always been theoretically possible to produce an asset with a predictably constant or low rate of supply growth to allow it to maintain its monetary role, but reality, as always, had proven far trickier than theory. Governments would never allow private parties to issue their own private currencies and transgress on the main way in which government funds itself and grows. So government would always want to monopolize money production and face too strong a temptation to engage in the increase of the money supply. But with the invention of bitcoin, the world had finally arrived at a synthetic form of money that had an iron-clad guarantee governing its low rate of supply growth. Bitcoin takes the macroeconomists, politicians, presidents, revolutionary leaders, military dictators, and TV pundits out of monetary policy altogether. Money supply growth is determined by a programmed function adopted by all members of the network. There may have been a time at the start of this currency when this inflation schedule could have been conceivably changed, but that time has well passed. For all practical intents and purposes, bitcoin's inflation schedule, like its record of transactions, is immutable.[7] While for the first few years of bitcoin's existence the supply growth was very high, and the guarantee that the supply schedule would not be altered was not entirely credible, as time went by the supply growth rate dropped and the credibility of the network in maintaining this supply schedule has increased and continues to rise with each passing day in which no serious changes are made to the network.

Bitcoin blocks are added to the shared ledger roughly every ten minutes. At the birth of the network, the block reward was programmed to be 50 bitcoins per block. Every four years, roughly, or after 210,000 blocks have been issued, the block reward drops by half. The first halving happened on November 28, 2012, after which the issuance of new bitcoins dropped to 25 per block. On July 9, 2016, it dropped again to 12.5 coins per block, and will drop to 6.25 in 2020. According to this schedule, the supply will continue to increase at a decreasing rate, asymptotically approaching 21 million coins sometime around the year 2140, at which point there will be no more bitcoins issued. (See Figure 14.)

Because new coins are only produced with the issuance of a new block, and each new block requires the solving of the proof-of-work problems, there is a real cost to the production of new bitcoins. As the price of bitcoins rises in the market, more nodes enter to compete for the solution

---

[7]See Chapter 10 for a discussion of bitcoin's immutability and resistance to change.

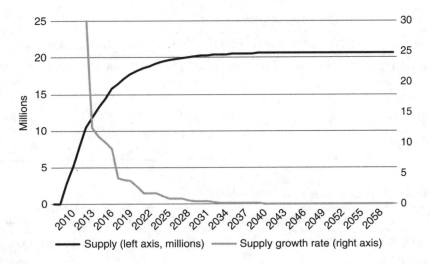

Figure 14 Bitcoin supply and supply growth rate assuming blocks are issued exactly every ten minutes.

of the PoW to obtain the block reward, which raises the difficulty of the PoW problems, making it more costly to obtain the reward. The cost of producing a bitcoin will thus generally rise along with the market price.

After setting this supply growth schedule, Satoshi divided each bitcoin into 100,000,000 units, which were later named satoshis in his pseudonymous honor. Dividing each bitcoin into 8 digits means that the supply will continue to grow at a decreasing rate until around the year 2140, when the digits all fill up and we reach 21,000,000 coins. The decreasing rate of growth, however, means that the first 20 million coins will be mined by around the year 2025, leaving 1 million coins to be mined over one more century.

The number of new coins issued is not exactly as predicted from the algorithm, because new blocks are not mined precisely every ten minutes, because the difficulty adjustment is not a precise process but a calibration that adjusts every two weeks and can overshoot or undershoot its target depending on how many new miners enter the mining business. In 2009, when very few people had used bitcoin at all, the issuance was far below schedule, while in 2010 it was above the theoretical number predicted from the supply. The exact numbers will vary, but this variance from the theoretical growth will decrease as the supply grows. What will not vary

Table 6 Bitcoin Supply and Growth Rate

Year	2009	2010	2011	2012	2013	2014	2015	2016	2017
Total BTC supply, millions	1.623	5.018	8.000	10.613	12.199	13.671	15.029	16.075	16.775
Annual growth rate, %		209.13	59.42	32.66	14.94	12.06	9.93	6.80	4.35

Table 7 Bitcoin Supply and Growth Rate (Projected)

Year	2018	2019	2020	2021	2022	2023	2024	2025	2026
Total BTC supply, millions	17.415	18.055	18.527	18.855	19.184	19.512	19.758	19.923	20.087
Annual growth rate, %	3.82	3.68	2.61	1.77	1.74	1.71	1.26	0.83	0.82

is the maximum cap of coins and the fact that the supply growth rate will continue to decline as an ever-decreasing number of coins is added onto an ever-increasing stock of coins.

By the end of 2017, 16.775 million coins were already mined, constituting 79.9% of all coins that will ever exist. The annual supply growth in 2017 was 4.35%, coming down from 6.8% in 2016. Table 6 shows the actual supply growth of BTC and its growth rate.[8]

A closer look at the bitcoin supply schedule over the coming years would give us these estimates for the supply and growth rate. The actual numbers will surely vary from this, but not by much. (See Table 7.[9])

Figure 15 extrapolates the growth rate of the main global reserve currencies' broad money supply and gold over the past 25 years into the next 25 years, and increases the supply of bitcoins by the programmed growth rates. By these calculations, the bitcoin supply will increase by 27% in the coming 25 years, whereas the supply for gold will increase by

---

[8] *Source*: blockchain.info.
[9] *Source*: author's calculations.

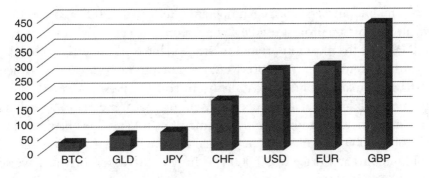

Figure 15 Projected bitcoin and national currency percentage growth in supply over 25 years.

52%, the Japanese yen by 64%, the Swiss franc by 169%, the U.S. dollar by 272%, the euro by 286%, and the British pound by 429%.

This exposition can help us appreciate the salability of bitcoin and how it fulfills the functions of money. With its supply growth rate dropping below that of gold by the year 2025, bitcoin has the supply restrictions that could make it have considerable demand as a store of value; in other words, it can have salability across time. Its digital nature that makes it easy to safely send worldwide makes it salable in space in a way never seen with other forms of money, while its divisibility into 100,000,000 satoshis makes it salable in scale. Further, bitcoin's elimination of intermediary control and the near-impossibility of any authority debasing or confiscating it renders it free of the main drawbacks of government money. As the digital age has introduced improvements and efficiencies to most aspects of our life, bitcoin presents a tremendous technological leap forward in the monetary solution to the indirect exchange problem, perhaps as significant as the move from cattle and salt to gold and silver.

Whereas traditional currencies are continuously increasing in supply and decreasing in purchasing power, bitcoin has so far witnessed a large increase in real purchasing power despite a moderate, but decreasing and capped, increase in its supply. Because miners who verify transactions are rewarded with bitcoins, these miners have a strong vested interest in maintaining the integrity of the network, which in turn causes the value of the currency to rise.

The bitcoin network began operating in January 2009 and was for a while an obscure project used by a few people in a cryptography mailing list. Perhaps the most important milestone in bitcoin's life was the first day that the tokens in this network went from being economically worthless to having a market value, validating that bitcoin had passed the market test: the network had operated successfully enough for someone to be willing to part with actual money to own some of its tokens. This happened in October 2009, when an online exchange named New Liberty Standard sold bitcoins at a price of $0.000994. In May 2010, the first real-world purchase with bitcoin took place, as someone paid 10,000 bitcoins for two pizza pies worth $25, putting the price of a bitcoin at $0.0025. With time, more and more people heard of bitcoin and became interested in purchasing it and the price continued to rise further.[10]

The market demand for a bitcoin token comes from the fact that it is needed to operate the first (and so far, arguably only) functional and reliable digital cash system.[11] The fact that this network was successfully operational in its early days gave its digital token a collectible value among tiny communities of cryptographers and libertarians, who tried mining it with their own PCs, and eventually even started purchasing it from one another.[12] That the tokens were strictly limited and could not be replicated helped create this initial collectible status. After being acquired by individuals to use on the bitcoin network, and gaining economic value, bitcoin began to get monetized through more people demanding it as a store of value. This sequence of activities conforms to Ludwig von Mises' Theory of Regression on the origins of money, which states that a monetary good begins as a market good and is then used as a medium of exchange. Bitcoin's collectible status among small communities is no different from seashells', Rai stones', and precious metals' ornamental value, from which they were to acquire a monetary role that raised their value significantly.

Being new and only beginning to spread, bitcoin's price has fluctuated wildly as demand fluctuates, but the impossibility of increasing the

---

[10]Details of both transactions can be found in Nathaniel Popper's *Digital Gold*.

[11]See Chapter 10 for a discussion of why bitcoin knockoffs cannot be described as digital cash.

[12]For a good discussion of this point, see Kyle Torpey, "Here's What Goldbugs Miss About Bitcoin's 'Intrinsic Value.'" *Forbes Digital Money*, 27 Oct. 2017, www.forbes.com/sites/ktorpey/2017/10/27/heres-what-gold-bugs-miss-about-bitcoins-intrinsic-value/2/#11b6a3b97ce0.

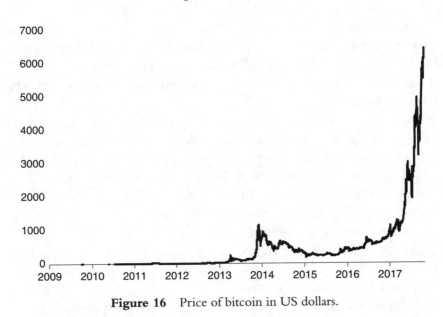

Figure 16   Price of bitcoin in US dollars.

supply arbitrarily by any authority in response to price spikes explains the meteoric rise in the purchasing power of the currency. When there is a spike in demand for bitcoins, bitcoin miners cannot increase production beyond the set schedule like copper miners can, and no central bank can step in to flood the market with increasing quantities of bitcoins, as Greenspan suggested central banks do with their gold. The only way for the market to meet the growing demand is for the price to rise enough to incentivize the holders to sell some of their coins to the newcomers. This helps explain why in eight years of existence, the price of a bitcoin has gone from $0.000994 on October 5, 2009, in its first recorded transaction, to $4,200 on October 5, 2017, an increase of 422,520,000% in eight years and a compound annual growth rate of 573% per year. (See Figure 16.[13])

For the bitcoin price to rise, people must hold it as a store of value, and not just spend it. Without a number of people willing to hold the currency for a significant period of time, continued selling of the currency will keep its price down and prevent it from appreciating.

---

[13] *Source*: Coindesk Bitcoin Price Index. Available at www.coindesk.com/price.

By November 2017, the total market value of all the bitcoins in circulation was in the range of $110 billion, giving it a value larger than the broad money supply of the national currencies of most countries. If bitcoin were a country, the value of its currency would be the 56th largest national currency worldwide, roughly in the range of the size of the money supply of Kuwait or Bangladesh, larger than that of Morocco and Peru, but smaller than Colombia and Pakistan. If it were to be compared to the narrow money supply, bitcoin's supply value would be ranked around the 33rd in the world, with a value similar to the narrow money supply of Brazil, Turkey, and South Africa.[14] It is perhaps one of the most remarkable achievements of the Internet that an online economy that spontaneously and voluntarily emerged around a network designed by an anonymous programmer has grown, in nine years, to hold more value than is held in the money supply of most nation-states and national currencies.[15]

This conservative monetary policy and the pursuant appreciation in the market value of bitcoins is vital to the successful operation of bitcoin, as it is the reason that miners have an incentive to expend electricity and processing power on honestly verifying transactions. Had bitcoin been created with an easy-money policy, such as what a Keynesian or Monetarist economist would recommend, it would have had its money supply grow in proportion to the number of users or transactions, but in that case it would have remained a marginal experiment among cryptography enthusiasts online. No serious amount of processing power would have gone to mining it, as there would be no point in investing heavily in verifying transactions and solving proof-of-work in order to get tokens that will get devalued as more people use the system. The expansionary monetary policies of modern fiat economies and economists have never won the market test of adoption freely, but have instead been imposed through government laws, as discussed earlier. As a voluntary system with no mechanism for forcing people to use it, bitcoin would fail to attract significant demand, and as a result its status as a successful digital cash

---

[14]CIA World Factbook. www.cia.gov/the-world-factbook/.

[15]These comparisons should be taken with a grain of salt, as they are not entirely accurate comparisons of like for like. Government money supply is created not just by the central bank, but also by the banks themselves, while no such process exists for bitcoin. The measures of money supply also differ from one country to another in terms of which financial assets they would include as part of the money supply.

Table 8   Annual Transactions and Average Daily Transactions

Year	Transactions	Average Daily Transactions
2009	32,687	90
2010	185,212	507
2011	1,900,652	5,207
2012	8,447,785	23,081
2013	19,638,728	53,805
2014	25,257,833	69,200
2015	45,661,404	125,100
2016	82,740,437	226,067
2017	103,950,926	284,797

would not be guaranteed. While the transactions could be carried out without need for trust in a third party, the network would be vulnerable to attack by any malicious actor mobilizing large amounts of processing power. In other words, without a conservative monetary policy and difficulty adjustment, bitcoin would only have succeeded theoretically as digital cash, but remained too insecure to be used widely in practice. In that case, the first competitor to bitcoin that introduced a hard money policy would make the updating of the ledger and production of new units progressively more expensive. The high cost of updating the ledger would give miners an incentive to be honest with their updating of the ledger, making the network more secure than easy money contenders.

The growth in the price is a reflection of the growing use and utility that the network offers its users. The number of transactions on the network has also grown rapidly: whereas 32,687 transactions were carried out in 2009 (at a rate of 90 transactions per day), the number grew to more than 103 million transactions in 2017 (at a daily rate of 284,797 transactions). The cumulative number of transactions is approaching 300 million transactions in January 2018. Table 8[16] and Figure 17[17] show the annual growth.

While the growth in transactions is impressive, it does not match the growth in the value of the total stock of the bitcoin currency, as can be

---

[16] *Source*: blockchain.info.
[17] *Source*: blockchain.info.

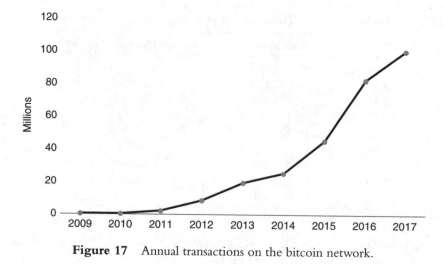

Figure 17   Annual transactions on the bitcoin network.

evidenced by the fact that the number of transactions is far less than what would be transacted in an economy whose currency had the value of the bitcoin supply; 300,000 daily transactions is the number of transactions that takes place in a small town, not in a medium-sized economy, which is around the value of the supply of bitcoin. Further, with the current size of bitcoin blocks being limited to 1 megabyte, 500,000 transactions per day is close to the upper limit that can be carried out by the bitcoin network and recorded by all peers on the network. Even as this limit is reached and its presence is well-publicized, the growth in the value of the currency and the value of daily transactions has not abated. This suggests that bitcoin adopters value it more as a store of value than a medium of exchange, as will be discussed in Chapter 9.

The market value of transactions has also increased over the network's lifetime. The peculiar nature of bitcoin transactions makes it hard to precisely estimate the exact value of transactions in bitcoins or U.S. dollars, but a lower-bound estimate sees an average daily volume of around 260,000 bitcoins in 2017, with highly volatile growth over bitcoin's lifetime. While the bitcoin value of transactions has not increased appreciably over time, the market value of these transactions in U.S. dollars has. The volume of transactions was $375.6 billion U.S. dollars in 2017. In total, by its ninth birthday, bitcoin had processed half

Table 9   Total Annual US Dollar Value of All
Bitcoin Network Transactions

Year	Total USD Value Transacted
2009	0
2010	985,887
2011	417,634,730
2012	607,221,228
2013	14,767,371,941
2014	23,159,832,297
2015	26,669,252,582
2016	58,188,957,445
2017	375,590,943,877
Total	**499,402,199,987**

a trillion US dollars' worth of transactions, with USD value calculated at the time of the transaction. (See Table 9.[18])

Another measure of the growth of the bitcoin network is the value of the transaction fees required to process the transactions. Whereas bitcoin transactions can theoretically be processed for free, it is incumbent on the miners to process them, and the higher the fee, the faster they are likely to pick them up. In the early days when the number of transactions was small, miners would process transactions that did not include a fee because the block subsidy of new coins itself was worth the effort. As demand for bitcoin transactions grew, miners could afford to be more selective and prioritize transactions with higher fees. Fees were under $0.1 per transaction up until late 2015, and started rising above $1 per transaction around early 2016. With the quick rise in bitcoin's price in 2017, the average daily transaction fee had reached $7 by the end of November. (See Figure 18.[19])

While the price of bitcoin has generally risen over time, this rise has been highly volatile. Figure 19 shows the 30-day standard deviation of daily returns for the past five years of bitcoin trading.[20] While the volatility appears to be declining, it remains very high compared

---

[18] *Source*: blockchain.info.
[19] *Source*: Ibid.
[20] *Source*: Author's calculations based on USD data from St. Louis Federal Reserve Economic Data, fred.stlouisfed.org/, and bitcoin data from coindesk.com.

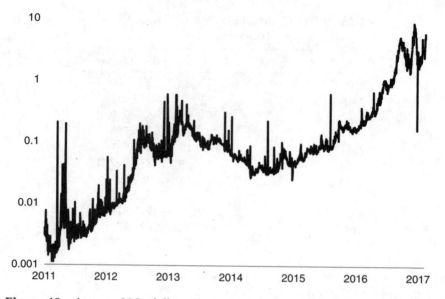

Figure 18 Average U.S. dollar value of transaction fees on bitcoin network, logarithmic scale.

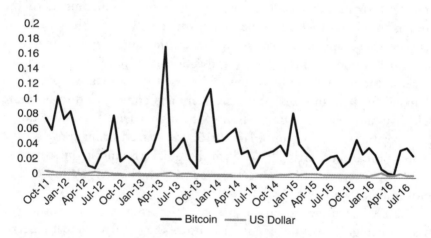

Figure 19 Monthly 30-day volatility for bitcoin and the USD Index.

to that of national currencies and gold, and the trend is still too weak to conclusively determine if it will continue to decline. The 30-day volatility of the U.S. Dollar Index is included in Figure 19 to provide perspective.

Table 10   Average Daily Percentage Change and Standard Deviation in the Market Price of Currencies per USD over the Period of September 1, 2011, to September 1, 2016

	Average Daily % Change	Standard Deviation
CNY	0.002	0.136
USD	0.015	0.305
GBP	0.005	0.559
INR	0.019	0.56
EUR	−0.013	0.579
JPY	0.02	0.61
CHF	0.003	0.699
Gold	−0.018	1.099
Bitcoin	0.37	5.072

Examining price data for gold and major national and crypto currencies shows a marked difference in the volatility in the market price of these currencies. Daily returns were collected for the previous five years for gold, major fiat currencies, and bitcoin. Bitcoin returns had a standard deviation more than seven times larger than that of national currencies. (See Table 10.[21])

Bitcoin's volatility derives from the fact that its supply is utterly inflexible and not responsive to demand changes, because it is programmed to grow at a predetermined rate. For any regular commodity, the variation in demand will affect the production decisions of producers of the commodity: an increase in demand causes them to increase their production, moderating the rise in the price and allowing them to increase their profitability, while a decrease in demand would cause producers to decrease their supply and allow them to minimize losses. A similar situation exists with national currencies, where central banks are expected to maintain relative stability in the purchasing power of their currencies by setting the parameters of their monetary policy to counteract market fluctuations. With a supply schedule utterly irresponsive to demand, and no central bank to manage the supply, there will likely be volatility,

[21]Prices of all currencies measured in USD while USD Index is used for the U.S. dollar. National currency data from St. Louis Federal Reserve Economic Data. Gold data from World Gold Council. Bitcoin data from coindesk.com.

particularly at the early stages when demand varies very erratically from day to day, and the financial markets that deal with bitcoin are still infant.

But as the size of the market grows, along with the sophistication and the depth of the financial institutions dealing with bitcoin, this volatility will likely decline. With a larger and more liquid market, the daily variations in demand are likely to become relatively smaller, allowing market makers to profit from hedging price variations and smoothing the price. This will only be achieved if and when a large number of market participants hold bitcoins with the intent of holding onto them for the long term, raising the market value of the supply of bitcoins significantly and making a large liquid market possible with only a fraction of the supply. Should the network reach a stable size at any point, the flow of funds in and out of it would be relatively equal and the price of bitcoin can stabilize. In such a case, bitcoin would gain more stability while also having enough liquidity to not move significantly with daily market transactions. But as long as bitcoin continues to grow in adoption, its appreciation attracts more adopters to it, leading to further appreciation, making this drop in volatility further away. As long as bitcoin is growing, its token price will behave like that of a stock of a start-up achieving very fast growth. Should bitcoin's growth stop and stabilize, it would stop attracting high-risk investment flows, and become just a normal monetary asset expected to appreciate slightly every year.

Appendix to Chapter 8

The following is a brief description of three technologies utilized by bitcoin:

Hashing is a process that can take any stream of data as an input and transform it into a dataset of fixed size (known as a hash) using a non-reversible mathematical formula. In other words, it is trivial to use this function to generate a uniform-sized hash for any piece of data, but it is not possible to determine the original string of data from the hash. Hashing is essential for the operation of bitcoin as it is used in digital signatures, proof-of-work, Merkle trees, transaction identifiers, bitcoin addresses, and various other applications. Hashing in essence allows identifying a piece of data in public without revealing anything about that data, which can be used to securely and trustlessly see if multiple parties have the same data.

Public key cryptography is a method for authentication that relies on a set of mathematically related numbers: a private key, a public key, and one or more signatures. The private key, which must be kept secret, can generate a public key that can be distributed freely because it is not possible to determine the private key by examining the public key. This method is used for authentication: after someone publicizes his public key, he can hash some data and then sign that hash with his private key to create a signature. Anyone with the same data can create the same hash and see that it was used to create the signature; then she can compare the signature to the public key she previously received and see that they're both mathematically related, proving that the person with the private key signed the data covered by the hash. Bitcoin utilizes public key cryptography to allow secure value exchange over an open unsecured network. A bitcoin holder can only access his bitcoins if he has the private keys attached to them, while the public address associated with them can be distributed widely. All network members can verify the validity of the transaction by verifying that the transactions sending the money came from the owner of the right private key. In bitcoin, the only form of ownership that exists is through the ownership of the private keys.

Peer-to-peer network is a network structure in which all members have equal privileges and obligations toward one another. There are no central coordinators who can change the rules of the network. Node operators that disagree with how the network functions cannot impose their opinions on other members of the network or override their privileges. The most well-known example of a peer-to-peer network is BitTorrent, a protocol for sharing files online. Whereas in centralized networks members download files from a central server that hosts them, in BitTorrent, users download files from each other directly, divided into small pieces. Once a user has downloaded a piece of the file, they can become a seed for that file, allowing others to download it from them. With this design, a large file can spread relatively quickly without the need for large servers and extensive infrastructure to distribute it, while also protecting against the possibility of a single point of failure compromising the process. Every file that is shared on the network is protected by a cryptographic hash that can be easily verified to ensure that any nodes sharing it have not corrupted it. After law enforcement had cracked down on centralized file-sharing websites such as Napster, BitTorrent's decentralized nature meant law enforcement could never shut it down. With a growing network of users worldwide, BitTorrent at some point represented about a third of all Internet traffic worldwide. Bitcoin utilizes a network similar to BitTorrent, but whereas in BitTorrent the network members share the bits of data that constitute a movie, song, or book, in bitcoin the network members share the ledger of all bitcoin transactions.

Chapter 9

What Is Bitcoin Good For?

Store of Value

The belief that resources are scarce and limited is a misunderstanding of the nature of scarcity, which is the key concept behind economics. The absolute quantity of every raw material present in earth is too large for us as human beings to even measure or comprehend, and in no way constitutes a real limit to what we as humans can produce of it. We have barely scratched the surface of the earth in search of the minerals we need, and the more we search, and the deeper we dig, the more resources we find. What constitutes the practical and realistic limit to the quantity of any resource is always the amount of human time that is directed toward producing it, as that is the only real scarce resource (until the creation of bitcoin). In his masterful book, *The Ultimate Resource*, the late economist Julian Simon explains how the only limited resource, and in fact the only thing for which the term *resource* actually applies, is

human time. Each human has a limited time on earth, and that is the
only scarcity we deal with as individuals. As a society, our only scarcity is
in the total amount of time available to members of a society to produce
different goods and services. More of any good can always be produced
if human time goes toward it. The real cost of a good, then, is always its
opportunity cost in terms of goods forgone to produce it.

In all human history, we have never run out of any single raw material or resource, and the price of virtually all resources is lower today than
it was in past points in history, because our technological advancement
allows us to produce them at a lower cost in terms of our time. Not
only have we not run out of raw materials, the proven reserves that exist
of each resource have only increased with time as our consumption
has gone up. If resources are to be understood as being finite, then the
existing stockpiles would decline with time as we consume more. But
even as we are always consuming more, prices continue to drop, and the
improvements in technology for finding and excavating resources allows
us to find more and more. Oil, the vital bloodline of modern economies,
is the best example as it has fairly reliable statistics. As Figure 20 shows,
even as consumption and production continue to increase year on

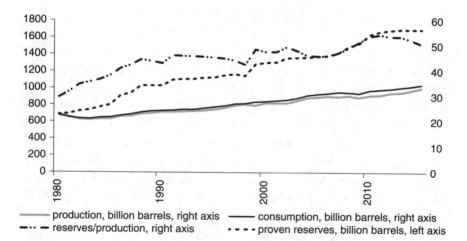

Figure 20 Global oil consumption, production, proven reserves, and ratio of
reserves over annual production, 1980–2015.

year, the proven reserves increase at an even faster rate.[1] According to data from BP's statistical review, annual oil production was 46% higher in 2015 than its level in 1980, while consumption was 55% higher. Oil reserves, on the other hand, have increased by 148%, around triple the increase in production and consumption.

Similar statistics can be produced for resources with varying degrees of prevalence in the earth's crust. The rarity of a resource determines the relative cost of extracting it from the earth. More prevalent metals like iron and copper are easy to find, and relatively cheap as a result. Rarer metals, such as silver and gold, are more expensive. The limit on how much we can produce of each of those metals, however, remains the opportunity cost of their production relative to one another, and not their absolute quantity. There is no better evidence for this than the fact that the rarest metal in the crust of the earth, gold, has been mined for thousands of years and continues to be mined in increasing quantities as technology advances over time, as shown in Chapter 3. If annual production of the rarest metal in the earth's crust goes up every year, then it makes no sense to talk of any natural element as being limited in its quantity in any practical sense. Scarcity is only relative in material resources, with the differences in cost of extraction being the determinant of the level of scarcity. The only scarcity, as Julian Simon brilliantly demonstrated, is in the time humans have to produce these metals, and that is why wages continue to rise worldwide, making products and materials continuously get cheaper in terms of human labor.

This is one the hardest economic concepts for people to understand, which fuels the endless hysteria that the environmental movement has foisted upon us through decades of apocalyptic scaremongering. Julian Simon did his best to combat this hysteria by challenging one of the foremost hysterics of the twentieth century to a famous 10-year bet. Paul Ehrlich had written several hysterical books arguing that the earth was on the edge of catastrophe from running out of vital resources, with precise dire predictions about the dates on which these resources would be exhausted. In 1980, Simon challenged Ehrlich to name any raw materials

---

[1] *Source*: BP Statistical Review.

and any period longer than a year, and bet him $10,000 that the price of each of these metals, adjusted for inflation, would be lower at the end of the period than before it. Ehrlich picked copper, chromium, nickel, tin, and tungsten, which were all materials he had predicted would run out. Yet, in 1990, the price of each of these metals had dropped, and the level of annual production had increased, even though the intervening decade had seen human population increase by 800 million people, the largest increase in a single decade before or since.

In reality, the more humans exist, the more production of all these raw materials can take place. More importantly, perhaps, as economist Michael Kremer[2] argues, the fundamental driver of human progress is not raw materials, but technological solutions to problems. Technology is by its nature both a *non-excludable good* (meaning that once one person invents something, all others can copy it and benefit from it) and a *non-rival good* (meaning that a person benefiting from an invention does not reduce the utility that accrues to others who use it). As an example, take the wheel. Once one person invented it, everyone else could copy it and make their own wheel, and their use of their wheel would not in any way reduce others' ability to benefit from it. Ingenious ideas are rare, and only a small minority of people can come up with them. Larger populations will thus produce more technologies and ideas than smaller populations, and because the benefit accrues to everyone, it is better to live in a world with a larger population. The more humans exist on earth, the more technologies and productive ideas are thought of, and the more humans can benefit from these ideas and copy them from one another, leading to higher productivity of human time and improving standards of living.

Kremer illustrates this by showing that as the population of the earth has increased, the rate of population growth has increased rather than declined. Had humans been a burden consuming resources, then the larger the population, the lower the quantity of resources available to each individual and the lower the rate of economic growth and thus population growth, as the Malthusian model predicts. But because humans

---

[2]Kremer, Michael. "Population Growth and Technological Change: One Million B.C. to 1990." *Quarterly of Journal of Economics*, vol. 108, no. 3, 1993, pp. 681–716.

are themselves the resource, and productive ideas are the driver of economic production, a larger number of humans results in more productive ideas and technologies, more production per capita, and a higher capacity for sustaining larger populations. Further, Kremer shows how isolated landmasses that were more heavily populated witnessed faster economic growth and progress than those that were sparsely populated.

It is a misnomer to call raw materials resources, because humans are not passive consumers of manna from heaven. Raw materials are always the product of human labor and ingenuity and thus humans are the ultimate resource, because human time, effort, and ingenuity can always be used to produce more output.

The eternal dilemma humans face with their time concerns how to store the value they produce with their time through the future. While human time is finite, everything else is practically infinite, and more of it can be produced if more human time is directed at it. Whatever object humans chose as a store of value, its value would rise, and because more of the object can always be made, others would produce more of the object to acquire the value stored in it. The Yapese had O'Keefe bringing explosives and advanced boats to make more Rai stones for them and acquire the value stored in the existing stones. Africans had Europeans bringing boats full of beads to acquire the value stored in their beads. Any metal other than gold that was used as a monetary medium was overproduced until its price collapsed. Modern economies have Keynesian central banks forever pretending to fight inflation while gradually or quickly eroding the value of their money, as discussed in Chapter 4. As Americans recently started using their homes as a medium for savings, the supply of housing was increased so much that prices came crashing down. As monetary inflation proceeds, the large number of bubbles can be understood as speculative bets for ways to find a useful store of value. Only gold has come close to solving this problem, thanks to its chemistry making it impossible for anyone to inflate its supply, and that resulted in one of the most glorious eras of human history. But the move toward government control of gold soon limited its monetary role by replacing it with government-issued money, whose record has been abysmal.

This sheds some light on an astonishing facet of the technical accomplishment that is bitcoin. For the first time, humanity has recourse to a

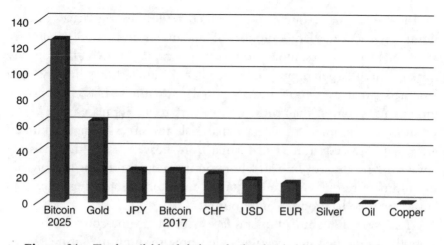

Figure 21   Total available global stockpiles divided by annual production.

commodity whose supply is *strictly limited*. No matter how many people use the network, how much its value rises, and how advanced the equipment used to produce it, there can only ever be 21 million bitcoins in existence. There is no technical possibility for increasing the supply to match the increased demand. Should more people demand to hold bitcoin, the only way to meet the demand is through appreciation of the existing supply. Because each bitcoin is divisible into 100 million satoshis, there is plenty of room for the growth of bitcoin through the use of ever-smaller units of it as the value appreciates. This creates a new type of asset well-suited for playing the role of store of value.

Until bitcoin's invention, all forms of money were unlimited in their quantity and thus imperfect in their ability to store value across time. Bitcoin's immutable monetary supply makes it the best medium to store the value produced from the limited human time, thus making it arguably the best store of value humanity has ever invented. To put it differently, bitcoin is the cheapest way to buy the future, because bitcoin is the only medium guaranteed to not be debased, no matter how much its value rises. (See Figure 21.[3])

---

[3] *Sources*: US Geological Survey data for gold. Silver Institute data for silver. blockchain.info. Author's calculations for bitcoin. BP Statistical Review of World Energy for oil. National currency data from Federal Reserve Economic Data, fred.stlouisfed.org. Author's estimates for copper.

In 2018, with bitcoin only nine years old, it has already been adopted by millions[4] worldwide and its current supply growth rate compares with that of the global reserve currencies. In terms of the stock-to-flow ratio discussed in Chapter 1, the existing stockpiles of bitcoin in 2017 were around 25 times larger than the new coins produced in 2017. This is still less than half of the ratio for gold, but around the year 2022, bitcoin's stock-to-flow ratio will overtake that of gold, and by 2025, it will be around double that of gold and continue to increase quickly into the future while that of gold stays roughly the same, given the dynamics of goldmining discussed in Chapter 3. Around the year 2140 there will be no new supply of bitcoin, and the stock-to-flow ratio becomes infinite, the first time any commodity or good has achieved this.

An important implication of the reduced supply of bitcoins and the continuously diminishing rate at which the supply grows is to make the supply of existing bitcoins very large compared to the new supply. In that sense, bitcoin mining is similar to goldmining, thus ensuring that as a monetary medium, relatively less time and effort would go toward securing new supplies of bitcoin than other moneys whose supply can be increased easily; and more time and effort is dedicated toward useful economic production which can then be exchanged for bitcoins. As the block subsidy declines, the resources dedicated to mining bitcoins will be mainly rewarded for processing the transactions and thus securing the network, rather than for the creation of new coins.

For most of human history, some physical object was used as the store of value. The function of value storage did not need a physical manifestation, but having one allowed for making the supply of the store of value harder to increase. Bitcoin, by not having any physical presence, and being purely digital, is able to achieve strict scarcity. No divisible and transportable physical material had ever achieved this before. Bitcoin allows humans to transport value digitally without any dependence on the physical world, which allows large transfers of sums across the world

---

[4]There are no simple ways of estimating the number of bitcoin users, as each individual user can have an arbitrary number of wallet addresses associated with them. Various attempts at estimating the number put it between 10 and 100 million holders in 2017, and I think this could be as accurate an estimate as we can get.

to be completed in minutes. The strict digital scarcity of the bitcoin tokens combines the best elements of physical monetary media, without any of the physical drawbacks to moving and transporting it. Bitcoin might have a claim to make for being the best technology for saving ever invented.

Individual Sovereignty

As the first form of digital cash, bitcoin's first and most important value proposition is in giving anyone in the world access to sovereign base money. Any person who owns bitcoin achieves a degree of economic freedom which was not possible before its invention. Bitcoin holders can send large amounts of value across the planet without having to ask for the permission of anyone. Bitcoin's value is not reliant on anything physical anywhere in the world and thus can never be completely impeded, destroyed, or confiscated by any of the physical forces of the political or criminal worlds.

The significance of this invention for the political realities of the twenty-first century is that, for the first time since the emergence of the modern state, individuals have a clear technical solution to escaping the financial clout of the governments they live under. Remarkably, the best description of the significance of such a technology can be found in a book written in 1997, a full 12 years before bitcoin's creation, which foresaw a digital currency remarkably similar to bitcoin, and the impact it would have on transforming human society.

In *The Sovereign Individual*, James Davidson and William Rees-Mogg argue that the modern nation-state, with its restrictive laws, high taxes, and totalitarian impulses, has grown to a level of burdensome repression of its citizens' freedom comparable to that of the Church in the European Middle Ages, and just as ripe for disruption. With its heavy burden of taxation, personal control, and rituals, the costs of supporting the Church became unbearable for Europeans, and newer more productive political and economic forms of organization emerged to replace it and consign it to insignificance. The rise of machinery, the printing press, capitalism, and the modern nation-state birthed the age of industrial society and modern conceptions of citizenship.

Five hundred years later, it is industrial society and the modern nation-state that have become repressive, sclerotic, and burdensome while new technology eats away at its power and raison d'être. "Microprocessors will subvert and destroy the nation-state" is the provocative thesis of the book. New forms of organization will emerge from information technology, destroying the capacity of the state to force citizens to pay more for its services than they wish. The digital revolution will destroy the power of the modern state over its citizens, reduce the significance of the nation-state as an organizing unit, and give individuals unprecedented power and sovereignty over their own lives.

We can already see this process taking place thanks to the telecommunication revolution. Whereas the printing press allowed the poor of the world to access knowledge that was forbidden them and monopolized by the churches, it still had the limitation of producing physical books which could always be confiscated, banned, or burned. No such threat exists in the cyber-world, where virtually all human knowledge exists, readily available for individuals to access without any possibility for effective government control or censorship.

Similarly, information is allowing trade and employment to subvert government restrictions and regulations, as best exemplified by companies like Uber and Airbnb, which have not asked for government permission to introduce their products successfully and subvert traditional forms of regulation and supervision. Modern individuals can transact with others they meet online via systems of identity and protection built on consent and mutual respect, without any need for resorting to coercive government regulations.

The emergence of cheap forms of telecommunication online has also subverted the importance of geographic location for work. Producers of many goods can now choose to be domiciled anywhere they prefer while the products of their labor, which are becoming increasingly informational and nonmaterial, can be transferred globally instantaneously. Government regulations and taxes are becoming less powerful as individuals can live or work where it suits them and deliver their work via telecommunication.

As more and more of the value of economic production takes the form of nontangible goods, the relative value of land and physical means of production declines, reducing returns on violently appropriating such physical means of production. Productive capital becomes more embodied in the individuals themselves, making the threat of violently appropriating it increasingly hollow, as individuals' productivity becomes inextricably linked to their consent. When peasants' productivity and survival was tied to the land that they did not own, the threat of violence was effective in getting them to be productive to benefit the landowner. Similarly, industrial society's heavy reliance on physical productive capital and its tangible output made expropriation by the state relatively straightforward, as the twentieth century so bloodily illustrated. But as the individual's mental capacities become the prime productive force of society, the threat of violence becomes far less effective. Humans can easily move to jurisdictions where they are not threatened, or can be productive on computers without governments being able to even know what they are producing.

There was one final piece in the puzzle of digitization that had been missing, and that is the transfer of money and value. Even as information technology could subvert geographic and governmental controls and restrictions, payments continued to be heavily controlled by governments and the state-enforced banking monopolies. Like all government-enforced monopolies, banking had for years resisted innovations and changes that benefit the consumers and restrict their ability to extract fees and rents. This was a monopoly that grew ever more burdensome as the global economy spread and became more global. Davidson and Rees-Mogg predict with remarkable prescience the form that the new digital monetary escape hatch will take: cryptographically secured forms of money independent of all physical restrictions that cannot be stopped or confiscated by government authorities. While this seemed like an outlandish prediction when the book was written, it is now a vivid reality already utilized by millions worldwide, though the significance of it is not widely understood.

Bitcoin, and cryptography in general, are defensive technologies that make the cost of defending property and information far lower than the cost of attacking them. It makes theft extremely expensive and uncertain, and thus favors whoever wants to live in peace without aggression toward others. Bitcoin goes a long way in correcting the imbalance of power that emerged over the last century when the government was able to appropriate money into its central banks and thus make individuals utterly reliant on it for their survival and well-being. The historical version of sound money, gold, did not have these advantages. Gold's physicality made it vulnerable to government control. That gold could not be moved around easily meant that payments using it had to be centralized in banks and central banks, making confiscation easy. With bitcoin, on the other hand, verifying transactions is trivial and virtually costless, as anyone can access the transactions ledger from any Internet-connected device for free.[5] While bitcoin's scaling will likely require the use of third-party intermediaries, this will be different from gold settlement in several very important respects. First, the dealings of the third parties will ultimately all be settled on a publicly accessible ledger, allowing for more transparency and auditing. Bitcoin offers the modern individual the chance to opt out of the totalitarian, managerial, Keynesian, and socialist states. It is a simple technological fix to the modern pestilence of governments surviving by exploiting the productive individuals who happen to live on their soil. If bitcoin continues to grow to capture a larger share of the global wealth, it may force governments to become more and more a form of voluntary organization, which can only acquire its "taxes" voluntarily by offering its subjects services they would be willing to pay for.

The political vision of bitcoin can be understood from a closer examination of the ideas of the cypherpunk movement from which it sprung. In the words of Timothy May:

> The combination of strong, unbreakable public key cryptography and virtual network communities in cyberspace will produce interesting and profound changes in the nature of economic and social systems. Crypto anarchy is the cyberspatial realization of anarcho-capitalism, transcending national boundaries and freeing individuals to make the economic arrangements they wish to make consensually... Crypto anarchy is liberating individuals from coercion by their physical neighbors—who cannot know who they are on the Net—and from governments. For libertarians, strong crypto provides the means by which government will be avoided.[6]

---

[5] And obtaining internet capable devices and an internet connection is cheap and continuously getting cheaper.

[6] May, Timothy C. "Crypto Anarchy and Virtual Communities." *Satoshi Nakamoto Institute*, 1994, nakamotoinstitute.org/virtual-communities/.

The vision of anarcho-capitalism May describes is the political philosophy developed by the American economist of the Austrian school, Murray Rothbard. In *The Ethics of Liberty* Rothbard explains libertarian anarcho-capitalism as the only logically coherent implication of the idea of free will and self-ownership:

> On the other hand, consider the universal status of the ethic of liberty, and of the natural right of person and property that obtains under such an ethic. For every person, at any time or place, can be covered by the basic rules: ownership of one's own self, ownership of the previously unused resources which one has occupied and transformed; and own-ership of all titles derived from that basic ownership—either through voluntary exchanges or voluntary gifts. These rules—which we might call the "rules of natural ownership"—can clearly be applied, and such ownership defended, regardless of the time or place, and regardless of the economic attainments of the society. It is impossible for any other social system to qualify as universal natural law; for if there is any coer-cive rule by one person or group over another (and all rule partakes of such hegemony), then it is impossible to apply the same rule for all; only a rulerless, purely libertarian world can fulfill the qualifications of natural rights and natural law, or, more important, can fulfill the conditions of a universal ethic for all mankind.[7]

The non-aggression principle is the foundation of Rothbard's anarcho-capitalism, and on its basis, any aggression, whether carried out by government or individual, cannot have moral justification. Bitcoin, being completely voluntary and relentlessly peaceful, offers us the monetary infrastructure for a world built purely on voluntary cooperation. Contrary to popular depictions of anarchists as hoodie-clad hoodlums, bitcoin's brand of anarchism is completely peaceful, pro-viding individuals with the tools necessary for them to be free from government control and inflation. It seeks to impose itself on nobody, and if it grows and succeeds, it will be for its own merits as a peaceful neutral technology for money and settlement, not through it being forced on others.

In the foreseeable future, as it is still at a very low level of general adoption, bitcoin provides a cost-effective option for people needing to

---

[7]Rothbard, Murray. *The Ethics of Liberty*. New York University Press, 1998, p. 43.

get around government restrictions on the banking sector, as well as to save wealth in a liquid store of value not subject to government inflation. If it were to be adopted widely, the cost of on-chain bitcoin transactions is likely to rise significantly, as discussed ahead in the section on scaling, making it less feasible for individuals to carry out the uncensorable on-chain transactions to get around government rules and regulations. In that situation, however, the wide adoption of bitcoin will have a far larger positive effect on individual freedom, by reducing government's ability to finance its operation through inflation. It was government money in the twentieth century that allowed for the birth of the heavily interventionist managerial state, with totalitarian and authoritarian tendencies. In a society run on hard money, government impositions that are not economically productive are unlikely to survive for long, as there is little incentive to continue financing them.

International and Online Settlement

Traditionally, gold was the medium of settlement of payments and store of value worldwide. The inability of any party to expand its supply in any significant quantities made it so. Its value was earned on the free market, and not a liability of anyone else. As the scope of communication and travel grew larger in the nineteenth century, requiring financial transactions over longer distances, gold moved out of people's hands and into the vaults of banks, and eventually, central banks. Under a gold standard, people held paper receipts in gold or wrote checks for it that cleared without physical gold having to be physically moved, vastly improving the speed and efficiency of global trade.

As governments confiscated gold and issued their own money, it was no longer possible for global settlements between individuals and banks to be done with gold, and instead they were conducted with national currencies fluctuating in value, creating significant problems for international trade, as discussed in Chapter 6. The invention of bitcoin has created, from the ground up, a new independent alternative mechanism for international settlement that does not rely on any intermediary and can operate entirely separate from the existing financial infrastructure.

The ability of any individual to run a bitcoin node and send his own money without permission from anyone, and without having to expose his identity, is a noteworthy difference between gold and bitcoin. Bitcoin does not have to be stored on a computer; the private key to a person's bitcoin hoard is a string of characters or a string of words the person remembers. It is far easier to move around with a bitcoin private key than with a hoard of gold, and far easier to send it across the world without having to risk it getting stolen or confiscated. Whereas governments confiscated people's gold savings and forced them to trade with money supposedly backed by that gold, people are able to keep the bulk of their bitcoin savings in storage away from government's hands and only use smaller amounts to transact through intermediaries. The very nature of the bitcoin technology puts governments at a severe disadvantage compared to all other forms of money and thus makes confiscation much harder.

Further, the ability of bitcoin holders to track all holdings of bitcoin on its blockchain makes it extremely impractical for any authority to play the role of a lender of last resort for banks dealing with bitcoin. Even in the heyday of the international gold standard, money was redeemable in gold, but central banks rarely had enough to cover the entire supply of currency they introduced, and thus always had a margin for increasing the supply of paper to back up the currency. This is much harder with bitcoin, which brings cryptographic digital certainty to accounting and can help expose banks engaging in fractional reserve banking.

The future use of bitcoin for small payments will likely not be carried out over the distributed ledger, as explained in the discussion on scaling in Chapter 10, but through second layers. Bitcoin can be seen as the new emerging reserve currency for online transactions, where the online equivalent of banks will issue bitcoin-backed tokens to users while keeping their hoard of bitcoins in cold storage, with each individual being able to audit in real time the holdings of the intermediary, and with online verification and reputation systems able to verify that no inflation is taking place. This would allow an infinite number of transactions to be carried out online without having to pay the high transaction fees for on-chain transactions.

As bitcoin continues to evolve in the direction of having a higher market value with higher transaction fees, it starts to look more and more like a reserve currency than a currency for everyday trading and transactions. Even at the time of writing, with bitcoin at a relatively small level of public adoption, the majority of bitcoin transactions are not recorded on-chain, but occur in exchanges and various types of bitcoin-based online platforms such as gambling and casino websites. These businesses will credit or debit bitcoins to their customers on their own internal records and then only make transactions on the bitcoin network when customers deposit or withdraw funds.

By virtue of being digital cash, bitcoin's comparative advantage may not lie in replacing cash payments, but rather in allowing for cash payments to be carried out over long distances. Payments in person, for small amounts, can be conducted in a wide variety of options: physical cash, barter, favors, credit cards, bank checks, and so on. Current state-of-the-art technology in payment settlements has already introduced a wide array of options for settling small-scale payments with very little cost. It is likely that bitcoin's advantage lies not in competing with these payments for small amounts and over short distances; bitcoin's advantage, rather, is that by bringing the finality of cash settlement to the digital world, it has created the fastest method for final settlement of large payments across long distances and national borders. It is when compared to these payments that bitcoin's advantages appear most significant. There are only a few currencies that are accepted for payment worldwide, namely the U.S. dollar, the euro, gold, and the IMF's Special Drawing Rights. The vast majority of international payments are denominated in one of these currencies, with only a tiny percentage shared by a few other major currencies. To send a few thousand dollars' worth of these currencies internationally usually costs dozens of dollars, takes several days, and is subject to invasive forensic examination by financial institutions. The high cost of these transactions lies primarily in the volatility of trading currencies and the problems of settlement between institutions in different countries, which necessitates the employment of several layers of intermediation.

In less than ten years of existence, bitcoin has already achieved a significant degree of global liquidity, allowing for international payments in prices that are currently much lower than existing international transfers. This is not to argue that bitcoin will replace the international money transfer market, but merely to point out its potential for international liquidity. As it stands, the volume of these international flows is far larger than what bitcoin's blockchain can handle, and if more such payments move to bitcoin, fees will rise to limit the demand for them. Yet, that would also not spell doom for bitcoin, because sending these individual payments is not the limit of bitcoin's capabilities.

Bitcoin is money free of counterparty risk, and its network can offer final settlement of large-volume payments within minutes. Bitcoin can thus be best understood to compete with settlement payments between central banks and large financial institutions, and it compares favorably to them due to its verifiable record, cryptographic security, and imperviousness to third-party security holes. Using the major national currencies (USD, euro) for settlement carries with it the risk of exchange rate fluctuation of these currencies and involves trust in several layers of existing intermediation. Settlements between central banks and large financial institutions take days, and sometimes weeks, to clear, during which time each party is exposed to significant foreign exchange and counterparty risk. Gold is the only traditional monetary medium that is not someone's liability, and is free of counterparty risk, but moving gold around is an extremely expensive operational task, fraught with risks.

Bitcoin, having no counterparty risk and no reliance on any third-party, is uniquely suited to play the same role that gold played in the gold standard. It is a neutral money for an international system that does not give any one country the "exorbitant privilege" of issuing the global reserve currency, and is not dependent on its economic performance. Being separated from any particular country's economy, its value will not be affected by the volume of trade denominated in it, averting all the exchange rate problems that have plagued the twentieth century. Further, the finality of settlement on bitcoin does not rely on any counterparty, and does not require any single bank to be the de facto arbiter, making it ideal for a network of global peers, rather than a global hegemonic centralized order. The bitcoin network is based on a form of money whose supply cannot be inflated by any single member bank, making it a more attractive store-of-value proposition than national currencies whose creation was precisely so their supply could be increased to finance governments.

Bitcoin's capacity for transactions is far more than what the current number of central banks would need even if they settled their accounts daily. Bitcoin's current capacity of around 350,000 transactions per day can allow a global network of 850 banks to each have one daily transaction with every other bank on the network. (The number of unique connections in a network equals $n(n-1)/2$, where n is the number of nodes.)

A global network of 850 central banks can perform daily final settlement with one another over the bitcoin network. If each central bank serves around 10 million customers, that would cover the entire world's population. This is offered as an absolute worst-case scenario in which bitcoin's capacity is not increased in any way whatsoever. As will be discussed in the next chapter, there are several ways in which capacity can be increased even without altering the architecture of bitcoin in a backward-incompatible way, potentially allowing for daily settlement between several thousands of banks.

In a world in which no government can create more bitcoins, these bitcoin central banks would compete freely with one another in offering physical and digital bitcoin-backed monetary instruments and payment solutions. Without a lender of last resort, fractional reserve banking becomes an extremely dangerous arrangement and it would be my expectation the only banks that will survive in the long run would be banks offering financial instruments 100% backed by bitcoin. This, however, is a point of contention among economists and time can only tell whether that will be the case. These banks would settle payments between their own customers outside of bitcoin's blockchain and then perform final daily settlement between each other over the blockchain.

While this view of bitcoin might sound like it is a betrayal of bitcoin's original vision of fully peer-to-peer cash, it is not a new vision. Hal Finney, the recipient of the first bitcoin transaction from Nakamoto, wrote this on the bitcoin forum in 2010:

> Actually there is a very good reason for bitcoin-backed banks to exist, issuing their own digital cash currency, redeemable for bitcoins. Bitcoin itself cannot scale to have every single financial transaction in the world be broadcast to everyone and included in the block chain. There needs to be a secondary level of payment systems which is lighter weight and more efficient. Likewise, the time needed for bitcoin transactions to finalize will be impractical for medium to large value purchases.

Bitcoin backed banks will solve these problems. They can work like banks did before nationalization of currency. Different banks can have different policies, some more aggressive, some more conservative. Some would be fractional reserve while others may be 100% bitcoin backed. Interest rates may vary. Cash from some banks may trade at a discount to that from others.

George Selgin has worked out the theory of competitive free banking in detail, and he argues that such a system would be stable, inflation resistant and self–regulating.

I believe this will be the ultimate fate of bitcoin, to be the "high–powered money" that serves as a reserve currency for banks that issue their own digital cash. Most bitcoin transactions will occur between banks, to settle net transfers. Bitcoin transactions by private individuals will be as rare as ... well, as bitcoin based purchases are today.[8]

The number of transactions in a bitcoin economy can still be as large as it is today, but the settlement of these transactions will not happen on bitcoin's ledger, whose immutability and trustlessness is far too valuable for individual consumer payments. Whatever the limitations of current payment solutions, they will stand to benefit immensely from the introduction of free market competition into the field of banking and payments, one of the most sclerotic industries in the modern world economy, because it is controlled by governments that can create the money on which it runs.

If bitcoin continues to grow in value and gets utilized by a growing number of financial institutions, it will become a reserve currency for a new form of central bank. These central banks could be primarily based in the digital or physical worlds, but it is becoming worth considering whether national central banks should supplement their reserves with bitcoin. In the current monetary global system, national central banks hold reserves mainly in U.S. dollars, euros, British pounds, IMF Standard Drawing Rights, and gold. These reserve currencies are used to settle accounts between central banks and to defend the market value of their local currencies. Should bitcoin's appreciation continue in the same manner it has

---

[8]Finney, Hal. *BitcoinTalk Forum*. 30 Dec. 2010, bitcointalk.org/index.php?topic=2500.msg34211#msg34211.

experienced over the past few years, it is likely to attract the attention of central banks with an eye on the future.

If bitcoin continues to appreciate significantly, it will provide the central bank more flexibility with their monetary policy and international account settlement. But perhaps the real case for central banks owning bitcoin is as insurance against the scenario of it succeeding. Given that the supply of bitcoins is strictly limited, it may be wise for a central bank to spend a small amount acquiring a small portion of bitcoin's supply today in case it appreciates significantly in the future. If bitcoin continues to appreciate while a central bank doesn't own any of it, then the market value of their reserve currencies and gold will be declining in terms of bitcoin, placing the central bank at a disadvantage the later it decides to acquire reserves.

Bitcoin is still viewed as a quirky Internet experiment for now, but as it continues to survive and appreciate over time, it will start attracting real attention from high-net-worth individuals, institutional investors, and then, possibly, central banks. The point at which central banks start to consider using it is the point at which they are all engaged in a reverse bank run on bitcoin. The first central bank to buy bitcoin will alert the rest of the central banks to the possibility and make many of them rush toward it. The first central bank purchase is likely to make the value of bitcoin rise significantly and thus make it progressively more expensive for later central banks to buy it. The wisest course of action in this case is for a central bank to purchase a small amount of bitcoin. If the central bank has the institutional capacity to purchase the currency without announcing it, that would be an even wiser course of action, allowing the central bank to accumulate it at low prices.

Bitcoin can also serve as a useful reserve asset for central banks facing international restrictions on their banking operations, or unhappy with the dollar-centric global monetary system. The possibility of adopting bitcoin reserves might itself prove a valuable bargaining chip for these central banks with U.S. monetary authorities, who would probably prefer not to see any central banks defect to bitcoin as a method of settlement, because that would then entice others to join.

While central banks have mostly been dismissive of the importance of bitcoin, this could be a luxury they may not afford for long. As hard as it might be for central bankers to believe it, bitcoin is a direct competitor to their line of business, which has been closed off from market competition for a century. Bitcoin makes global processing of payments and final clearance available for anyone to perform at a small cost, and it replaces human-directed monetary policy with superior and perfectly predictable algorithms. The modern central bank business model is being disrupted. Central banks now have no way of stopping competition by just passing laws as they have always done. They are now up against a digital competitor that most likely cannot be brought under the physical world's laws. Should national central banks not use bitcoin's instant clearance and sound monetary policy, they would leave the door open for digital upstarts to capture more and more of this market for a store of value and settlement.

If the modern world is ancient Rome, suffering the economic consequences of monetary collapse, with the dollar our aureus, then Satoshi Nakamoto is our Constantine, bitcoin is his solidus, and the Internet is our Constantinople. Bitcoin serves as a monetary lifeboat for people forced to transact and save in monetary media constantly debased by governments. Based on the foregoing analysis, the real advantage of bitcoin lies in it being a reliable long-term store of value, and a sovereign form of money that allows individuals to conduct permissionless transactions. Bitcoin's main uses in the foreseeable future will follow from these competitive advantages, and not from its ability to offer ubiquitous or cheap transactions.

Global Unit of Account

This final application of bitcoin is not one that is likely to materialize any time soon, but is nonetheless intriguing given bitcoin's unique properties. Since the end of the gold standard era, global trade has been hampered by the differences in currency value across different countries. This destroyed people's ability to conduct indirect exchange using a single medium of exchange and instead created a world where buying something across borders has to be preceded by buying the currency of the producer, almost mimicking barter. This has severely hampered people's ability to conduct economic calculation across borders and resulted in the growth of a massive foreign exchange industry. That industry produces little of value but an amelioration of the terrible consequences of monetary nationalism.

The gold standard offered a solution to this problem, wherein a single form of money, independent of the control of any single government or authority, was the monetary standard worldwide. Prices could be calibrated against gold and expressed in it, facilitating calculation across borders. The physical heft of gold, however, meant that it had to be centralized and settlement had to be carried out between central banks. Once the gold was centralized, its lure proved irresistible for governments, who took control of it and eventually replaced it with fiat money whose supply they control. Sound money became unsound as a result.

It is an open question whether bitcoin could potentially play the role of a global unit of account for trade and economic activity. For this possibility to materialize, bitcoin would need to be adopted by an extremely large number of people in the world, most likely indirectly, through its use as a reserve currency. It would then remain to be seen whether the stability of bitcoin's supply would make it also stable in value, as daily transactions in it would be marginal compared to the quantities held. As it stands, given that bitcoin constitutes less than 1% of the global money supply, large individual transactions in bitcoin can have a large impact on price, and small variations in demand can cause large swings in price. This, however, is a feature of the current situation where bitcoin as a global settlement network and currency is still a tiny fraction of global settlement payments and money supply. Buying a bitcoin token today can be considered an investment in the fast growth of the network and currency as a store of value, because it is still very small and able to grow many multiples of its size and value very quickly. Should bitcoin's share of the global money supply and international settlement transactions become a majority share of the global market, the level of demand for it will become far more predictable and stable, leading to a stabilization in the value of the currency. Hypothetically, should bitcoin become the only money used around the world, it will no longer have large room for growth in value. At that point, demand for it will simply be demand for holding liquid money, and the speculative investment aspect of the demand we see today would disappear. In such a situation, the value of bitcoin would vary along with the time preference of the entire world's population, with increasing demand for holding bitcoin as a store of value leading to only small appreciation of its value.

In the long run, the absence of any authority that can control bitcoin's supply will likely go from creating volatility in the price to reducing it. The predictability of the supply combined with growth in the number of users could make daily fluctuations in demand less significant determinants of price, as market makers are able to hedge and smooth supply-and-demand fluctuations and create a more stable price.

The situation would be similar to gold under the gold standard, as detailed in Jastram's study referenced in Chapter 6. For centuries during which gold was used as money, the steady and gradual increase in its supply meant that its value did not increase or decrease significantly, making it the perfect unit of account across space and time.

But this scenario ignores one fundamental difference between gold and bitcoin, and that is that gold has large and highly elastic demand for use in a multitude of industrial and ornamental applications. Gold's unique chemical properties have ensured that it is always in high demand regardless of its monetary role. Even as monetary demand for gold changes, industry stands ready to utilize essentially limitless quantities of gold should the price drop due to a decrease in monetary demand. Gold's properties make it the best choice for many applications, for which inferior substitutes are only chosen due to gold's high price. Even in a scenario where all global central banks dispose of all their gold reserves, jewelry and industrial demand is likely to absorb all that excess supply with only temporary reductions in price. The rarity of gold in the earth's crust will always ensure it will remain expensive relative to other materials and metals. This property has been instrumental in the rise of gold as money because it ensured a relative stability of value for gold over time, regardless of global changes in monetary demand through countries going on or off the gold standard. This relative stability in turn solidified gold's appeal as a monetary asset and ensured demand for it, and can be understood as the real reason central banks do not sell their gold reserves decades after their currencies stopped being redeemable in it. Should central banks sell their gold reserves, the net effect will be that tons more gold will be utilized in industrial applications over the coming few years, with a small impact on gold's price. In this trade, the central bank would only gain a fiat currency it can print itself, and would lose an asset which will likely gain value over its own currency.

The equivalent nonmonetary demand for bitcoin can be understood as the demand for the coins not as a store of value, but as a necessary prerequisite to using the network. But unlike industrial demand for gold, which is completely independent of its monetary demand, demand for bitcoin to operate the network is inextricably linked to demand for it as a store of value. It thus cannot be expected to play a significant role in ameliorating the volatility of bitcoin's market value as it is growing in its monetary role.

On the one hand, bitcoin's strict scarcity makes it a very attractive choice for a store of value, and an ever-growing number of holders could tolerate the volatility for long periods of time if it is heavily skewed to the upside, as has been the case so far. On the other hand, the persistence of volatility in bitcoin's value will prevent it from playing the role of a unit of account, at least until it has grown to many multiples of its current value and in the percentage of people worldwide who hold and accept it.

Yet, considering that the world's population today has only lived in a world of volatile fiat currencies shifting against each other, bitcoin holders should be far more tolerant of its volatility than generations reared under the certainty of the gold standard. Only the best fiat currencies have been stable in the short-term, but the devaluation in the long term is evident. Gold, on the other hand, has maintained long-term stability, but it is relatively unstable in the short term. Bitcoin's lack of stability does not seem like a fatal flaw that would prevent its growth and adoption given that all its alternatives are also relatively unstable.

Such questions cannot be answered definitively at this point, and only the real world will tell how these dynamics will unfold. Monetary status is a spontaneously emergent product of human action, not a rational product of human design.[9] Individuals act out of self-interest, and technological possibilities and the economic realities of supply and demand shape the outcomes of their actions, providing them incentives

---

[9]For more on this very important distinction, see Adam Ferguson, *An Essay on the History of Civil Society*. London, T. Cadell, 1782. See also Vernon Smith, *Rationality in Economics*. New York, Cambridge University Press, 2008.

to persist, adapt, change, or innovate. A spontaneous monetary order emerges from these complex interactions; it is not something that is conferred through academic debate, rational planning, or government mandate. What might appear like a better technology for money in theory may not necessarily succeed in practice. Bitcoin's volatility may make monetary theorists dismiss it as a monetary medium, but monetary theories cannot override the spontaneous order that emerges on the market as a result of human actions. As a store of value, bitcoin may continue to attract more savings demand, causing it to continue appreciating significantly compared to all other forms of money until it becomes the prime choice for anyone looking to get paid.

Should it achieve some sort of stability in value, bitcoin would be superior to using national currencies for global payment settlements, as is the case today, because national currencies fluctuate in value based on each nation's and government's conditions, and their widespread adoption as a global reserve currency results in an "exorbitant privilege" to the issuing nation. An international settlement currency should be neutral to the monetary policy of different countries, which is why gold played this role with excellence during the international gold standard. Bitcoin would have an advantage over gold in playing this role because its settlement can be completed in minutes, and the authenticity of the transactions can be trivially verified by anyone with an Internet connection, at virtually no cost. Gold, on the other hand, takes more time to transport, and its clearance relies on varying degrees of trust in intermediaries responsible for settling it and transferring it. This might preserve gold's monetary role for in-person cash transactions while bitcoin specializes in international settlement.

Chapter 10

Bitcoin Questions

With the economic basics of the operation of bitcoin explained in Chapter 8, and the main potential use cases of bitcoin discussed in Chapter 9, a few of the most salient questions surrounding bitcoin's operation are examined here.

Is Bitcoin Mining a Waste?

Anyone who joins the bitcoin network generates a *public address* and a *private key*. These are analogous to an email address and its password: people can send you bitcoins to your public address while you use your private key to send bitcoins from your balance. These addresses can also be presented in Quick Response (QR) code format.

When a transaction is made, the sender broadcasts it to all other network members (nodes), who can verify the sender has enough bitcoins to fulfill it, and that he has not spent these coins on another transaction. Once the transaction is validated by a majority of the CPU behind the network, it is inscribed onto the common ledger shared by all network members, allowing all members to update the balance of the two transacting members. While it is easy for any network member to verify the validity of a transaction, a system of voting based on giving each member one vote could be gamed by a hacker creating a lot of nodes to vote to validate their fraudulent transactions. Only by making accuracy based on CPU cycles expended by members, in other words, employing a proof-of-work system, can bitcoin solve the double-spending problem without a trusted third party.

In its essence, proof-of-work involves network members competing to solve mathematical problems that are hard to solve but whose solution is easy to verify. All bitcoin transactions verified in a ten-minute interval are transcribed and grouped together into one block. Nodes compete to solve the PoW math problems for a block of transactions, and the first node to produce the correct solution broadcasts it to network members, who can very quickly verify its correctness. Once the validity of the transactions and PoW are verified by a majority of the network nodes, a set quantity of bitcoin is issued to reward the node that correctly solved the PoW. This is known as the *block subsidy*, and the process of generating the new coins has been referred to as *mining*, because it is the only way that the supply of coins is increased, in the same way that mining is the only way to increase the supply of gold. On top of the block subsidy, the node that correctly solved the PoW also gets the *transaction fees* included by senders. The sum of the transaction fees and the block subsidy is the *block reward*.

Although solving these problems might initially seem a wasteful use of computing and electric power, proof-of-work is essential to the operation of bitcoin.[1] By requiring the expenditure of electricity and processing power to produce new bitcoins, PoW is the only method so far

---

[1] The question of whether bitcoin wastes electricity is at its heart a misunderstanding of the fundamentally subjective nature of value. Electricity is generated worldwide in large quantities to satisfy the needs of consumers. The only judgment about whether this electricity has gone to waste or not lies with the consumer who pays for it. People who are willing to pay the cost of the operation of the bitcoin network for their transactions are effectively financing this electricity consumption, which means the electricity is being produced to satisfy consumer needs and has not been wasted. Functionally speaking, PoW is the only method humans have invented for creating digital hard money. If people find that worth paying for, the electricity has not been wasted.

discovered for making the production of a digital good reliably expensive, allowing it to be a hard money. By ensuring that finding the solution to the mathematical problem consumes large quantities of processing power and electricity, nodes who expend that processing power have a very strong incentive to not include any invalid transactions in their blocks to receive the block reward. Because it is far cheaper to verify the validity of transactions and the PoW than it is to solve the PoW, nodes attempting to enter invalid transactions into a block are almost certainly doomed to failure, ensuring that their expended processing power goes unrewarded.

PoW makes the cost of writing a block extremely high and the cost of verifying its validity extremely low, almost eliminating the incentive for anyone to try to create invalid transactions. If they tried, they would be wasting electricity and processing power without receiving the block reward. Bitcoin can thus be understood as a technology that converts electricity to truthful records through the expenditure of processing power. Those who expend this electricity are rewarded with the bitcoin currency, and so they have a strong incentive to maintain its integrity. As a result of attaching a strong economic incentive for honesty, bitcoin's ledger has been practically incorruptible for the period of its operation so far, with no example of a successful double-spend attack on a confirmed transaction. This integrity of the bitcoin ledger of transactions is achieved without having to rely on any single party being honest. By relying entirely on verification, bitcoin dooms fraudulent transactions to failure and obviates the need for trust in anyone for transactions to be completed.

For an attacker to try to insert fraudulent transactions into the bitcoin ledger, he would need to have a majority of the processing power behind the network to accept his fraud. Honest nodes that are part of the network would have no incentive to do so, because it would undermine the integrity of bitcoin and devalue the rewards they are receiving, wasting the electricity and resources they have expended on it. So an attacker's only hope would be to mobilize a quantity of processing power that constitutes more than 50% of the network to verify his fraud and build on it as if it were valid. Such a move could have been possible in the early days of bitcoin when the total processing power behind the network was very small. But because the economic value held in the network at the time was nonexistent or insignificant, no such attacks materialized. As the network continued to grow and more members brought processing power to it, the cost to attack the network rose.

The reward to nodes for verifying transactions has proven to be a profitable use of processing power. In January 2017, the processing power behind the bitcoin network is equivalent to that of 2 trillion consumer laptops. It is more than two million times larger than the processing power of the world's largest supercomputer, and more than 200,000 times larger than the world's top 500 supercomputers combined. By monetizing processing power directly, bitcoin has become the largest single-purpose computer network in the world.

Another contributing factor in this growth in processing power is that the verification of transactions and the solving of the PoW problems has moved from being conducted by personal computers to specialized processers built specifically to be optimally efficient at running the bitcoin software. These Application Specific Integrated Circuits (ASICs) were first introduced in 2012, and their deployment has made adding processing power to the bitcoin network more efficient, because no electricity is wasted on any irrelevant computing processes that would be present in any other, non-bitcoin-specific computing unit. A global distributed network of independent dedicated miners now protects the integrity of the bitcoin ledger. All of these miners have no conceivable purpose but verifying bitcoin transactions and solving proof-of-work. Should bitcoin fail for whatever reason, these ASICs would be rendered useless and their owners' investment would be lost, so they have a strong incentive to maintain the honesty of the network.

For someone to alter the record of the network they would need to invest hundreds of millions, if not billions, of dollars building new ASIC chips to alter it. Should an attacker succeed in altering the record, he would be highly unlikely to gain any economic benefit from it, as compromising the network would probably reduce the value of bitcoins to close to nothing. In other words, to destroy bitcoin, an attacker needs to expend very large sums of money with no return at all. And in fact, even if such an attempt succeeded, the honest nodes on the network can effectively go back to the record of transactions before the attack and resume operation. The attacker would then need to continue incurring significant running costs to keep attacking the consensus of the honest nodes.

In its early years, bitcoin users would run nodes and use them to carry out their own transactions and to verify each other's transactions, making each node a wallet and a verifier/miner. But with time, these functions have been separated. ASIC chips are now specialized only in verifying transactions to receive reward coins (which is why they are commonly referred to as miners). Node operators can now generate unlimited wallets, allowing businesses to offer convenient wallets for users who can send and receive bitcoins without operating a node or spending processing power on verifying transactions. This has moved bitcoin away from being a pure peer-to-peer network between identical nodes, but the main functional importance of the decentralized and distributed nature of the network has arguably remained intact, as a large number of nodes still exists and no single party is relied on to operate the network. Further, specialized mining has allowed for the processing power backing the network to grow to the astoundingly large size it has reached.

In its early days, when the tokens had little or no value, the network could have been conceivably hijacked and destroyed by attackers, but as the network had little economic value, nobody seems to have bothered. As the economic value held on the network increased, the incentive to attack the network may have increased, but the cost of doing so rose much more, resulting in no attacks materializing. But perhaps the real protection of the bitcoin network at any point in time is that the value of its tokens is entirely dependent on the integrity of the network. Any attack that succeeds in altering the blockchain, stealing coins, or double-spending them would be of little value to the attacker, as it would become apparent to all network members that it is possible to compromise the network, severely reducing demand for using the network and holding the coins, crashing the price. In other words, the defense of the bitcoin network is not just that attacking it has become expensive, but that the attack succeeding renders the attacker's loot worthless. Being an entirely voluntary system, bitcoin can only operate if it is honest, as users can very easily leave it otherwise.

The distribution of the bitcoin processing power, and the strong resistance of the code to change, combined with the intransigency of the monetary policy, are what has allowed bitcoin to survive and grow in value to the extent to which it has today. It is hard for people new to bitcoin to appreciate just how many logistical and security challenges bitcoin has had to endure over the years to arrive at where it is today. Bearing in mind that the Internet has created opportunities for hackers to attack all sorts of networks and websites for fun and profit, this achievement becomes more startling. The ever-growing number of security breaches that happen to computer networks and email servers across the world on a daily basis have occurred to systems which offer the attackers not much more than data or opportunities to score political points. Bitcoin, on the other hand, contains billions of dollars of value, but continues to operate safely and reliably because it was built, from day one, to operate in a highly adversarial setting, subject to relentless attack. Programmers and hackers worldwide have tried to tear it apart using all sorts of techniques, and yet it has continued to operate according to the exact essence of its specification.

Out of Control: Why Nobody Can Change Bitcoin

> "The nature of Bitcoin is such that once version 0.1 was released, the core design was set in stone for the rest of its lifetime."
> —*Satoshi Nakamoto, 6/17/2010*[2]

Bitcoin's resilience has so far not been restricted to successfully repelling attacks; it has also ably resisted any attempt at changing it or altering its characteristics. The true depth of this statement and its implications has not yet been fully realized by most skeptics. If bitcoin's currency were to be compared to a central bank, it would be the world's most independent central bank. If it were to be compared to a nation-state, it would be the most sovereign nation-state in the world. The sovereignty of bitcoin is derived from the fact that, as far as anyone can tell, the operation of its consensus rules makes it very resistant to alteration by individuals. It is no exaggeration to say nobody controls bitcoin, and that the only option available to people is to use it as it is or not use it.

This immutability is not a feature of the bitcoin software, which is trivial to change for anyone with coding skills, but rather is grounded in the economics of the currency and network, and stems from the difficulty of getting every member of the network to adopt the same changes

---

[2]Nakamoto, Satoshi. *BitcoinTalk Forum*. 17 June 2010, bitcointalk.org/index.php?topic=195.msg1611# msg1611.

to the software. The software implementation that allows an individual to run a node that connects to the bitcoin network is open source software, which was initially made available by Satoshi Nakamoto in collaboration with the late Hal Finney and some other programmers. Since then, any person has been free to download and use the software as he or she pleases, and to make changes to it. This creates a freely competitive market in bitcoin implementations, with anyone free to contribute changes or improvements to the software and present them to users for adoption.

Over time, hundreds of computer programmers from around the world have volunteered their time to improve the node software and in the process improve the capabilities of individual nodes. These coders have formed several different implementations, the largest and most popular of which is known as "Bitcoin Core." Several other implementations exist, and users are free to alter the source code at any point. The only requirement for a node to be a part of the network is that it follows the consensus rules of the other nodes. Nodes which break the consensus rules by altering the structure of the chain, the validity of the transaction, the block reward, or any one of many other parameters in the system end up having their transactions rejected by the rest of the nodes.

The process of what defines the parameters of bitcoin is an example of what Scottish philosopher Adam Ferguson called "the product of human action, and not of human design."[3] Although Satoshi Nakamoto and Hal Finney and others had produced a working model of the software in January 2009, the code has evolved significantly since then through the contributions of hundreds of developers as chosen by thousands of users who run nodes. There is no central authority that determines the evolution of the bitcoin software and no single programmer is able to dictate any outcome. The key to running an implementation that gets adopted has proven to be the adherence to the parameters of the original design. To the extent that changes have been made to the software, these changes can be best understood as improvements to the way in which an individual node interacts with the network, but not alterations to the bitcoin network or its consensus rules. While it is outside the scope of the book to discuss which

---

[3] Ferguson, Adam. *An Essay on the History of Civil Society*. London, T. Cadell, 1782.

parameters these are, suffice it to specify this criterion: a change that puts the node who adopts it out of consensus with other nodes requires all other nodes to update in order for the node initiating the change to remain on the network. Should a number of nodes adopt the new consensus rules, what emerges is referred to as a hard fork.

Bitcoin's coders, then, for all their competence, cannot control bitcoin, and are only bitcoin coders to the extent that they provide node operators with software the node operators want to adopt. But coders aren't the only ones who cannot control bitcoin. Miners, too, for all of the hashing power they can marshal, also cannot control bitcoin. No matter how much hashing power is expended on processing blocks that are invalid, they will not be validated by a majority of bitcoin nodes. Therefore, if miners attempted to change the rules of the network, the blocks they generate would simply be ignored by the network members who operate the nodes, and they would be wasting their resources on solving proof-of-work problems without any reward. Miners are only bitcoin miners to the extent that they produce blocks with valid transactions according to the current consensus rules.

It would be tempting here to say that node operators control bitcoin, and that is true in an abstract collective manner. More realistically, node operators can only control their own nodes and decide for themselves which network rules to join and which transactions they deem valid or invalid. Nodes are severely restricted in their choice of consensus rules because if they enforced rules inconsistent with the consensus of the network, their transactions would be rejected. Each node has a strong incentive to maintain network consensus rules and to stay compatible with nodes on these consensus rules. Each individual node is powerless to force other nodes to change their code, and that creates a strong collective bias to remain on the current consensus rules.

In conclusion, the bitcoin coders face a strong incentive to abide by consensus rules if they are to have their code adopted. The miners have to abide by the network consensus rules to receive compensation for the resources they spend on proof-of-work. The network members face a strong incentive to remain on the consensus rules to ensure they can clear their transactions on the network. Any individual coder, miner, or node operator is dispensable to the network. If they stray away from consensus rules, the most likely outcome is that they will individually waste resources. As long as the network provides positive rewards to its participants, it's likely that replacement participants will come up. The consensus parameters of bitcoin can thus be understood as being sovereign. To the extent that bitcoin will exist, it will exist according to these parameters and specifications. This very strong status–quo bias in bitcoin's operation makes alterations to its money supply schedule, or important economic parameters, extremely difficult. It is only because of this stable equilibrium that bitcoin can be considered hard money. Should bitcoin deviate from these consensus rules its value proposition as hard money would be seriously compromised.

To the best of this author's knowledge, there have been no significant coordinated attempts to alter the monetary policy of bitcoin,[4] but even far simpler attempts at altering some of the technical specifications of the code have so far failed. The reason that even seemingly innocuous changes to the protocol are extremely hard to carry out is the distributed nature of the network, and the need for many disparate and adversarial parties to agree to changes whose impact they cannot fully understand, while the safety and tried-and-tested familiarity of the status quo remains fully familiar and dependable. Bitcoin's status quo can be understood as a stable Schelling point,[5] which provides a useful incentive for all participants to stick to it, while the move away from it will always involve a significant risk of loss.

If some members of the bitcoin network decided to change a parameter in the bitcoin code by introducing a new version of the software that is incompatible with the rest of the network members, the result would be a fork, which effectively creates two separate currencies and networks. For as long as any members stay on the old network, they would benefit from the infrastructure of the network as it exists, the mining equipment, the network effect, and name recognition. In order for the new fork to succeed it would need an overwhelming majority

---

[4] After the first halving of coin rewards in 2012, some miners attempted to continue to mine blocks with 50 coin rewards, but the attempt was thwarted quickly as nodes rejected the blocks mined by these miners, forcing them to switch back to the original inflation schedule.

[5] A Schelling point is a strategy which individuals will use in the absence of communication with others because the point appears natural, and because they expect others to also choose this strategy. Given that there is no formal way of even assessing how many bitcoin nodes there are, the Schelling point for each node member is stick to the existing set of consensus rules and avoid defecting to a new set.

of users, mining hashing power, and all of the related infrastructure to migrate at the same time. If it doesn't get that overwhelming majority, the likeliest outcome is that the two bitcoins would trade versus one another on exchanges. Should the people behind the fork hope for their fork to succeed, they will have to sell their coins on the old fork and hope everyone else does the same, so that the price of it collapses and the price of the new fork rises, thus driving all the mining power and economic network to the new network. But because any change in any parameter in bitcoin's operation is likely to have beneficial effects on some network members at the expense of others, it is unlikely that a consensus would form to shift to the new coin. More broadly, the majority of bitcoin holders only hold it because they were attracted to the automated nature of its rules and their imperviousness to direction by third parties. Such individuals are highly unlikely to want to risk giving discretion for fundamental changes to the network to a new group proposing a new incompatible codebase. Whether such a majority exists or not is a moot point; what matters is that enough of them exist to make it always certain that they will continue with the current system parameters, unless their operation is compromised for some reason.

Barring such catastrophic failure in the current design, it is a safe bet that there will be a significant percentage of nodes choosing to stay with the old implementation, which automatically makes that choice far safer for anyone considering going onto a fork. The problem with deciding to go onto a fork is that the only way to help it succeed is by selling your coins on the old chain. Nobody wants to sell their coins on the old network to move to the new network, only to find that not everybody moved and the value of the coins on the new network collapses. In summation, no move to a new implementation with consensus rules can take place unless the vast majority is willing to shift together, and any shift without the majority shifting is almost certain to be economically disastrous for everyone involved. Because any such move to a new implementation likely gives the party proposing the change significant control over the future direction of bitcoin, bitcoin holders, who are needed for this shift to succeed, are to a large extent ideologically opposed to any such group having authority over bitcoin and are highly unlikely to support such a move. The existence of this group makes supporting a fork highly risky for everybody else. This analysis may help explain why bitcoin has resisted all attempts to change it significantly so far. The coordination problem of organizing a simultaneous shift among people with adversarial interests, many of whom are strongly vested in the notion of immutability for its own sake, is likely intractable barring any pressing reason for people to move away from current implementations.

For instance, an edit to increase the issuance rate of the currency to raise the coins that reward miners might appeal to miners, but it would not appeal to current holders, and so they are unlikely to go with such a proposal. Similarly, an edit to increase the size of the bitcoin network blocks would likely benefit miners by allowing them to run more transactions per block and possibly collect more transaction fees to maximize return on their investment in their mining equipment. But it would likely not appeal to long-term holders of bitcoin, who would worry that larger blocks would cause the size of the blockchain to grow much bigger, and thus make running a full node more expensive, thereby dropping the number of nodes in the network, making the network more centralized and thus more vulnerable to attack. The coders who develop software to run bitcoin nodes are powerless to impose changes on anybody; all they can do is propose code, and users are free to download whichever code and version they like. Any code that is compatible with the existing implementations will be far more likely to be downloaded than any code that is not compatible, because the latter would only succeed if the overwhelming majority of the network also ran it.

As a result, bitcoin exhibits extremely strong status-quo bias. Only minor and uncontroversial changes to the code have been implemented so far, and every attempt to alter the network significantly has ended with resounding failure, to the delight of long-term bitcoin stalwarts who like nothing more about their currency than its immutability and resistance to change. The highest-profile of these attempts have concerned increasing the size of individual blocks to increase transaction throughput. Several projects have gathered the names of some very prominent and old-time bitcoiners, and spent a lot on trying to gain publicity for the coin. Gavin Andresen, who was one of the faces most publicly associated with bitcoin, has pushed very aggressively for several attempts to fork bitcoin into having bigger blocks, along with many stakeholders, including some skilled developers and deep-pocketed entrepreneurs.

Initially, bitcoin XT was proposed by Andresen and a developer by the name of Mike Hearn in June 2015, aiming at increasing the size of a block from 1MB to 8MB. But the majority of nodes refused to update to their software and preferred to stay on the 1-megabyte blocks. Hearn was then hired by a "blockchain consortium of financial institutions" to bring blockchain technology to the financial markets, and published a blogpost to coincide with a glowing profile of him in the *New York Times* which hailed him as desperately trying to save bitcoin while painting bitcoin as now being doomed to failure. Hearn proclaimed "the resolution of the bitcoin experiment," citing the lack of growth in transaction capacity as a lethal roadblock to bitcoin's success and announcing he had sold all his coins. The bitcoin price on that day was around $350. Over the following two years, the price was to increase more than forty-fold while the "blockchain consortium" he joined is yet to produce any actual products.

Undeterred, Gavin Andresen immediately proposed a new attempt to fork bitcoin under the name of "bitcoin classic," which would have raised the blocksize to 8 megabytes. This attempt fared no better, and by March 2016 the number of nodes supporting it began to fizzle. Yet, supporters of increasing the blocksize regrouped into bitcoin unlimited in 2017, an even wider coalition that included the largest maker of bitcoin mining chips, as well as a wealthy individual who controls the bitcoin.com domain name and has spent enormous resources trying to promote larger blocks. A lot of media hype was generated and the sense of crisis was palpable to many who follow bitcoin news on mainstream media and social media; yet the reality remained that no fork was attempted, as the majority of nodes continued to run on the 1MB-compatible implementations.

Finally, in August 2017, a group of programmers proposed a new fork of bitcoin under the name of "bitcoin cash," which included many of the earlier advocates of increasing the block size. The fate of bitcoin cash is a vivid illustration of the problems with a bitcoin fork that does not have consensus support. Because a majority chose to stay with the original chain, and the economic infrastructure of exchanges and businesses supporting bitcoin is still largely focused on the original bitcoin, this has kept the value of bitcoin's coins much higher than that of bitcoin cash, and the price of bitcoin cash continued to drop until it hit a low of

5% of bitcoin's value in November 2017. Not only is the fork unable to gain economic value, it is also dogged with a serious technical problem that renders it almost unusable. Seeing as the new chain has the same hashing algorithm as bitcoin, miners can utilize their processing power on both chains and receive rewards in both. But because bitcoin's coins are far more valuable than bitcoin cash, the processing power behind bitcoin remains far higher than that of bitcoin cash, and bitcoin miners can shift to bitcoin cash any time the rewards get high. This leaves bitcoin cash in an unfortunate dilemma: if the mining difficulty is too high, then there will be a long delay for blocks to be produced and transactions to process. But if the difficulty is set too low, the coin is mined very quickly and the supply increases quickly. This increases the supply of the bitcoin cash coins faster than the bitcoin chain, and would lead to the coin reward for bitcoin cash running out very quickly, thus reducing the incentive for future miners to mine it. Most likely, this will have to lead to a hard fork that adjusts the supply growth to continue offering rewards to miners. This problem is unique to a chain breaking off from bitcoin, but was never true for bitcoin itself. Bitcoin mining was always utilizing the largest amount of processing power for its algorithm, and the increase in processing power was always incremental as miners employed more mining capacity. But with a coin that breaks off from bitcoin, the lower value of the coin and the lower difficulty makes the coin constantly vulnerable for quick mining by the much larger mining capacity of the more valuable chain.

After the failure of this fork to challenge bitcoin's prime position, another attempt at a fork to double the blocksize, negotiated between various startups active in the bitcoin economy, was canceled in mid-November as its promoters realized they were highly unlikely to achieve consensus for their move and would instead most likely end up with another coin and network. Bitcoin stalwarts have learned to shrug at such attempts, realizing that no matter how much hype is generated, any attempt to change the consensus rules of bitcoin will lead to the generation of yet another bitcoin copycat, like the altcoins which copy bitcoin's incidental details but do not have its only important characteristic: immutability. From the discussion above it should be clear that bitcoin's advantages lie not in its speed, convenience, or friendly user experience. Bitcoin's value comes from it having an immutable monetary policy precisely because nobody can easily change it. Any coin that begins with a group of individuals changing bitcoin's specification has with its creation lost arguably the only property that makes bitcoin valuable in the first place.

Bitcoin is straightforward to use, but virtually impossible to alter. Bitcoin is voluntary, so nobody has to use it, but those who want to use it have no choice but to play by its rules. Changing bitcoin in any meaningful way is not really possible, and should it be attempted, will produce another pointless knock-off to be added to the thousands already out there. Bitcoin is to be taken as it is, accepted on its own terms and used for what it offers. For all practical intents and purposes, bitcoin is *sovereign*: it runs by its own rules, and there are no outsiders who can alter these rules. It might even be helpful to think of the parameters of bitcoin as being similar to the rotation of the earth, sun, moon, or stars, forces outside of our control which are to be lived, not altered.

Antifragility

Bitcoin is an embodiment of the idea of *antifragility*, which is understood as gaining from adversity and disorder. Bitcoin is not just robust to attack, but it can be said to be antifragile on both a technical and economic level. While attempts to kill bitcoin have so far failed, many of them have made it stronger by ending up allowing coders to identify weaknesses and patch them up. Further, every thwarted attack on the network is a notch on its belt, another testament and advertisement to participants and outsiders of the security of the network.

A global team of volunteer software developers, reviewers, and hackers have taken a professional, financial, and intellectual interest in working on improving or strengthening the bitcoin code and network. Any exploits or weaknesses found in the specification of the code will attract some of these coders to offer solutions, debate them, test them, and then propose them to network members for adoption. The only changes that have happened so far have been operational changes that allow the network to run more efficiently, but not changes that alter the essence of the coin's operation. These coders can own bitcoin tokens, and so have a financial incentive to work on ensuring bitcoin grows and succeeds.

In turn, the continued success of bitcoin rewards these coders finan-
cially and thus allows them to dedicate more time and effort to the
maintenance of bitcoin. Some of the prominent developers working
on maintaining bitcoin have become wealthy enough from investing in
bitcoin that they can make it their prime occupation without receiving
pay from anyone.

In terms of media coverage, bitcoin appears to be a good embodiment of the adage "all publicity is good publicity." As a new technology
that is not easy to understand, bitcoin was always going to receive inaccurate and downright hostile media coverage, as was the case with many
other technologies. The website 99bitcoins.com has collected more than
200 examples of prominent articles announcing the death of bitcoin over
the years. Some of these writers found bitcoin to be a contravention to
their worldview—usually related to the state theory of money or Keynesian faith in the importance of an elastic supply of money—and refused to
consider the possibility they might be wrong. Instead, they concluded
that it must be bitcoin whose existence is wrong, and therefore they
predicted it would die soon. Others believed strongly in the need for
bitcoin to change to maintain its success, and when they failed to get
it to change in the way they desired, they concluded it must die. These
people's attacks on bitcoin led them to write about it and bring it to the
attention of ever-wider audiences. The more obituaries intensified, the
more its processing power, transactions, and market value grew. Many
bitcoiners, this author included, only came around to appreciating the
importance of bitcoin by noticing how many times it had been written
off, and how it continued to operate successfully. The bitcoin obituaries
were powerless to stop it, but they seem to have helped it gain more
publicity and awaken the public's curiosity to the fact that it continues
to operate in spite of all the hostility and bad press it gets.

A good example of bitcoin's antifragility came in the fall of 2013,
when the FBI arrested the alleged owner of the Silk Road website, which
was a truly free online market allowing users to sell and buy anything
they wanted online, including illegal drugs. With bitcoin's association in
the public's mind with drugs and crime, most analysts predicted the closing of the website would destroy bitcoin's utility. The price on that day
dropped from around the $120 range to the $100 range, but it rebounded
quickly and began a very fast rise, reaching $1,200 per bitcoin within a

few months. At the time of writing, the price had never again dropped to the level it was at before the closing of the Silk Road website. By surviving the closing of the Silk Road unscathed, bitcoin demonstrated that it is far more than a currency for crime, and in the process it benefited from the free publicity from the Silk Road media coverage.

Another example of bitcoin's antifragility came in September 2017, after the Chinese government announced the closure of all Chinese exchanges that traded bitcoin. Whereas the initial reaction was one of panic that saw the price drop by around 40%, it was only a matter of hours before the price started recovering, and within a few months the price had more than doubled from where it was before the government's ban. While banning exchanges from trading bitcoin could be viewed as an impediment to bitcoin's adoption through a reduction in its liquidity, it seems to have only served to reinforce bitcoin's value proposition. More transactions started happening off exchanges in China, with volume on websites like localbitcoins.com exploding. It may just be that the suspension of trading in China caused the opposite of the intended effect, as it drove Chinese to hold onto their bitcoin for the long term rather than trade it for the short term.

Can Bitcoin Scale?

At the time of writing, one of the most high-profile debates surrounding bitcoin concerns the question of scaling, or increasing the transaction capacity. Bitcoin's 1-megabyte blocks mean that the capacity for transactions as it stands is around fewer than 500,000 transactions per day. Bitcoin has already approached these levels of transactions, and as a result, transaction fees have risen significantly over the past few months. The implementation of a technology called SegWit could result in a quadrupling of this daily capacity, but it is nonetheless becoming clear that there will be a hard limit to how many transactions can be processed over the bitcoin blockchain, due to the decentralized and distributed nature of bitcoin. Each bitcoin transaction is recorded with all network nodes, who are all required to keep a copy of the entire ledger of all transactions. This necessarily means that the cost of recording transactions will be far higher than for any centralized solution which only needs one record and a few backups. The most efficient payment processing systems are all centralized for a good reason: it is cheaper to keep a central record than to keep several distributed records and have to worry about them updating in sync, a process which so far can only be achieved using bitcoin proof-of-work.

Centralized payment solutions, such as Visa or MasterCard, employ one centralized ledger to which all transactions are committed, as well as a backup that is entirely separate. Visa can process around 3,200 transactions per second, or 100.8 billion transactions per year.[6] Bitcoin's current 1-megabyte blocks are able to process a maximum of four transactions per second, 350,000 transactions per day, or around 120 million transactions per year. For bitcoin to process the 100 billion transactions that Visa processes, each block would need to be around 800 megabytes, meaning every ten minutes, each bitcoin node would need to add 800 megabytes of data. In a year, each bitcoin node would add around 42 terabytes of data, or 42,000 gigabytes, to its blockchain. Such a number is completely outside the realm of possible processing power of commercially available computers now or in the foreseeable future. The average consumer computer, or the average external hard drive, has a capacity in the order of 1 terabyte, about a week's worth of transactions at Visa volumes. For some perspective, it is worth examining the sort of computing infrastructure that Visa employs to process these transactions.

In 2013, a report showed that Visa owns a data center described as a "digital Fort Knox" containing 376 servers, 277 switches, 85 routers, and 42 firewalls.[7] Granted, Visa's centralized system is a single point of failure, and so it employs very large amounts of redundancy and spare capacity to protect from unforeseen circumstances, whereas in the case of bitcoin, the presence of many nodes would make each one of them non-critical, and so requiring less security and capacity. Nonetheless, a node that can add 42 terabytes of data every year would require a very expensive computer, and the network bandwidth required to process all of these transactions every day would be an enormous cost that would be

---

[6] *Facts and Figures*. Visa, Inc., Nov. 2015, usa.visa.com/content/dam/VCOM/download/corporate/media/VisaInc_factsheet_11012015%20(002).pdf.
[7] Kontzer, Tony. "Inside Visa's Data Center." *Network Computing*, 29 May 2013, www.networkcomputing.com/networking/inside-visas-data-center/1599285558.

clearly unworkably complicated and expensive for a distributed network to maintain.

There are only a handful of such centers in existence worldwide: those employed by Visa, MasterCard, and a few other payment processors. Should bitcoin attempt to process such a capacity, it could not possibly compete with these centralized solutions by having thousands of distributed centers on a similar scale; it would have to become centralized and employ only a few such data centers. For bitcoin to remain distributed, each node on the network must cost something reasonable for thousands of individuals to run it on commercially available personal computers, and the transfer of data between the nodes has to be at scales that are supported by regular consumer bandwidth.

It is inconceivable that bitcoin could run the same scale of transactions on-chain that a centralized system can support. This explains why transaction costs are rising, and in most likelihood, will continue to rise if the network continues to grow. The biggest scope for scaling bitcoin transactions will likely come off-chain, where many simpler technologies can be used for small and unimportant payments. This ensures there can be no compromise of bitcoin's two most significant properties for which using extensive processing power is justified: digital sound money and digital cash. There are no alternative technologies that can offer these two functions, but there are many technologies that can offer small payments and consumer spending at low costs, and the technology for these choices is very simple to implement relatively reliably with current banking technologies. Bitcoin mass use for merchant payments is not even very feasible given that it takes anywhere from 1 to 12 minutes for a transaction to receive its first confirmation. Merchants and customers cannot wait that long on payments, and even though the risk of a double-spend attack is not significant enough for one small payment, it is significant enough for merchants who receive large numbers of transactions as in the example of the attack on Betcoin Dice, discussed later in the section on attacks on bitcoin.

For people who want to use bitcoin as a digital long-term store of value, or for people who want to carry out important transactions without having to go through a repressive government, the high transaction fees are a price well worth paying. Saving in bitcoin by its very nature will not require many transactions, and so a high transaction fee is worth paying for it. And for transactions that cannot be carried out through the regular banking system, such as people trying to get their money out of a country suffering inflation and capital controls, bitcoin's high transaction fees will be a price well worth paying. Even at current low levels of adoption, the demand for digital cash and digital sound money has already raised transaction fees to the point where they cannot compete with centralized solutions like PayPal and credit cards for small payments. This has not stalled bitcoin's growth, however, which indicates that the market demand for bitcoin is driven by its use as a digital cash and digital store of value, rather than small digital payments.

If bitcoin's popularity continues to grow, there are some potential scaling solutions that do not involve creating any changes to the structure of bitcoin, but which take advantage of the way transactions are structured to increase the number of payments possible. Each bitcoin transaction can contain several inputs and outputs, and using a technique called CoinJoin, several payments can be grouped together into one transaction, allowing several inputs and outputs for only a fraction of the space that would have been needed otherwise. This could potentially raise the transaction volume of bitcoin to the millions of payments per day, and as the transaction costs rise higher, this is more and more likely to become a popular option.

Another possibility for scaling bitcoin is digital mobile USB wallets, which can be made to be physically tamper-proof and can be checked for their balance at any time. These USB drives would carry the private keys to specific amounts of bitcoins, allowing whoever holds them to withdraw the money from them. They could be used like physical cash, and each holder could verify the value in these drives. As fees have been rising on the network, there has been no respite in the growth of demand for bitcoin, as evidenced by its rising price, indicating that users value the transactions more than the transaction costs they have to pay for them. Instead of the rising fees slowing bitcoin's adoption, all that is happening is that the less important transactions are being moved off-chain and the on-chain transactions are growing in importance. The most important use cases of bitcoin, as a store of value and uncensorable payments, are well worth the transaction fees. When people buy bitcoin to hold it for the long-term, a one-off small transaction fee is to be expected and is usually dwarfed by the commission and the premium placed by the sellers. For people looking to escape capital controls or send money to countries facing economic difficulties, the transaction fee is well worth paying considering bitcoin is the only alternative. As bitcoin adoption spreads, and transaction fees rise high enough that they will matter to the people paying them, there will be economic pressure to utilize more of the above scaling solutions which can increase transaction capacity without making changes that compromise the rules of the network and force a chain split.

Beyond these possibilities, the majority of bitcoin transactions today are already carried out off-chain, and only settled on-chain. Bitcoin-based businesses, such as exchanges, casinos, or gaming websites, will only use bitcoin's blockchain for customer deposits and withdrawals, but within their platforms, all transactions are recorded on their local databases, denominated in bitcoin. It is not possible to make accurate estimates of the number of these transactions due to the very large number of businesses, the lack of public data on the transactions taking place in their proprietary platforms, and the quickly shifting dynamics of the bitcoin economy, but a conservative estimate would put them as being more than ten times the number of transactions carried out on the bitcoin blockchain. In effect, bitcoin is already being used as a reserve asset in the majority of the transactions in the bitcoin economy. Should bitcoin's growth continue it is only natural to see the number of off-chain transactions increase faster than the on-chain transactions.

Such an analysis may contradict the rhetoric that accompanied the rise of bitcoin, which promotes bitcoin as putting an end to banks and banking. The idea that millions, let alone billions, could use the bitcoin network directly for carrying out their every transaction is unrealistic as it would entail that every network member needs to be recording every other member's transactions. As the numbers grow, these records become larger and constitute a significant computing burden. On the other hand, bitcoin's unique properties as a store of value are likely to continue to increase demand for it, making it hard for it to survive as a purely peer-to-peer network. For bitcoin to continue to grow there will have to be payment processing solutions handled off the bitcoin blockchain, and such solutions are emerging out of the grind of competitive markets.

Another important reason why banking as an institution is not going away is the convenience of banking custody. While many bitcoin purists value the freedom accorded to them by being able to hold their own money and not rely on a financial institution to access it, the vast majority of people would not want this freedom and prefer to not have their money under their responsibility for fear of theft or abduction. In the midst of the very common anti-bank rhetoric that is popular these days, particularly in bitcoin circles, it is easy to forget that deposit banking is a legitimate business which people have demanded for hundreds of years around the world. People have happily paid to have their money stored safely so they only need to carry a small amount of money on them and face little risk of loss. In turn, the widespread use of banking cards instead of cash allows people to carry small sums of money on them at all times, which likely makes modern society safer than it would be otherwise, because most potential assailants these days realize they are not likely to come across a victim carrying significant amounts of cash, and theft of banking cards is unlikely to yield significant sums before the victim is able to cancel them.

Even if it were possible for bitcoin's network to support billions of transactions per day, obviating the need for second-layer processing, many, if not most, bitcoiners with significant holdings will eventually resort to keeping them in one of the growing number of services for safe custody of bitcoin. This is an entirely new industry and it is likely to evolve significantly to provide technical solutions for storage with different degrees of safety and liquidity. Whatever shape this industry takes, the services it provides and how it evolves will shape the contours of a bitcoin-based banking system in the future. I make no prediction as to what shape these services will take, and what technological capabilities they will have, except to say that it will likely utilize cryptographic proof mechanisms on top of establishing market reputation in order to operate successfully. One possible technology for how this might be achieved is known as the Lightning Network, a technology under development that promises increasing transaction capacity significantly by allowing nodes to run payment channels off-chain, which only use the bitcoin ledger for verification of valid balances rather than transfers.

In 2016 and 2017, as bitcoin approached the maximum number of daily transactions, the network continued to grow, as is clear from the data in Chapter 8. Bitcoin is scaling through an increase in the value of on-chain transactions, not through a rise of their number. More and more transactions are being carried out off-chain, settled on exchanges or websites that handle bitcoin, turning bitcoin into more of a settlement network than a direct payment network. This does not represent a move away from bitcoin's function as cash, as is commonly believed. While the term *cash* has come to denote the money used for small consumer transactions today, the original meaning of the term refers to money that is a bearer instrument, whose value can be transferred directly without resort to settlement by, or liability of, third parties. In the nineteenth century, the term *cash* referred to central bank gold reserves, and cash settlement was the transfer of physical gold between banks. If this analysis is correct, and bitcoin continues to grow in value and off-chain transactions while on-chain transactions do not grow as much, bitcoin would be better understood as cash in the old meaning of the term, similar to gold cash reserves, rather than the modern term for cash as paper money for small transactions.

In conclusion, there are many possibilities for increasing the number of bitcoin transactions without having to alter the architecture of bitcoin as it is, and without requiring all current node operators to upgrade simultaneously. Scaling solutions will come from node operators improving the way they send data on bitcoin transactions to other network members. This will come through joining transactions together, off-chain transactions, and payment channels. On-chain scaling solutions are unlikely to be enough to meet the growing demand for bitcoin over time, and so second-layer solutions are likely to continue to grow in importance, leading to the emergence of a new kind of financial institution similar to today's banks, using cryptography, and operating primarily online.

Is Bitcoin for Criminals?

One of the very common misconceptions about bitcoin from its inception is that it would make a great currency for criminals and terrorists. A long list of press articles have been published with unsubstantiated claims that terrorists or criminal gangs are using bitcoin for their activity. Many of these articles have been retracted,[8] but not before they have imprinted the idea into the minds of many people, including misguided criminals.

The reality is that bitcoin's ledger is globally accessible and immutable. It will carry the record of every transaction for as long as bitcoin is still operational. It is inaccurate to really say bitcoin is anonymous, as it is rather pseudonymous. It is possible, though not guaranteed, to establish links between real-life identities and bitcoin addresses, thus allowing the full tracking of all transactions by an address once its identity is established. When it comes to anonymity, it is useful to think of bitcoin as being as anonymous as the Internet: it depends on how well you hide, and how well the others look. Yet bitcoin's blockchain makes hiding that much more difficult on the Web. It is easy to dispose of a device, email address, or IP address and never use it again, but it is harder to completely erase the trail of funds to one bitcoin address. By its very nature, bitcoin's blockchain structure is not ideal for privacy.

All of this means that for any crime that actually has a victim, it would be inadvisable for the criminal to use bitcoin. Its pseudonymous nature means that addresses could be linked to real-world identities, even many years after the crime is committed. The police, or the victims and any investigators they hire, might well be able to find a link to the identity of the criminal, even after many years. The bitcoin trail of payments itself has been the reason that many online drug dealers have been identified and caught as they fell for the hype of bitcoin as completely anonymous.

Bitcoin is a technology for money, and money is something that can be used by criminals at all times. Any form of money can be used by criminals or to facilitate crime, but bitcoin's permanent ledger makes it particularly unsuited to crimes with victims likely to try to investigate. Bitcoin can be useful in facilitating "victimless crimes," where the absence of the victim will mean nobody trying to establish the identity of the "criminal." In reality, and once one overcomes the propaganda of the twentieth-century state, there is no such thing as a victimless crime. If an action has no victims, it is no crime, regardless of what some self-important voters or bureaucrats would like to believe

---

[8]Stein, Mara Lemos. "The Morning Risk Report: Terrorism Financing via Bitcoin May Be Exaggerated." *Wall Street Journal*, 2017.

about their prerogative to legislate morality for others. For these illegal but perfectly moral actions, bitcoin could be useful because there are no victims to try to hunt down the perpetrator. The harmless activity carried out shows up on the blockchain as an individual transaction which could have a multitude of causes. So one can expect that victimless crimes, such as online gambling and evading capital controls, would use bitcoin, but murder and terrorism would more likely not. Drug dealing seems to happen on the bitcoin blockchain, though that is likely more down to addicts' cravings than sound judgment, as evidenced by the large number of bitcoin drug purchasers that have been identified by law enforcement. While statistics on this matter are very hard to find, I would not be surprised to find buying drugs with bitcoin is far more dangerous than with physical government money.

In other words, bitcoin will likely increase individuals' freedom while not necessarily making it easier for them to commit crimes. It is not a tool to be feared, but one to be embraced as an integral part of a peaceful and prosperous future.

One high-profile type of crime that has indeed utilized bitcoin heavily is ransomware: a method of unauthorized access to computers that encrypts the victims' files and only releases them if the victim makes a payment to the recipient, usually in bitcoin. While such forms of crime were around before bitcoin, they have become more convenient to carry out since bitcoin's invention. This is arguably the best example of bitcoin facilitating crime. Yet one can simply understand that these ransomware crimes are being built around taking advantage of lax computer security. A company that can have its entire computer system locked up by anonymous hackers demanding a few thousand dollars in bitcoin has far bigger problems than these hackers. The incentive for the hackers may be in the thousands of dollars, but the incentive for the firm's competitors, clients, and suppliers for gaining access to this data can be much higher. In effect, what bitcoin ransomware has allowed is the detection and exposition of computer security flaws. This process is leading firms to take better security precautions, and causing computer security to grow as an industry. In other words, bitcoin allows for the monetizing of the computer security market. While hackers can initially benefit from this, in the long run, productive businesses will command the best security resources.

How to Kill Bitcoin: A Beginners' Guide

Many bitcoiners have developed quasi-religious beliefs in the ability of bitcoin to survive come what may. The amount of processing power behind it and the large number of nodes distributed worldwide verifying transactions means that it is highly resistant to change and likely to remain as such. Most of those unfamiliar with bitcoin will frequently believe that it is doomed because it will inevitably get hacked, like everything digital seems to. Once bitcoin's operation is understood, it becomes clear that "hacking" it is not a straightforward task. There are several other possible threats to bitcoin. Computer security is a fundamentally intractable problem, as it involves unpredictable attackers finding new angles of attack. It is beyond the scope of this book to elucidate all potential threats to bitcoin and assess them. This section examines only some of the more high-profile threats and the ones most relevant to the focus of this book on bitcoin as sound money.

Hacking

Bitcoin's resistance to attack is rooted in three properties: its barebones simplicity, the vast processing power that does nothing but ensure the safety of this very simple design, and the distributed nodes which need to achieve consensus on any change for it to take effect. Imagine the digital equivalent of placing the entirety of the U.S. military's infantry and equipment around a school playground to protect it from invasion and you begin to get an idea of how overly fortified bitcoin is.

Bitcoin is at its essence a ledger of ownership of virtual coins. There are only 21 million of these coins, and a few million addresses that own them, and every day no more than 500,000 transactions move some of these coins around. The computing power necessary to operate such a system is minuscule. A laptop for $100 could do it while also surfing the Web. But the reason bitcoin is not run on one laptop is that such an arrangement would require trust in the owner of the laptop while also being a relatively simple target for hacking.

All computer networks rely for their security on making some computers impenetrable to attackers and using these as the definitive record. Bitcoin, on the other hand, takes an entirely different approach to computer security: it does not bother to secure any of its computers individually, and operates under the working assumption that all computer nodes are hostile attackers. Instead of establishing trust in any network member, bitcoin verifies everything they do. That process of verification, through proof-of-work, is what consumes large amounts of processing power, and it has proven very effective because it makes bitcoin security dependent on brute processing power, and as such, invulnerable to problems of access or credentials. If everyone is assumed dishonest, everyone must pay a large cost to commit transactions to the common record, and everyone will lose these costs if their fraud is detected. The economic incentives make dishonesty extremely expensive and highly unlikely to succeed.

To hack bitcoin, in the sense of corrupting the ledger of transactions to fraudulently move coins to a specific account, or to make it unusable, would require a node to post an invalid block to the blockchain, and the network to adopt it and continue to build on it. Because nodes have a very low cost of detecting fraud, while the cost of adding a block of transactions is high and continuously rising, and because the majority of nodes in the network have an interest in bitcoin surviving, this battle is unlikely to be won by attackers, and continues to get harder as the cost of adding blocks gets higher.

At the heart of bitcoin's design there is a fundamental asymmetry between the cost of committing a new block of transactions and the cost of verifying the validity of these transactions. This means while forging the record is technically possible, the economic incentives are highly stacked against it. The ledger of transactions as a result constitutes an undisputable record of valid transactions so far.

The 51% Attack

The 51% attack is a method of using large amounts of hashrate to generate fraudulent transactions, by spending the same coin twice, thus having one of the transactions canceled and defrauding the recipient. In essence, if a miner who controls a large percentage of the hashrate manages to solve proof-of-work problems quickly, he could spend a bitcoin on a public chain that receives confirmations while mining another fork of the blockchain with another transaction of the same bitcoin to another address, belonging to the attacker. The recipient of the first transaction receives confirmations, but the attacker will attempt to use his processing power to make the second chain longer. If he succeeds in making the second chain longer than the first one, the attack succeeds, and the recipient of the first transaction will find the coins they received vanish.

The more hashrate the attacker is able to command, the more likely he is to make the fraudulent chain longer than the public one, and then reverse his transaction and profit. While this may sound simple in principle, in practice it has been much harder. The longer the recipient waits for confirmation, the less likely it is that the attacker can succeed. If the recipient is willing to wait for six confirmations, the probability of an attack succeeding shrinks infinitely low.

In theory, the 51% percent attack is feasible technically. But in practice, the economic incentives are heavily aligned against it. A miner who successfully executes a 51% attack would severely undermine the economic incentives for anyone to use bitcoin, and with that the demand for bitcoin tokens. As bitcoin mining has grown to become a heavily capital-intensive industry with large investments dedicated to producing coins, miners have grown to have a vested long-term interest in the integrity of the network, as the value of their rewards depends on it. There have been no successful double-spend attacks on any bitcoin transactions that have been confirmed at least once.

The closest thing to a successful double-spend attack that bitcoin has witnessed was in 2013, when a bitcoin betting site called Betcoin Dice had a sum in the range of 1,000 bitcoins (valued at around $100,000 at the time) stolen from it through double-spend attacks utilizing significant mining resources. That attack, however, only succeeded because Betcoin Dice was accepting transactions with zero confirmations, making the cost of attack relatively low. Had they accepted transactions with one confirmation, it would have been much harder to pull off the attack. This is another reason bitcoin's blockchain is not ideal for mass consumer payments: it takes somewhere in the range of 1 to 12 minutes for a new block to be generated to produce one confirmation for a transaction. Should a large payment processor want to accept taking the risk of approving payments with zero confirmations, it constitutes a lucrative target for coordinated double-spend attacks that utilize heavy mining resources.

In conclusion, a 51% attack is theoretically possible to execute if the recipients of the payment are not waiting for a few blocks to confirm the validity of the transaction. In practice, however, the economic incentives are heavily against owners of hashpower utilizing their investments in this avenue, and as a result, there have been no successful 51% attacks on node members that have waited for at least one confirmation.

A 51% attack would likely not be successful if done for a profit motive, but such an attack could also be carried out with no profit motive, but with the intention of destroying bitcoin. A government or private entity could decide to acquire bitcoin mining capacity to commandeer a majority of the bitcoin network and then proceed to use that hashrate to launch continuous double-spend attacks, defrauding many users and destroying confidence in the safety of the network. Yet the economic nature of mining is heavily stacked against this scenario materializing. Processing power is a highly competitive global market, and bitcoin mining is one of the largest, most profitable, and fastest growing uses of processing power in the world. An attacker may look at the cost of commandeering 51% of current hashing power and be willing to dedicate that cost to purchasing the hardware necessary for this. But if such an enormous amount of resources were mobilized to buy bitcoin equipment, manufacturers of this equipment would be able to expand their operation, acquire more capital for producing miners, and produce more mining equipment for anyone on the market to buy, thus inadvertently raising the bitcoin difficulty and hashrate, making the attack more expensive. As an outsider entering the market, the attacker is at a constant disadvantage as his own purchasing of mining equipment leads to the faster growth of the mining processing power not controlled by him. In turn, the more resources are expended on building processing power to attack bitcoin, the faster the growth of the processing power of bitcoin and the harder it becomes to attack. So, yet again, while technically possible, the economics of the network makes it highly unlikely that such an attack would succeed.

An attacker, particularly a state, could attempt to attack bitcoin through taking control of existing mining infrastructure and using it unprofitably in order to undermine the safety of the network. The fact that bitcoin mining is widely distributed geographically makes this a challenging prospect that would require collaboration from various governments worldwide. A better way to implement this might be not through physically taking over mining equipment but commandeering it through hardware backdoors.

Hardware Backdoors

Another possibility for disrupting or destroying the bitcoin network is through corrupting hardware that runs bitcoin software to be accessible by outside parties. Nodes that perform mining could, for example, be fitted with undetectable malware that allows outsiders to commandeer the hardware. This equipment could then be deactivated or remotely controlled at a time when a 51% attack is launched.

Another example would be through spying technology installed on user computers allowing access to users' bitcoins by accessing their private keys. Such attacks on a mass scale could severely undermine confidence in bitcoin as an asset and demand for it.

Both types of attack are feasible technically, and unlike the previous two kinds of attacks, they do not have to succeed entirely in order to create enough confusion to hurt bitcoin's reputation and demand. Such an attack on mining equipment is more likely to succeed given that there are only a few manufacturers of mining equipment, and this constitutes one of bitcoin's most critical points of failure. However, as bitcoin mining is growing, it is likely to start attracting more hardware makers to manufacture its equipment, which would reduce the disastrous impact on the network from the compromise of one manufacturer's operations.

With individual computers, this risk is less systematic to the network because there is a large and potentially unlimited number of manufacturers worldwide that produce equipment capable of accessing the bitcoin network. Should any one producer turn out to be compromised, it is just likely to lead to consumers shifting to other producers. Further, users can generate the private keys to their addresses on offline computers which they will never connect to the Internet. The extra-paranoid can even generate their addresses and private keys on offline computers which are then immediately destroyed. Coins stored on these virtual private keys will survive any kind of attack on the network.

Particularly important defenses against these kinds of attacks are bitcoiners' anarchist and cypherpunk tendencies, which lead them to believe much more in verification than trust. Bitcoiners are generally far more technically competent than the average population, and they are very meticulous about examining the hardware and software they utilize. The open source peer review culture also acts as a significant defense against these sorts of attacks. Given the distributed nature of the network, it is far more likely that such attacks could cause significant costs and losses to individuals, and perhaps even systemic disruptions of the network, but it will be very hard to cause the network to come to a standstill or to destroy demand for bitcoin completely. The reality is that the economic incentives of bitcoin are what make it valuable, not any type of hardware. Any individual piece of equipment is dispensable to the operation of bitcoin and can be replaced with other equipment. Nonetheless, bitcoin's survival and robustness will be enhanced if it can diversify its hardware providers to not make any of them systemically important.

Internet and Infrastructure Attacks

One of the most commonly held misconceptions about bitcoin is that it can be shut down by shutting down important communications infrastructure on which bitcoin relies, or shutting down the Internet. The problem with these scenarios is that they misunderstand bitcoin as if it is a network in the traditional sense of dedicated hardware and infrastructure with critical points that can be attacked and compromised. But bitcoin is a software protocol; it is an internal process that can be carried out on any one of billions of computer machines that are distributed worldwide. Bitcoin has no single point of failure, no single indispensable hardware structure anywhere in the world on which it relies. Any computer that runs bitcoin's software can connect to the network and carry out operations on it. It is in that sense similar to the Internet, in that it is a protocol that allows computers to connect together; it is not the infrastructure which connects them. The quantity of data that is required to pass on information about bitcoin is not very large, and a tiny fraction of the total amount of Internet traffic. Bitcoin does not need as extensive an infrastructure as the rest of the Internet, because its blockchain is really only about transmitting 1 megabyte of data every ten minutes. There are countless wired and wireless technologies for the transmission of data worldwide, and any particular user only needs one of these to be working to connect to the network. In order to create a world in which no bitcoin user is able to connect to other users, the kind of damage that would be needed to be done to the world's information, data, and connectivity infrastructure would be absolutely devastating. The life of modern society depends to a very large degree on connectivity, and many vital services and matters of life and death rely on these communication infrastructures continuing. To begin trying to turn off all of the Internet infrastructure simultaneously would likely cause significant damage to any society that tries it while likely failing to stem the flow of bitcoin, as dispersed machines can always connect to one another using protocols and encrypted communications. There are simply far too many computers and connections spread out all over the world, utilized by far too many people, for any force to be able to make them all stop functioning simultaneously. The only conceivable scenario where this could happen would be through the sort of apocalyptic scenario after which there would be nobody left to even wonder if bitcoin is operational or not. Of all the threats that are often mentioned against bitcoin, I find this to be the least credible or meaningful.

Rise in Cost of Nodes and Drop in Their Numbers

Rather than imagining futuristic sci-fi scenarios involving the destruction of humanity's telecommunication infrastructure in a futile attempt at eradicating a software program, there are far more realistic threats to bitcoin grounded in the fundamentals of its design. Bitcoin's property as hard money whose supply cannot be tampered with, and as uncensorable digital cash without the possibility for third-party intervention, is dependent upon the consensus rules of the network remaining very hard to change, especially the money supply. What achieves this stable status quo, as discussed earlier, is that it is a highly risky and likely negative move for a network member to move out of the current consensus rules if the other members of the network do not also move to the new consensus rules. But what keeps that move highly risky and unlikely is that the number of nodes running the software is large enough that coordination between them is not practical. Should the cost of running a bitcoin node increase significantly, it would make running a node harder for more and more users, and as a result it would decrease the number of nodes on the network. A network with a few dozen nodes stops being an effectively decentralized network as it becomes very possible for the few nodes that operate it to collude to alter the rules of the network to their own benefit, or even to sabotage it.

This remains in my opinion the most serious technical threat to bitcoin in the medium and long term. As it stands, the main constraint on individuals being able to run their own nodes is the Internet connection bandwidth. As blocks remain under 1 megabyte, this should be generally manageable. A hard fork that increases the size of the block would cause a rise in the cost of running a node and lead to a reduction in the number of operational nodes. And just like with the previous threats, while this is certainly technically possible, it remains unlikely to materialize because the economic incentives of the system militate against it, as evidenced by the widespread rejection of attempts to increase the blocksize so far.

The Breaking of the SHA-256 Hashing Algorithm

The SHA-256 hashing function is an integral part of the operation of the bitcoin system. Briefly, hashing is a process that takes any stream of data as an input and transforms it into a dataset of fixed size (known as a hash) using a nonreversible mathematical formula. In other words, it is trivial to use this function to generate a hash for any piece of data, but it is not possible to determine the original string of data from the hash. With improvements in processing power, it might become possible for computers to reverse-calculate these hashing functions, which would render all bitcoin addresses vulnerable to theft.

It is not possible to ascertain if and when such a scenario might unfold, but if it does, it would constitute a very serious technical threat to bitcoin. The technical fix to counter this is to switch to a stronger form of encryption, but the tricky part is to coordinate a hard fork that brings most of the nodes of the network to abandon the old consensus rules for a new set of rules with a new hashing function. All of the problems previously discussed in the difficulty of coordinating a fork apply here, but this time, because the threat is real, and any bitcoin holder who chooses to stay on the old implementation will be vulnerable to hacking, it is likely that an overwhelming majority of users will take part in a hard fork. The only interesting question that remains is whether this hard fork will be orderly and witness all users migrate to the same chain, or if it will lead to the chain splitting into several branches using different encryption methods. While it is certainly possible that the SHA-256 encryption may be broken, the economic incentives of network users are to switch from it to a stronger algorithm, and to switch together to one algorithm.

A Return to Sound Money

While most discussions of how bitcoin could fail or get destroyed focus on technical attacks, a far more promising way of attacking bitcoin is through undermining the economic incentives to its use. To attempt to attack or destroy bitcoin in any of the ways mentioned earlier is highly unlikely to succeed because it conflicts with the economic incentives that drive the use of bitcoin. The situation is analogous to trying to ban the wheel or a knife. As long as the technology is useful for people, attempts at banning it will fail as people will continue to find ways of utilizing it, legally or not. The only way that a technology can be stopped is not by banning it, but by inventing a better replacement or by obviating the need for its use. The typewriter could never be banned or legislated out of existence, but the rise of the PC did effectively kill it.

The demand for bitcoin stems from the need of individuals all over the world to carry out transactions that bypass political controls and to have an inflation-resistant store of value. For as long as political authorities impose restrictions and limitations on individuals transferring money, and for as long as government money is easy money whose supply can be easily expanded according to the whims of politicians, demand for bitcoin will continue to exist, and its diminishing supply growth is likely to lead to its value appreciating over time, thus attracting ever-larger numbers of people to use it as a store of value.

Hypothetically, if the entire world's banking and monetary systems were replaced with those of the gold standard in the late nineteenth century, where individual freedom and hard money were paramount, the demand for bitcoin would likely subside significantly. It might just be the case that such a move would cause a large enough reduction in demand for bitcoin that brings its price significantly down, hurting current holders significantly, increasing the volatility of the currency, and setting it back many years. With the increased volatility and the availability of a reliable and relatively stable hard-money international monetary standard, the incentive for using bitcoin drops significantly. In a world in which governments' restrictions and inflationary tendencies are disciplined by the gold standard, it might just be the case that gold's first-mover advantage and relative purchasing power stability would constitute an insurmountable hurdle for bitcoin to overcome, by depriving bitcoin of the fast growth in users and thus preventing it from reaching a large enough size with any semblance of stability in price.

In practice, however, the possibility of a global return to sound money and liberal government is extremely unlikely as these concepts are largely alien to the vast majority of politicians and voters worldwide, who have been reared for generations to understand government control of money and morality as necessary for the functioning of any society. Further, even if such a political and monetary transformation were possible, bitcoin's diminishing supply growth rate is likely to continue to make it an attractive speculative bet for many, which would in itself cause it to grow further and acquire a larger monetary role. In my assessment, a global monetary return to gold might be the most significant threat to bitcoin, yet it is both unlikely to happen and unlikely to destroy bitcoin completely.

Another possibility for derailing bitcoin would be through the invention of a new form of sound money that is superior to bitcoin. Many seem to think that the other cryptocurrencies that mimic bitcoin could achieve this, but it is my firm belief that none of the coins that copy bitcoin's design can compete with bitcoin on being sound money, for reasons discussed at length in the next section of the chapter, primarily: Bitcoin is the only truly decentralized digital currency which has grown spontaneously as a finely balanced equilibrium between miners, coders, and users, none of whom can control it. It was only ever possible to develop one currency based on this design, because once it became obvious that it is workable, any attempt at copying it will have been a top-down and centrally controlled network which will never escape the control of its creators.

So when it comes to bitcoin's structure and technology, it is highly unlikely that any coin that copies it could replace bitcoin. A new design and technology for implementing digital cash and hard money might produce such a competitor, although it is not possible to predict the emergence of such a technology before it is created, and a familiarity with the problem of digital cash over the years will make it clear that this is not an invention that would be easy to devise.

Altcoins

While bitcoin was the first example of a peer-to-peer electronic cash, it was certainly not the last. Once Nakamoto's design was out in the open, and the currency succeeded in gaining value and adopters, many copied it to produce similar currencies. Namecoin was the first such currency, which used bitcoin's code and started operation in April 2011. At least 732 digital currencies were created by February 2017, according to coinmarketcap.com.

While it is common to think that these currencies exist in competition with bitcoin, and that one of them might overtake bitcoin in the future, in reality they are not in competition with bitcoin because they can never have the properties that make bitcoin functional as digital cash and sound money. In order for a digital system to function as digital cash, it has to be outside the control of any third party; its operation needs to conform to the will of its user according to the protocol, with no possibility for any third party to stop these payments. After years of watching altcoins get created, it seems impossible that any coin will recreate the adversarial standoff that exists between bitcoin stakeholders and prevents any party from controlling payments in it.

Bitcoin was designed by a pseudonymous programmer whose real identity is still unknown. He posted the design to an obscure mailing list for computer programmers interested in cryptography, and after receiving feedback on it over a few months, he launched the network with the late programmer Hal Finney, who passed away in August 2014. After a few days of transacting with Finney and experimenting with the software, more members began to join the network to transact and mine. Nakamoto disappeared in mid-2010, citing "moving to new projects" and has most likely never been heard from since.[9] In all likelihood, there are around 1 million bitcoins that are held in an account that is or was controlled by Nakamoto, but these coins have not moved once. Nakamoto did, however, take extreme caution to ensure that he will not be identified, and until this day there is no compelling evidence to identify who the real Nakamoto is. Had he wanted to be identified, he would already have come forward. Had he left any evidence that could lead to the tracing of his identity, it would have likely already been used to do so. All of his writings and communications have been pored over obsessively by investigators and journalists to no avail. It is high time for everyone involved in bitcoin to stop concerning themselves with the question of the identity of Nakamoto, and accept that it does not matter to the operation of the technology, in the same way that the identity of the inventor of the wheel no longer matters.

Because Nakamoto and Finney are no longer with us, bitcoin has not had any central authority figure or leader who could dictate its direction or exercise influence over the course of its development. Even Gavin Andresen, who was in close contact with Nakamoto, and one of the most identifiable faces of bitcoin, has failed repeatedly at exercising influence on the direction of bitcoin's evolution. An email is often quoted in the press, claiming to be the last email ever sent by Nakamoto, which says, "I've moved on to other things. It's in good hands with Gavin and everyone."[10] Andresen has repeatedly tried to increase the size of bitcoin's

---

[9]Two further communications were possibly made by Nakamoto since then. One was to deny that his real identity was that of a Japanese-American engineer with the real name Dorian Prentice Satoshi Nakamoto, who was identified by *Newsweek* magazine as the real Nakamoto based on no more evidence than a coincidence of names and a knowledge of computers. The other was to offer an opinion on the way the debate for scaling bitcoin had been proceeding. It is not clear whether these posts were by Nakamoto himself or whether someone had compromised his account, particularly as it is a known fact that the email account which he had used to communicate was in fact compromised.

[10]Nakamoto, Satoshi. "Re: I had a few other things on my mind (as always) . . ." Received by Mike Hearn, 23 Apr. 2011. Note: The author is unable to establish the veracity of this email, but it is telling enough that the email is widely quoted, to the point that the MIT Technology Review ran a long feature piece on Andresen entitled "The Man Who Really Built Bitcoin," claiming Andresen was more important to bitcoin's development than even Nakamoto.

blocks, but all his proposals to do so have failed to gain traction with the operators of the nodes.

Bitcoin has continued to grow and thrive in all the metrics mentioned in Chapter 8, while the authority of any individual or party over it has diminished to insignificance. Bitcoin can be understood as a sovereign piece of code, because there is no authority outside of it that can control its behavior. Only bitcoin's rules control bitcoin, and the possibility of changing these rules in any substantive way has become extremely impractical as the status-quo bias continues to shape the incentives of everyone involved in the project.

It is the sovereignty of bitcoin code, backed by proof-of-work, which makes it a genuinely effective solution to the double-spending problem, and a successful digital cash. And it is this trustlessness which other digital currencies cannot replicate. Facing any digital currency built after bitcoin is a deep existential crisis: because bitcoin is already in existence, with more security, processing power and an established user base, anybody looking to use digital cash will naturally prefer it over smaller and less secure alternatives. Because the replication of the code to generate a new coin is almost costless, and the imitation coins proliferate, no single coin is likely to develop any sort of significant growth or momentum unless there is an active team dedicated to nurturing it, growing it, coding it, and securing it. Being the first such invention, bitcoin demonstrating its value as digital cash and hard money was enough to secure growing demand for it, allowing it to succeed when the only person behind it was an anonymous programmer who practically spent no money on promoting it. Being fundamentally knock-offs that are very easy to recreate, all altcoins do not have this luxury of real-world demand, and must actively build and increase this demand.

This is why virtually all altcoins have a team in charge; they began the project, marketed it, designed the marketing material, and plugged press releases into the press as if they were news items, while also having the advantage of mining a large number of coins early before anybody had heard of the coins. These teams are publicly known individuals, and no matter how hard they might try, they cannot demonstrate credibly that they have no control over the direction of the currency, which undermines any claims other currencies might have to being a form of digital cash that cannot be edited or controlled by any third party. In other words, after the bitcoin genie got out of the bottle, anybody trying to build an alternative to bitcoin will only succeed by investing heavily in the coin, making them effectively in control of it. And as long as there is a party with sovereign power over a digital currency, then that currency cannot be understood as a form of digital cash, but rather, a form of intermediated payment—and a very inefficient one at that.

This presents a dilemma facing designers of alternative currencies: without active management by a team of developers and marketers, no digital currency will attract any attention or capital in a sea of 1,000+ currencies. But with active management, development, and marketing by a team, the currency cannot credibly demonstrate that it is not controlled by these individuals. With a group of developers in control of the majority of coins, processing power, and coding expertise, the currency is practically a centralized currency where the interests of the team dictate its development path. There is nothing wrong with a centralized digital currency, and we may well get such competitors in a free market without government restrictions. But there is something deeply and fundamentally wrong about a centralized currency that adopts a highly cumbersome and inefficient design whose only advantage is the removal of a single point of failure.

This problem is more pronounced for digital currencies that begin with an Initial Coin Offering, which creates a highly visible group of developers communicating publicly with investors, making the entire project effectively a centralized project. The trials and tribulations of Ethereum, the largest coin in terms of market value after bitcoin, illustrate this point vividly.

The Decentralized Autonomous Organization (DAO) was the first implementation of smart contracts on the Ethereum network. After more than $150 million was invested in this smart contract, an attacker was able to execute the code in a way that diverted around one-third of all the DAO's assets to his own account. It would be arguably inaccurate to describe this attack as a theft, because all the depositors had accepted that their money will be controlled by the code and nothing else, and the attacker had done nothing but execute the code as it was accepted by the depositors. In the aftermath of the DAO hack, Ethereum developers created a new version of Ethereum where this inconvenient mistake never occurred, confiscating the attacker's funds and distributing them to his victims. This re-injection of subjective human management is at odds with the objective of making code into law, and questions the entire rationale of smart contracts.

If the second largest network in terms of processing power can have its blockchain record altered when the transactions do not go in a way that suits the interests of the development team, then the notion that any of the altcoins is truly regulated by processing power is not tenable. The concentration of currency holding, processing power, and programming skills in the hands of one group of people who are effectively partners in a venture defeats the entire purpose of employing a blockchain structure.

Further, it is extremely difficult to foresee such privately issued currencies rise to the status of a global currency when they have a visible team behind them. Should the currencies appreciate significantly, a small team of creators will become extremely rich, and endowed with the power to collect seigniorage, a role reserved for nation-states in the modern world. Central banks and national governments will not take kindly to this undermining of their authority. It would be relatively easy for central banks to get any of the teams behind this currency to destroy it, or alter its operation in a way that prevents it from competing with national currencies. No single altcoin has demonstrated anything near bitcoin's impressive resilience to change, which is due to its truly decentralized nature and the strong incentives for everyone to abide by the status quo consensus rules. Bitcoin can only make this claim after growing in the wilds of the internet for nine years without any authority controlling it, and very ably repelling some highly coordinated and well-funded campaigns to alter it. In comparison, altcoins have the unmistakable friendly culture of nice people working together on a team project. While this would be great for a new start-up, it is anathema to a project that wants to demonstrate credible commitment to a fixed monetary policy. Should the teams behind any particular altcoin decide to change its monetary policy, it would be a relatively straightforward thing to achieve. Ethereum, for instance, does not yet have a clear vision of what it wants its monetary policy to be in the future, leaving the matter up to community discussion. While this may work wonders for the community spirit of Ethereum, it is no way to build a global hard money, which, to be fair, Ethereum does not claim to do. Whether it is because they are aware of this point, or to avoid run-ins with political authority, or as a marketing gimmick, most altcoins do not market themselves as competitors to bitcoin, but as performing tasks different to bitcoin.

There is nothing about bitcoin's design that suggests it would be good for any of the multitude of use cases that other coins claim they will be able to do, and no coin other than bitcoin has delivered any differentiating capabilities or features which bitcoin does not have. Yet they all have a freely trading currency which is somehow essential for their complex system for performing some online applications.

But the notion that new web apps require their own decentralized currency is the desperately naïve hope that somehow unsolving the problem of lack of coincidence of wants could be economically profitable. There is a reason real-world businesses don't issue their own currency, and that is that nobody wants to hold currency that is only spendable in one business. The point of holding money is holding liquidity which can be spent as easily as possible. Holding forms of money which can only be spent in particular vendors offers very little liquidity and serves no purpose. People will naturally prefer to hold the liquid means of payment, and any business that insists on payment in its own freely trading currency is just introducing significantly high costs and risks to its potential customers.

Even in businesses which require some form of token operationally, such as amusement parks or casinos, the token is always fixed in value compared to liquid money so customers know exactly what they are getting and can make accurate economic calculations. Should any of these supposedly revolutionary decentralized currencies offer any real-world valuable application, it is completely inconceivable that it would be paid for with its own freely trading currency.

In reality, after examining this space for years, I have yet to identify a single digital currency that offers any product or service that has any market demand. The highly vaunted decentralized applications of the future never seem to arrive, but the tokens that are supposedly essential to their operation continue to proliferate by the hundreds every month. One cannot help but wonder if the only use of these revolutionary currencies is the enriching of their makers.

No coin other than bitcoin can lay a credible claim to being outside the control of anyone, and as such, the entire point of utilizing the extremely complex structure underpinning bitcoin is moot. There is nothing original or difficult about copying bitcoin's design and producing a slightly different copycat, and thousands have done this so far. With time, one can expect more and more of these coins to enter the market, diluting the brand of all the other altcoins. Non-bitcoin digital currencies are, in the aggregate, easy money. No single altcoin can be considered on its own merits, because they are all indistinguishable in what they perform, which is also what bitcoin performs, but very distinguishable from bitcoin in that their supply and design can easily be altered, whereas bitcoin's monetary policy is for all intents and purposes set in stone.

It is an open question if any of these currencies will succeed in offering a market-demanded service other than the one offered by bitcoin, but it appears patently clear that they cannot compete with bitcoin on being trustless digital cash. That they have all chosen to ape bitcoin's rituals while pretending to be solving something extra does not inspire confidence in them achieving anything more than enriching their makers. The thousands of imitations of Nakamoto's design are perhaps the sincerest form of flattery, but their continued failure to ever deliver anything more than what Nakamoto delivered is a testament to how singular his accomplishment is. The only worthwhile additions to bitcoin's design were done by the competent selfless volunteer coders who contributed long hours to making the bitcoin code better. Many less competent coders have gotten massively rich by repackaging Nakamoto's design with marketing and pointless buzzwords, but have all failed in adding any functional capabilities to it that have any real-world demand. The growth of these altcoins cannot be understood outside the context of easy government money looking for easy investment, forming large bubbles in massive malinvestments.

Blockchain Technology[11]

As a result of bitcoin's startling rise in value, and the difficulty in understanding its operating procedure and technicalities, there has been a significant amount of confusion surrounding it. Perhaps the most persistent

---

[11] This section draws heavily on my paper: "Blockchain Technology: What Is It Good For?" *Banking and Finance Law Review*, iss. 1, vol. 33.3, 2018.

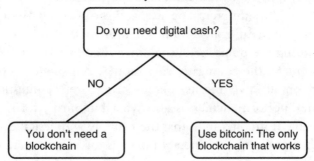

Figure 22 Blockchain decision chart.

and high-profile confusion is the notion that a mechanism that is part of bitcoin's operation—putting transactions into blocks which are chained together to form the ledger—can somehow be deployed to solve or improve economic or social problems, or even "revolutionize" them, as is the wont of every newfangled overhyped toy invented these days. "Bitcoin is not important, but the underlying blockchain technology is what holds promise" is a mantra that has been repeated ad nauseam between 2014 and 2017 by banking executives, journalists, and politicians, who all share one thing in common: a lack of understanding of how bitcoin actually works. (See Figure 22.)

The fixation with blockchain technology is a great example of "cargo cult science," an idea popularized by physicist Richard Feynman. The story goes that the U.S. military established airplane landing strips to aid in military operations on an island in the South Pacific Ocean during World War II. The airplanes would usually bring gifts to the local inhabitants of the island, who used to enjoy them immensely. After the war ended and the airplanes stopped landing on the strip, the locals tried their best to bring the airplanes and their cargo back. In their desperation, they would mimic the behavior of the long-gone military airport ground controllers, thinking that if they put a man in a hut with an antenna and light a fire, as the military ground controllers used to do, then the airplanes would come back and bring them the gifts. Clearly such a strategy could not work, because the procedures of the ground controllers were not creating airplanes out of thin air; they were but one integral part of an elaborate technological process, beginning with the manufacturing of the airplanes and their departure from their bases, which the South Pacific islanders could not comprehend.

Like these islanders, the people touting blockchain technology as a process that could generate economic benefits on its own do not understand the larger process of which it is a part. Bitcoin's mechanism for establishing the authenticity and validity of the ledger is extremely complex and complicated, but it serves an explicit purpose: issuing a currency and moving value online without the need for a trusted third party. "Blockchain technology," to the extent that such a thing exists, is not an efficient or cheap or fast way of transacting online. It is actually immensely inefficient and slow compared to centralized solutions. The *only* advantage that it offers is eliminating the need to trust in third-party intermediation. The only possible uses of this technology are in avenues where removing third-party intermediation is of such paramount value to end users that it justifies the increased cost and lost efficiency. And the only process for which it actually can succeed in eliminating third-party intermediation is the process of moving the native token of the network itself, as the code of the blockchain has no integrated control over anything taking place outside it.

A comparison will help give a sense of just how inefficient bitcoin is as a method for running transactions. If we strip away the trappings of decentralization, proof-of-work verification, mining, and trustlessness, and run a centralized version of bitcoin, it would essentially consist of an algorithm for generating coins, and a database for coin ownership that processes around 300,000 transactions per day. Such tasks are trivial, and any modern personal computer could perform them reliably. In fact, a regular off-the-shelf consumer laptop can be made to process around 14,000 transactions per second, or all of bitcoin's current daily transaction volume in 20 seconds.[12] To process bitcoin's entire yearly transaction volume, a personal laptop would need little more than two hours.

The problem with running such a currency on a personal laptop, however, is that it requires trust in the owner of the laptop and in the

---

[12] See Peter Geoghegan's blogpost explaining how he managed to achieve this on his personal computer: "Towards 14,000 write transactions per second on my laptop." *Peter Geoghegan's blog*, 4 Jun 2012, pgeoghegan.blogspot.com/2012/06/towards-14000-write-transactions-on-my.html.

laptop's security and safety from attack. In order to make such a trivial software system run without requiring trust in any single party to not defraud the record of transactions or alter the rate of currency issuance, the only design anyone has found is bitcoin's decentralized peer-to-peer network with proof-of-work verification. This is not a trivial software problem, and it took decades of computer programmers attempting different designs before one was found that could demonstrably achieve this. Whereas a good consumer laptop today has a hashrate around 10 megahashes per second, the bitcoin network collectively processes around 20 exahashes per second, or the equivalent of 2 trillion laptops. In other words, to remove the need for trust, the processing power to run a simple currency and database software needs to be increased roughly by a factor of 2 trillion. It is not the currency and its transactions that require so much processing power; making the entire system trustless does. For any other computing process to be run using blockchain technology, it would need to fulfill two criteria:

First, the gains from decentralization need to be compelling enough to justify the extra costs. For any process which will still require some form of trust in a third party to implement any small part of it, the extra costs of decentralization cannot be justified. For implementing contracts dealing with real-world businesses under legal jurisdictions, there will still be legal oversight relating to the real-world implementation of these contracts that can override the network consensus, making the extra cost of decentralization pointless. The same applies for decentralizing databases of financial institutions that will remain as trusted third parties in their own operations with one another or with their clients.

Second, the initial process itself needs to be simple enough to ensure the ability to run the distributed ledger on many nodes, without the blockchain becoming too heavy to be distributed. As the process continues to repeat over time, the size of the blockchain will grow and become more and more unmanageable for distributed nodes to hold a full copy of the blockchain, ensuring that only a few large computers can operate the blockchain and rendering decentralization obsolete. Note here the distinction between nodes that carry the ledger and dedicated miners who solve the proof-of-work, which is discussed in Chapter 8: miners need to expend enormous processing power to commit transactions to the joint ledger, whereas nodes need very little power to keep a copy of the ledger with which to verify the accuracy of miners' transactions. This is why nodes can be run on personal computers, whereas individual miners have the processing power of hundreds of personal computers. Should the operation of the ledger itself become too complex, nodes will need to be large servers instead of personal computers, destroying the possibility of decentralization.

The bitcoin blockchain has placed a 1-megabyte limit on the size of each block, which has limited the pace at which the blockchain has grown. That limit allows simple computers to be able to maintain and run a node. Should the size of each block increase, or should the blockchain be used for more sophisticated processes such as those touted by blockchain enthusiasts, it would become too large to be run on individual computers. Centralizing the network over a few large nodes owned and operated only by large institutions defeats the entire point of decentralization.

Trustless digital cash has so far been the only successful implementation for blockchain technology precisely because it is a clean and simple technological process to operate, leading to its ledger growing relatively slowly over time. This means that being a member of the bitcoin network is possible for a residential computer and connection in most of the world. Predictable controlled inflation also requires little processing power, but is a process whose decentralization and trustlessness offers enormous value to end users, as explained in Chapter 8. All other monetary media today are controlled by parties who can inflate the supply in order to profit from increased demand. This is true for fiat currencies and nonprecious metals, but also for gold, which is held in large quantities by central banks ready to sell it onto the market to prevent it from appreciating too quickly and thus displacing fiat currencies. For the first time since the abolition of the gold standard, bitcoin has made sound money easily available to anyone in the world who wants it. This highly unlikely combination of lightweight computing load and heavy economic significance is why it has made sense to grow the size of the bitcoin network's processing power to the largest network in history. It has proven impossible over eight years to find one other use case that is valuable enough to justify being distributed over thousands of node members while also being lightweight enough to allow for that decentralization.

The first implication of this analysis is that any change to bitcoin's protocol that increases the size of the blockchain is highly unlikely to pass, not just for the reasons of immutability mentioned before, but also because it would likely prevent most node operators from managing to run their own nodes, and because they are the ones who decide which software runs, it is safe to assume a significant intransigent minority of node operators will continue to run the current software, holding their current bitcoins, making any attempt to upgrade the bitcoin software effectively just another worthless altcoin like the hundreds of others that already exist.

The second implication is that all the "blockchain technology" applications being touted as revolutionizing banking or database technology are utterly doomed to fail in achieving anything more than fancy demos that will never transfer to the real world, because they will always be a highly inefficient way for the trusted third parties that operate them to conduct their business. It is outside the realm of possibility that a technology designed specifically to eliminate third-party intermediation could end up serving any useful purpose to the intermediaries it was created to replace.

There are many easier and less cumbersome ways of recording transactions, but this is the only method that eliminates the need for a trusted third party. A transaction is committed to the blockchain because many verifiers compete to verify it for profit. Yet not one of them is relied upon or trusted for the transaction to go through. Rather, fraud is immediately detected and reversed by other network members who have strong incentives to ensure the integrity of the network. In other words, bitcoin is a system built entirely on cumbersome and expensive verification so it can eliminate the need for any trust or accountability between all parties: it is 100% verification and 0% trust.

Contrary to a lot of the hype surrounding bitcoin, eliminating the need for trust in third parties is not an unquestionably good thing to do in all avenues of business and life. Once one understands the mechanism of bitcoin's operation, it is clear that there is a trade-off involved in moving to a system that does not rely on any trusted third parties. The advantages lie in individual sovereignty over the protocol, censorship-resistance, and immutability of the money supply growth and technical parameters. The disadvantages lie in the need for much larger processing power expenditure to perform the same amount of work. There is no reason, outside of naïve futuristic hype, to believe that this is a trade-off that is worthwhile for much. It may well be that the only place where this trade-off is worthwhile is the managing of a global homogeneous supranational sound money, for two important reasons. First, the excessive costs of operating the system can be recouped from slowly capturing parts of the global currency market, which runs at around 80 trillion U.S. dollars in value. Second, the nature of sound money, as explained earlier, lies precisely in the fact that no human is able to control it, and hence, a predictable immutable algorithm is uniquely suited for this task. Having thought of this question for years, in no other avenue of business can I find a similar process that is at once so important as to be worth the extra costs for disintermediation, as well as being so transparently simple that removing all human discretion would be a massive advantage.

An analogy with the automobile is instructive here. In 1885, when Karl Benz added an internal combustion engine to a carriage to produce the first autonomously powered vehicle, the express purpose of that move was to remove horses from carriages and free people from having to constantly deal with horse excrement. Benz was not trying to make horses faster. Burdening a horse with a heavy metal engine will not make it go faster; it will only slow it down while doing nothing to reduce the amount of excrement it produces. Similarly, as Chapter 8 explained, the colossal processing power needed to make the bitcoin network operate eliminates the need for a trusted third party to process payments or determine the supply of money. If the third party remains, then all of that processing power is a pointless waste of electricity.

Only time will tell whether this model for bitcoin will continue to grow in popularity and adoption. It is possible that bitcoin will grow to displace many financial intermediaries. It is also possible that bitcoin will stagnate or even fail and disappear. What cannot happen is bitcoin's blockchain benefiting the intermediation it was specifically designed to replace.

For any trusted third party carrying out payments, trading, or recordkeeping, the blockchain is an extremely costly and inefficient technology to utilize. A non-bitcoin blockchain combines the worst of both worlds: the cumbersome structure of the blockchain with the cost and security risk of trusted third parties. It is no wonder that eight years after its invention, blockchain technology has not yet managed to break through in a successful, ready-for-market commercial application other than the one for which it was specifically designed: bitcoin.

Instead, an abundance of hype, conferences, and high-profile discussions in media, government, academia, industry, and the World Economic Forum on the potential of blockchain technology has emerged. Many millions of dollars have been invested in venture capital, research, and marketing by governments and institutions that are seduced by the hype, without any practical result.

Blockchain consultants have built prototypes for stock trading, asset registry, voting, and payment clearance. But none of them have been commercially deployed because they are more expensive than simpler methods relying on established database and software stacks, as the government of Vermont recently concluded.[13]

Meanwhile, banks don't have a great track record in applying earlier technological advances for their own use. While JPMorgan Chase's CEO Jamie Dimon was touting blockchain technology in Davos in January 2016, his bank's Open Financial Exchange interfaces—a technology from 1997 to provide aggregators a central database of customer information—had been down for two months.

In contrast, the bitcoin network was born from the blockchain design two months after Nakamoto presented the technology. To this day, it has been operating uninterrupted and growing to more than $150 billion worth of bitcoins. The blockchain was the solution to the electronic cash problem. Because it worked, it grew quickly while Nakamoto worked anonymously and only communicated curtly via email for about two years. It did not need investment, venture capital, conferences, or advertisement.

As will become apparent from this exposition, the notion that a "blockchain technology" exists and can be deployed to solve any specific problems is highly dubious. It is far more accurate to understand the blockchain structure as an integral part of the operation of bitcoin and its testnets and copycats. Nevertheless, the term blockchain technology is used for simplicity in elucidation. The next section of this

---

[13] Higgins, Stan. "Vermont Says Blockchain Record-Keeping System Too Costly." *Coindesk.com*, 20 Jan. 2016, www.coindesk.com/report-blockchain-record-keeping-system-too-costly-for-vermont.

chapter examines the most commonly touted use-cases for blockchain technology, while the section after it identifies the main impediments to its application to these problems.

Potential Applications of Blockchain Technology

An overview of startups and research projects related to blockchain technology concludes that the potential applications of blockchains can be divided into three main fields:

Digital Payments

Current commercial mechanisms for payment clearance rely on centralized ledgers to record all transactions and maintain account balances. In essence, the transaction is transmitted once from the transacting parties to the intermediary, checked for validity, and accordingly both accounts are adjusted. In a blockchain, the transaction is transmitted to all network nodes, which involves many more transmissions and more processing power and time. The transaction also becomes part of the blockchain, copied onto every member computer. This is slower and more expensive than centralized clearance, and helps explain why Visa and MasterCard clear 2,000 transactions per second while bitcoin can at best clear four. Bitcoin has a blockchain not because it allows for faster and cheaper transactions, but because it removes the need to trust in third-party intermediation: transactions are cleared because nodes compete to verify them, yet no node needs to be trusted. It is unworkable for third-party intermediaries to imagine they could improve their performance by employing a technology that sacrifices efficiency and speed precisely to remove third-party intermediaries. For any currency controlled by a central party, it will always be more efficient to record transactions centrally. What can be clearly seen is that blockchain payment applications will have to be with the blockchain's own decentralized currency, and not with centrally controlled currencies.

Contracts

Currently, contracts are drafted by lawyers, judged by courts, and enforced by the police. Smart contract cryptographic systems such as Ethereum encode contracts into a blockchain to make them self-executing, with no possibility for appeal or reversal and beyond the reach of courts and police. "Code is law" is a motto used by smart contract programmers. The problem with this concept is that the language lawyers use to draft contracts is understood by far more people than the code language used by smart contract drafters. There are probably only a few hundred people worldwide with the technical expertise to fully understand the implications of a smart contract, and even they could miss glaring software bugs. Even as more people become proficient in the programming languages necessary to operate these contracts, the few people who are most proficient at it will by definition continue to have an advantage over the rest. Code competence will always offer a strategic advantage to the most proficient over everyone else.

This all became apparent with the first implementation of smart contracts on the Ethereum network, the Decentralized Autonomous Organization (DAO). After more than $150 million was invested in this smart contract, an attacker was able to execute the code in a way that diverted around a third of all the DAO's assets to his own account. It would be arguably inaccurate to describe this attack as a theft, because all the depositors had accepted that their money would be controlled by the code and nothing else, and the attacker had done nothing but execute the code as it was accepted by the depositors. In the aftermath of the DAO hack, Ethereum developers created a new version of Ethereum where this inconvenient mistake never occurred. This re-injection of subjective human management is at odds with the objective of making code into law, and questions the entire rationale of smart contracts.

Ethereum is the second largest blockchain after bitcoin in terms of its processing power, and while the bitcoin blockchain cannot effectively be rolled back, that Ethereum can be rolled back means that all blockchains smaller than bitcoin's are effectively centralized databases under the control of their operators. It turns out code is not really law, because the operators of these contracts can override what the contract executes. Smart contracts have not replaced courts with code, but they have replaced courts with software developers with little experience, knowledge, or accountability in arbitrating. It remains to be seen whether courts and lawyers will remain uninvolved as the ramifications of such forks continue to be explored.

The DAO was the first and so far only sophisticated application of a smart contract on a blockchain, and the experience suggests wider implementation is still a long way off, if it ever were to occur. All other applications currently only exist in prototype. Perhaps in a hypothetical future where code literacy is far more common and code more predictable and reliable, such contracts might become more commonplace. But if operating such contracts only adds processing power requirements while still leaving them subject to editing, forking, and overruling by the blockchain's engineers, then the entire exercise serves no purpose but the generation of buzzwords and publicity. A far more likely future for smart contracts is that they will exist over secured centralized computers operated by trusted third parties with the ability to override them. This formalizes the reality of blockchain smart contracts as editable while reducing the processing power requirement and reducing the attack vectors possible to compromise this.

For actual operational blockchains, demand will likely only be found for simple contracts whose code can be easily verified and understood. The only rationale for employing such contracts on a blockchain rather than a centralized computer system would be for the contracts to utilize the blockchain's native currency in some form, as all other contracts are better enforced and supervised without the extra burden of a blockchain distributed system. The only existing meaningful blockchain contract applications are for simple time-programmed payments and multi-signature wallets, all of which are performed with the currency of the blockchain itself, mostly on the bitcoin network.

Database and Record Management

Blockchain is a reliable and tamper-proof database and asset register, but only for the blockchain's native currency and only if the currency is valuable enough for the network to have strong enough processing power to resist attack. For any other asset, physical or digital, the blockchain is only as reliable as those responsible for establishing the link between the asset and what refers to it on the blockchain. There are no efficiency or transparency gains from using a permissioned blockchain here, as the blockchain is only as reliable as the party that grants permission to write to it. Introducing blockchain to that party's recordkeeping is only going to make it slower while adding no security or immutability, because there is no proof-of-work. Trust in third-party intermediaries must remain while the processing power and time required for running the database increases. A blockchain secured with a token could be used as a notary service, where contracts or documents are hashed onto a block of transactions, allowing any party to access the contract and be sure that the version displayed is the one that was hashed at the time. Such a service will provide a market for scarce block space, but is unworkable with any blockchain without a currency.

The Economic Drawbacks of Blockchain Technology

From examining the previous three potential applications of blockchain technology, five main obstacles to wider adoption are identified.

1. Redundancy

Having every transaction recorded with every member of the network is a very costly redundancy whose only purpose is to remove intermediation. For any intermediary, whether financial or legal, there is no sense in adding this redundancy while remaining an intermediary. There is no good reason for a bank to want to share a record of all its transactions with all banks, nor is there a reason for a bank to want to expend significant resources on electricity and processing power to record the transactions of other financial institutions with one another. This redundancy offers increased costs for no conceivable benefit.

2. Scaling

A distributed network where all nodes record all transactions will have its common transaction ledger grow exponentially faster than the number of network members. The storage and computational burden on members of a distributed network will be far larger than a centralized network of the same size. Blockchains will always face this barrier to effective scaling, and this explains why as bitcoin developers search for solutions for scaling, they are moving away from the pure decentralized blockchain model toward having payments cleared on second layers, such as the Lightning Network, or off the blockchain with intermediaries. There is a clear trade-off between scale and decentralization. Should a blockchain be made to accommodate larger volumes of transactions, the blocks need to be made larger, which would raise the cost of joining the network and result in fewer nodes. The network will tend toward centralization as a result. The most cost-effective way to have a large volume of transactions is centralization in one node.

3. Regulatory Compliance

Blockchains with their own currency, such as bitcoin, exist orthogonally to the law; there is virtually nothing that any government authority can do to affect or alter their operation. The Federal Reserve chair has even said as much: it has no authority to regulate bitcoin at all.[14] Roughly every ten minutes on the bitcoin network, a new block is released containing all the valid transactions made in these ten minutes, and nothing else. Transactions will clear if valid, and will not clear if not valid, and there is nothing that regulators can do to overturn the consensus of the network processing power. Applying blockchain technology in heavily regulated industries such as law or finance, with currencies other than bitcoin, will result in regulatory problems and legal complications. Regulations were designed for an infrastructure much different from that of blockchain and the rules cannot be easily tailored to fit blockchain operation, with the radical openness of having all records distributed to all network members. Further, a blockchain operates online across jurisdictions with different regulatory rules, so compliance with all rules is difficult to ensure.

4. Irreversibility

With payments, contracts, or databases operated by intermediaries, human or software errors can be easily reversed by appealing to the intermediary. In a blockchain, things are infinitely more complicated. Once a block has been confirmed and new blocks are being attached to it, it is only possible to reverse any of its transactions by marshalling 51% of the processing power of the network to roll back the network, where all these nodes agree to move simultaneously to an amended blockchain, and hope that the other 49% will not want to start their own network and

---

[14]Russolillo, S. "Yellen on Bitcoin: Fed Doesn't Have Authority to Regulate It in Any Way." *Wall Street Journal*, 27 Feb. 2014.

will join the new one. The larger the network, the harder it is to reverse any mistaken transaction. Blockchain technology, after all, is meant to replicate cash transactions online, which includes the irreversibility of cash transactions and none of the benefits of custodial intermediation in redress and revision. Human and software errors constantly occur in banking, and employing a blockchain structure will only result in these errors being far more costly to fix. The DAO incident revealed just how expensive and protracted such a reversal would be on a blockchain, requiring weeks of coding and public relations campaigns to get network members to agree to adopt the new software. And even after all that, the old chain continued to exist and took away a significant amount of the value and hashing power of the old network. This loss created a situation where two records of the previous transactions exist, one in which the DAO attack succeeded, and another in which it did not.

If the second largest network in terms of processing power can have its blockchain record altered when the transactions do not go in a way that suits the interests of the development team, then the notion that any other blockchain is truly regulated by processing power is not tenable. The concentration of currency holding, processing power, and programming skills in the hands of one group of people who are de facto colleagues in a private venture defeats the purpose of implementing this elaborate structure.

Such a reversal is extremely impractical and unlikely in bitcoin, for the reasons discussed in Chapter 9, mainly that every party in the bitcoin network is only capable of joining the network by agreeing to existing consensus rules. The adversarial interests of different members of the ecosystem have always meant that the network only grew through attracting the voluntary contributions of people who are willing to accept the consensus rules. In bitcoin, the consensus rules are constant and the users can choose to come and go. For every other blockchain project which was established by imitating bitcoin's design, there was always a single group responsible for setting the rules of the system, and thus having the ability to change them. Whereas bitcoin grew around the set of established consensus rules through human action, all other projects grew by active human design and management. Bitcoin has earned its reputation as being immutable after years of resisting alteration. No other blockchain project can make such a claim.

A blockchain that is alterable is a functionally pointless exercise in engineering sophistry: it uses a complex and expensive method for clearance to remove intermediaries and establish immutability, but then grants an intermediary the ability to overturn that immutability. Current best practice in these fields contains reversibility and supervision by legal and regulatory authorities, but employs cheaper, faster, and more efficient methods.

5. Security

The security of a blockchain database is entirely reliant on the expenditure of processing power on verification of transactions and proof-of-work. Blockchain technology can best be understood as the conversion of electric power to verifiable undisputed records of ownership and transactions. For this system to be secure, the verifiers who expend the processing power have to be compensated in the currency of the payment system itself, to align their incentive with the health and longevity of the network. Should payment for the processing power be made in any other currency, then the blockchain is essentially a private record maintained by whoever pays for the processing power. The security of the system rests on the security of the central party funding the miners, but it is compromised by operating on a shared ledger, which opens up many possibilities for security breaches to take place. An open decentralized system built on verification by processing power is more secure the more open the system and the larger the number of network members expending processing power on verification. A centralized system reliant on a single point of failure is less secure with a larger number of network members able to write to the blockchain as each added network member is a potential security threat.

Blockchain Technology as a Mechanism for Producing Electronic Cash

The only commercially successful application of blockchain technology so far is electronic cash, and in particular, bitcoin. The most common potential applications touted for blockchain technology—payments, contracts, and asset registry—are only workable to the extent that they run using the decentralized currency of the blockchain. All blockchains without currencies have not moved from the prototype stage to commercial implementation because they cannot compete with current best practice in their markets. Bitcoin's design has been freely available online for nine years, and developers can copy and improve on it to introduce commercial products, but no such products have appeared.

The market test shows that the redundancies of transaction recording and proof-of-work can only be justified for the purpose of producing electronic cash and a payment network without third-party intermediation. Electronic cash ownership and transactions can be communicated in very small quantities of data. Other economic cases which need more data requirements, such as mass payments and contracts, become unworkably cumbersome in the blockchain model. For any applications which involve intermediaries, the blockchain will offer an uncompetitive solution. There cannot be wide adoption of blockchain technology in industries reliant on trust in intermediaries, because the mere presence of intermediaries makes all the costs associated with running a blockchain superfluous. Any application of blockchain technology will only make commercial sense if its operation is reliant on the use of electronic cash, and only if electronic cash's disintermediation provides economic benefits outweighing the use of regular currencies and payment channels.

Good engineering begins with a clear problem and attempts to find the optimal solution for it. An optimal solution not only solves the problem, but by definition does not contain within it any irrelevant or superfluous excess. Bitcoin's creator was motivated by creating a "peer-to-peer electronic cash," and he built a design for that end. There is no reason, except for ignorance of its mechanics, to expect that it would be suited for other functions. After nine years and millions of users, it is safe to say his design has succeeded in producing digital cash, and, unsurprisingly, nothing else. This electronic cash can have commercial and digital applications, but it is not meaningful to discuss blockchain technology as a technological innovation in its own right with applications in various fields. Blockchain is better understood as an integral cog in the machine that creates peer-to-peer electronic cash with predictable inflation.

Acknowledgments

This manuscript benefited immensely from the help, guidance, and technical expertise of bitcoin developer David Harding, who has an admirable gift for communicating complex technical topics effectively. At Wiley I have been very fortunate to work with an editor who believed in my book and pushed me to relentlessly improve it, and for that, I am extremely thankful to Bill Falloon, as well as the entire Wiley team for their professionalism and efficiency. I also thank Rachael Churchill for her thorough and quick proofreading.

Earlier drafts of this book were read by a number of friends who gave me excellent feedback to improve it, for which I am very thankful. In particular, I thank Ahmad Ammous, Stefano Bertolo, Afshin Bigdeli, Andrea Bortolameazzi, Michael Byrne, Napoleon Cole, Adolfo Contreras, Rani Geha, Benjamin Geva, Michael Hartl, Alan Krassowski, Russell Lamberti, Parker Lewis, Alex Millar, Joshua Matettore, Daniel Oliver, Thomas Schellen, Valentin Schmit, Omar Shams, Jimmy Song, Luis Torras, and Hachem Yassine.

This book is the result of a learning process over many years, during which, I have been fortunate to learn from some very bright minds. In particular, I thank Tuur Demeester, Ryan Dickherber, Pete Dushenski, Michel Fahed, Akin Fernandez, Viktor Geller, Michael Goldstein, Konrad Graf, Stacy Herbert, Max Keiser, Pontus Lindblom, Mircea Popescu, Pierre Rochard, Peter Šurda, Nick Szabo, Kyle Torpey, and Curtis Yarvin for writings and discussions that were instrumental in developing my understanding of bitcoin.

The research and editing for this book benefited from the work of my very able research assistants, Rebecca Daher, Ghida Hajj Diab, Maghy Farah, Sadim Sbeity, and Racha Khayat, to whom I am very thankful. Professor George Hall graciously provided me data from his research paper, for which I am grateful.

The 2021 reprint of this book benefited from astute comments from Ross Ulbricht, David Killion, and Angelino Demset, as well thorough proofreading by Alexander Bradbury.

Finally, neither this book nor bitcoin would be possible without the tireless work of the volunteer developers who have dedicated their time for the development and maintenance of the protocol. I am grateful for their selflessness and dedication to this project.

Bibliography

Ahamed, Liaquat. *Lords of Finance: The Bankers Who Broke the World*. Penguin Press, 2009.

Ammous, Saifedean. "Blockchain Technology: What Is It Good For?" *Banking and Finance Law Review*, iss. *1*, vol. 33.3, 2018.

Anderson, William. "Dollar or Dinar?" *Mises Daily Articles*, Mises Institute, 4 Mar. 2003, mises.org/library/dollar-or-dinar.

Barzun, Jacques. *From Dawn to Decadence: 500 Years of Cultural Life, 1500 to the Present*. HarperCollins, 2000, p. 679, 688.

Bly, Nellie. *Around the World in Seventy-Two Days*. New York, Pictorial Weeklies, 1890.

Böhm-Bawerk, Eugen von. *Capital and Interest*. London, MacMillan and Co., 1890.

Brown, Malcolm, and Shirley Seaton. *Christmas Truce: The Western Front, December 1914*. London, PanMacmillan, 2014.

Buchanan, James M., and Gordon Tullock. *The Calculus of Consent: Logical Foundations of Constitutional Democracy*. Ann Arbor, University of Michigan Press, 1962.

Bunch, Bryan, and Alexander Hellemans. *The History of Science and Technology:A Browser's Guide to the Great Discoveries, Inventions, and the People Who Made Them, from the Dawn of Time to Today*. Houghton Mifflin Harcourt, 2014.

CIA World Factbook. www.cia.gov/the-world-factbook/.

Coase, Ronald. "The Nature of the Firm." *Economica*, vol. 4, no. 16, 1937, pp. 386–405.

Courtois, Stéphane, Nicolas Werth, Karel Bartosek, Andrzej Paczkowski, Jean-Louis Panné, and Jean-Louis Margolin. *The Black Book of Communism: Crimes, Terror, Repression*. Harvard University Press, 1997.

Davidson, James, and William Rees-Mogg. *The Sovereign Individual: Mastering the Transition to the Information Age*. New York, Simon and Schuster, 1999.

Deflation: Making Sure "It" Doesn't Happen Here. Remarks by Governor Ben S. Bernanke before the National Economists Club, Washington, D.C., 21 Nov. 2002.

Diamond, D. W., and P. H. Dybvig. "Bank Runs, Deposit Insurance, and Liquidity." *Journal of Political Economy*, vol. 91, no. 3, 1983, pp. 401–19.

Facts and Figures. Visa, Inc., Nov. 2015, usa.visa.com/content/dam/VCOM/download/corporate/media/VisaInc_factsheet_11012015%20(002).pdf.

Fekete, Antal. *Whither Gold?* Winner of the 1996 International Currency Prize, Sponsored by Bank Lips, 1997, www.professorfekete.com/articles/AEFWhitherGold.pdf.

Felix, David. *Keynes: A Critical Life*. Santa Barbara, CA, ABC-Clio, 1999, p. 112.

Ferguson, Adam. *An Essay on the History of Civil Society*. London, T. Cadell, 1782.

Finney, Hal. *BitcoinTalk Forum*. 30 Dec. 2010, bitcointalk.org/index.php?topic=2500.msg34211#msg34211.

Fisher, Irving. "Fisher Sees Stocks Permanently High." *New York Times*, 16 Oct. 1929, p. 8.

Friedman, Milton, and Anna Schwartz. *The Monetary History of the United States*. Princeton University Press, 1963, table 10, p. 206.

Galbraith, John Kenneth. *The Great Crash, 1929*. Boston, Houghton Mifflin Harcourt, 1997, p. 133.

Geoghegan, Peter. "Towards 14,000 write transactions per second on my laptop." Peter Geoghegan's blog, 4 Jun 2012, pgeoghegan.blogspot.com/2012/06/towards-14000-write-transactions-on-my.html.

Gilder, George. *The Scandal of Money: Why Wall Street Recovers but the Economy Never Does*. Washington, D.C., Regnery, 2016.

Glubb, John. *The Fate of Empires and Search for Survival*. Edinburgh, Scotland, William Blackwood and Sons, 1978.

Graf, Konrad. "On the Origins of Bitcoin: Stages of Monetary Evolution." *Konrad S. Graf*, 2013, www.konradsgraf.com.

Grant, James. *The Forgotten Depression: 1921: The Crash that Cured Itself*. New York, Simon & Schuster, 2014.

Greaves, Bettina Bien. *Ludwig von Mises on Money and Inflation: A Synthesis of Several Lectures*. Auburn, AL, Ludwig von Mises Institute, 2010, p. 32.

Halévy, Élie and May Wallas. "The Age of Tyrannies." *Economica*, New Series, vol. 8, no. 29, Feb. 1941, pp. 77–93.

Hall, George. "Exchange Rates and Casualties During the First World War." *Journal of Monetary Economics*, vol. 51, no. 8, Elsevier, Nov. 2004, pp. 1711–42.

Hanke, Steve, and Charles Bushnell. "Venezuela Enters the Record Book: The 57th Entry in the Hanke-Krus World Hyperinflation Table." *Studies in Applied Economics, no. 69*, Dec. 2016.

Hayek, Friedrich. *Denationalisation of Money: The Argument Refined*. London, Institute of Economic Affairs, 1976.

Hayek, Friedrich. "The Intellectuals and Socialism." *The University of Chicago Law Review* 16, no. 3, 1949, 417–33.

Hayek, Friedrich. *Monetary Nationalism and International Stability*. London, Longmans, Green and Company, 1937.

Hayek, Friedrich. "Monetary Policy, the Gold Standard, Deficits, Inflation, and John Maynard Keynes." Interview by James U. Blanchard III, University of Freiburg, Germany, *Libertarianism*, 1984, www.libertarianism .org/media/video-collection/interview-f-hayek.

Hayek, Friedrich. *Monetary Theory and the Trade Cycle*. New York, Sentry Press, 1933.

Hayek, Friedrich. *A Tiger by the Tail*. 3rd ed., compiled by Sudha Shenoy, Institute of Economic Affairs, and Ludwig von Mises Institute, 2009, p. 126.

Hayek, Friedrich. "The Use of Knowledge in Society." *The American Economic Review*, vol. 35, no. 4, Sep. 1945, pp. 519–30.

Hazlitt, Henry. *The Failure of the "New Economics."* New York, Van Nostrand, 1959, p. 277.

Higgins, Stan. "Vermont Says Blockchain Record-Keeping System Too Costly." *Coindesk.com*, 20 Jan. 2016, www.coindesk.com/report-blockchain-record-keeping-system-too-costly-for-vermont.

Higgs, Robert. *World War II and the Triumph of Keynesianism*. Independent Institute, 2001, www.independent.org/publications/article.asp?id=317.

His Majesty O'Keefe. Directed by Byron Haskin, performances by Burt Lancaster, Joan Rice, and André Morell, Warner Bros, 1954.

Holroyd, Michael. *Lytton Strachey: The New Biography*. vol. I, Portsmouth, NH, Heinemann, 1994, p. 80.

Hoppe, Hans-Hermann, *Democracy: The God That Failed*. Rutgers, NJ, Transaction Publishers, 2001, pp. 6, 1–43.

Hoppe, Hans-Hermann. "How Is Fiat Money Possible?" *Review of Austrian Economics*, vol. 7, no. 2, 1994.

Huebner, Jonathan. "A Possible Declining Trend for Worldwide Innovation." *Technological Forecasting and Social Change*, vol. 72, no. 8, Elsevier, Oct. 2005, pp. 980–6.

Human Development Report 2005: International Cooperation at a Crossroads: Aid, Trade and Security in an Unequal World. United Nations Development Program, New York, 2005, hdr.undp.org/en/content/human-development-report-2005.

Ibn Khaldun, Abd Alrahman. *Al-Muqaddima*. 1377.

Jastram, Roy. *The Golden Constant: The English and American Experience 1560–2007*. Cheltenham, UK, Edward Elgar, 2009.

Kent, R. "The Edict of Diocletian Fixing Maximum Prices." *University of Pennsylvania Law Review*, vol. 69, 1920, p. 35.

Keynes, J. M. "The End of Laissez-Faire." *Essays in Persuasion*, London, The Royal Economic Society, 1931, pp. 272–95.

Keynes, J. M. *Essays in Persuasion*. W. W. Norton, 1963.

Keynes, J. M. *The General Theory of Employment, Money, and Interest*. Palgrave Macmillan, 1936.

Keynes, J. M. *A Tract on Monetary Reform*. London, Macmillan and Co., 1923, p. 80.

Klingman, Lawrence Lewis, and Gerald Green. *His Majesty O'Keefe*. Scribner, 1950.

Koning, J. P. "Orphaned Currency: Odd Case of Somali Shillings." *Moneyness: The Blog of J. P. Koning*, 1 Mar. 2013, jpkoning.blogspot.com/2013/03/orphaned-currency-odd-case-of-somali.html.

Kontzer, Tony. "Inside Visa's Data Center." *Network Computing*, 29 May 2013, www.networkcomputing.com/networking/inside-visas-data-center/1599285558.

Kremer, Michael. "Population Growth and Technological Change: One Million B.C. to 1990." *Quarterly of Journal of Economics*, vol. 108, no. 3, 1993, pp. 681–716.

Krugman, Paul. "Secular Stagnation, Coalmines, Bubbles, and Larry Summers." *New York Times*, 16 Nov. 2003.

Levy, David and Sandra Peart. "Soviet Growth and American Textbooks: An Endogenous Past." *Journal of Economic Behavior & Organization*, vol. 78, iss. 1–2, Apr. 2011, pp. 110–25.

Lips, Ferdinand. *Gold Wars: The Battle Against Sound Money as Seen from a Swiss Perspective*. New York, Foundation for the Advancement of Monetary Education, 2001.

Luscombe, David, and Jonathan Riley-Smith. *The New Cambridge Medieval History: Volume 4, C.1024–1198*. Cambridge University Press, 2008, p. 255.

Mallery, Otto. *Economic Union and Durable Peace*. New York, Harper and Brothers, 1943, p. 10.

Matonis, John. "Bitcoin Obliterates 'The State Theory of Money.'" *Forbes*, 3 Apr. 2013, www.forbes.com/sites/jonmatonis/2013/04/03/bitcoin-obliterates-the-state-theory-of-money/#6b93e45f4b6d.

May, Timothy C. "Crypto Anarchy and Virtual Communities." *Satoshi Nakamoto Institute*, 1994, nakamotoinstitute.org/virtual-communities/.

McConnell, Campbell, Stanley Brue, and Sean Flynn. *Economics: Principles, Problems, and Policies*. McGraw-Hill, 2009, p. 535.

Mencken, H. L. *A Carnival of Buncombe*, edited by Malcolm Moos, Baltimore, MD, Johns Hopkins Press, 1956, p. 325.

Menger, Carl. "On the Origins of Money." Trans. C. A. Foley. *Economic Journal,* vol. 2, 1892, pp. 239–55.

Merkle, Ralph. "DAOs, Democracy and Governance." *Cryonics*, vol. 37, no. 4, Jul.–Aug. 2016, Alcor, pp. 28–40, www.alcor.org.

Mischel, Walter, Ebbe Ebbesen, and Antonette Raskoff Zeiss. "Cognitive and Attentional Mechanisms in Delay of Gratification." *Journal of Personality and Social Psychology*, vol. 21, no. 2, 1972, pp. 204–18.

Mises, Ludwig von. *Socialism: An Economic and Sociological Analysis*. Auburn, AL, Ludwig von Mises Institute, 1922.

Mises, Ludwig von. *Human Action: The Scholar's Edition.* Auburn, AL, Ludwig von Mises Institute, 1998, pp. 250, 421, 472–3, 473, 474, 476–533, 560, 575, 703–4.

Mises, Ludwig von. *The Theory of Money and Credit*. 2nd ed., Irvington-on-Hudson, NY, Foundation for Economic Education, 1971, pp. 414–6.

Nakamoto, Satoshi. *BitcoinTalk Forum.* 17 June 2010, bitcointalk.org/index.php?topic=195.msg1611#msg1611.

Nakamoto, Satoshi. "Re: Bitcoin P2P e-cash paper." Received by The Cryptography Mailing List, 31 Oct. 2008.

Nakamoto, Satoshi. "Re: I had a few other things on my mind (as always) . . . " Received by Mike Hearn, 23 Apr. 2011.

New Liberty Standard. newlibertystandard.wikifoundry.com/.

Philippon, Thomas, and Ariell Reshef. "An International Look at the Growth of Modern Finance." *Journal of Economic Perspectives*, vol. 27, no. 2, 2013, pp. 73–96.

Popper, Nathaniel. *Digital Gold: Bitcoin and the Inside Story of the Misfits and Millionaires Trying to Reinvent Money*. HarperCollins, 2015.

Proceedings and Documents of the United Nations Monetary and Financial Conference. vol. 1, Bretton Woods, NH, US Department of State, 1944.

The Regulation of OTC Derivatives. Testimony of Chairman Alan Greenspan before the Committee on Banking and Financial Services, US House of Representatives, 24 Jul. 1998.

Rooney, Ben. "Copper Strikes After Chile Quake." *CNN Money,* 1 Mar. 2010.

Rothbard, Murray. *America's Great Depression*. 5th ed., Auburn, AL, Ludwig von Mises Institute, 2000, p. 186.

Rothbard, Murray. "The Austrian Theory of Money." *The Foundations of Modern Austrian Economics*, edited by Edwin Dolan, Kansas City, Sheed and Ward, 1976, pp. 160–84.

Rothbard, Murray. "A Conversation with Murray Rothbard." *Austrian Economics Newsletter,* vol. 11, no. 2, Auburn, AL, Mises Institute, Summer 1990.

Rothbard, Murray. *Economic Depressions: Their Cause and Cure.* Auburn, AL, Ludwig von Mises Institute, 2009.

Rothbard, Murray. "The End of Socialism and the Calculation Debate Revisited." *Review of Austrian Economics,* vol. 5, no. 2, 1991.

Rothbard, Murray. *The Ethics of Liberty.* New York University Press, 1998, p. 43.

Rothbard, Murray. *Man, Economy, and State, with Power and Market.* Auburn, AL, Ludwig von Mises Institute, 1962, pp. 367–450.

Rudolph, Barbara. "Big Bill for a Bullion Binge." *TIME,* 29 Aug. 1988.

Ruoti, Scott, Ben Kaiser, Arkady Yerukhimovich, Jeremy Clark, and Robert Cunningham. "Blockchain Technology: What Is It Good For?" *Banking and Finance Law Review,* iss. 1, vol. 33.3, 2018.

Russolillo, S. "Yellen on Bitcoin: Fed Doesn't Have Authority to Regulate It in Any Way." *Wall Street Journal,* 27 Feb. 2014.

Salerno, Joseph. *Money: Sound and Unsound.* Auburn, AL, Ludwig von Mises Institute, 2010, pp. xiv–xv.

Samuelson, Paul. *Economics: An Introductory Analysis.* McGraw-Hill, 1948.

Samuelson, Paul. "Full Employment After the War." *Postwar Economic Problems,* edited by Seymour Harris, McGraw-Hill, 1943, pp. 27–53.

Saunders, Frances Stonor. *The Cultural Cold War: The CIA and the World of Arts and Letters.* New York, The New Press, 2000.

Schuettinger, Robert, and Eamonn Butler. *Forty Centuries of Price and Wage Controls: How Not to Fight Inflation.* Washington, D.C., Heritage Foundation, 1978.

Simon, Julian. *The Ultimate Resource.* Princeton University Press, 1981.

Skousen, Mark. "The Perseverance of Paul Samuelson's Economics." *Journal of Economic Perspectives,* vol. 11, no. 2, 1997, pp. 137–52.

Smith, Vernon. *Rationality in Economics.* New York, Cambridge University Press, 2008.

Steil, Benn. *The Battle of Bretton Woods: John Maynard Keynes, Harry Dexter White, and the Making of a New World Order.* Princeton University Press, 2013.

Stein, Mara Lemos. "The Morning Risk Report: Terrorism Financing Via Bitcoin May Be Exaggerated." *Wall Street Journal,* 2017.

Stevenson, Betsy, and Justin Wolfers. "The Paradox of Declining Female Happiness." *American Economic Journal: Economic Policy,* vol. 1, no. 2, 2009, pp. 190–225.

Sutton, Antony. *Wall Street and the Bolshevik Revolution*. Crown Publishing Group, 1974.

Symonds, John Addington. *The Sonnets of Michael Angelo Buonarroti*. London, Smith Elder & Co., 1904.

Szabo, Nick. "Shelling Out: The Origins of Money." *Satoshi Nakamoto Institute*, 2002, nakamotoinstitute.org/shelling-out/.

Szabo, Nick. "Trusted Third Parties Are Security Holes." *Satoshi Nakamoto Institute*, 2001, nakamotoinstitute.org/trusted-third-parties/.

Taylor, Simon. "The True Meaning of 'In the Long Run We Are All Dead.'" *Simon Taylor: Behind Blue Eyes*, 5 May 2013, www.simontaylors blog.com/2013/05/05/the-true-meaning-of-in-the-long-run-we-are-all-dead/.

Thiel, Peter, and Blake Masters. *Zero to One: Notes on Startups, or How to Build the Future*. New York, Crown Business, 2014.

Torpey, Kyle. "Here's What Goldbugs Miss About Bitcoin's 'Intrinsic Value.'" *Forbes Digital Money*, 27 Oct. 2017, www.forbes.com/sites/ktorpey/2017/10/27/heres-what-gold-bugs-miss-about-bitcoins-intrinsic-value/2/#11b6a3b97ce0.

Triennial Central Bank Survey: Foreign Exchange Turnover in April 2016. Basel, CH, Bank of International Settlements, 2016.

Vaillant, George. *Triumphs of Experience: The Men of the Harvard Grant Study*. Cambridge, MA, Harvard University Press, 2012.

Online Resources

bitcoin.org: The original domain used by Nakamoto to announce bitcoin, share the white paper, and distribute the code. It continues to be run by several contributors and serves as a good resource for information.

nakamotoinstitute.org: The Satoshi Nakamoto Institute curates primary source literature on cryptography and society, with a focus on the history and economics of bitcoin. It also maintains an archive of all of Nakamoto's known writings: the bitcoin white paper, the emails he sent, and the forum posts he made.

Saifedean.com: The author's education platform teaching courses on the economics of bitcoin and the Austrian School tradition.

lopp.net/bitcoin.html: An excellent, comprehensive, and regularly updated page listing bitcoin resources maintained by Jameson Lopp.

List of Figures

Figure 1   Global gold stockpiles and annual stockpile growth
rate   22

Figure 2   Existing stockpiles as a multiple of annual
production   24

Figure 3   Price of gold in silver ounces, 1687–2017   33

Figure 4   Central bank official gold reserves, tons   40

Figure 5   Major national exchange rates vs. Swiss Franc
during WWI. Exchange rate in June 1914 = 1   45

Figure 6   Broad money average annual growth rate for 167
currencies, 1960–2015   63

Figure 7   Annual broad money growth rate in Japan, U.K.,
United States, and Euro area   65

Figure 8   Purchasing power of gold and wholesale
commodity index in England, 1560–1976   86

Figure 9   Price of commodities in gold and in U.S. dollars,
in log scale, 1792–2016   87

Figure 10 Major currencies priced in gold, 1971–2017   88

Figure 11 Oil priced in U.S. dollars and ounces of gold, 1861–2017, as multiple of price in 1971   88

Figure 12 National savings rates in major economies, 1970–2016, %   91

Figure 13 Unemployment rate in Switzerland, %   120

Figure 14 Bitcoin supply and supply growth rate assuming blocks are issued exactly every ten minutes   179

Figure 15 Projected bitcoin and national currency percentage growth in supply over 25 years   181

Figure 16 Price of bitcoin in US dollars   183

Figure 17 Annual transactions on the bitcoin network   186

Figure 18 Average U.S. dollar value of transaction fees on bitcoin network, logarithmic scale   188

Figure 19 Monthly 30-day volatility for bitcoin and the USD Index   188

Figure 20 Global oil consumption, production, proven reserves, and ratio of reserves over annual production, 1980–2015   194

Figure 21 Total available global stockpiles divided by annual production   198

Figure 22 Blockchain decision chart   258

List of Tables

Table 1   Major European Economies' Periods Under the
Gold Standard   35

Table 2   Depreciation of National Currency Against the
Swiss Franc During World War I   46

Table 3   The Ten Countries with Highest Average Annual
Broad Money Supply Growth, 1960–2015   63

Table 4   Average Annual Percent Increase in Broad Money
Supply for the Ten Largest Global Currencies   64

Table 5   Conflict Deaths in the Last Five Centuries   148

Table 6   Bitcoin Supply and Growth Rate   180

Table 7   Bitcoin Supply and Growth Rate (Projected)   180

Table 8   Annual Transactions and Average Daily Transactions   185

Table 9   Total Annual US Dollar Value of All Bitcoin
Network Transactions   187

Table 10 Average Daily Percentage Change and Standard
Deviation in the Market Price of Currencies per
USD over the Period of September 1, 2011, to
September 1, 2016   189

Index

51% attack, 242–245

aggry beads, 13
altcoins, 251–257
anarcho-capitalism, 203–204
antifragility, 230–232
art, 98–104
aureus, 25
Austrian school of economics, 3, 70, 106,
     142–145, 204

barter, 1
bezant, 28–29
bitcoin, 33–34, 167
block subsidy, 187, 199, 218
blockchain, 257–272
breakdown of the family, 95
Bretton Woods conference, 56–57
business cycle, 116, 119, 145
Byzantine empire, 28–29
Byzantium, *see* Byzantine empire

capital goods, 9, 75, 109–116
capitalism, 92, 109–111, 118, 200
cargo cult science, 258
cash, 169, 171, 207, 238
cash, digital, *see* digital cash
central banks, 39–40, 56–57, 59, 69, 89,
     117–119, 210–212
coin clipping, 25
coincidence of wants, 2
coins, 18

comparative advantage, 108
Constantine, 28
counterparty risk, 208
crime, 238–240
Croesus, 18, 25
cypherpunk, 203, 246

DAO, *see* Decentralized Autonomous
     Organization
Dark Ages, 29–30
Decentralized Autonomous Organization, 254,
     266–267
deflation, 121, 140–141
denarius, 25
depression, economic, 49–53, 120–124
depression, psychological, 95
digital cash, 168–170, 182, 200, 207, 238
digital goods, 201–202
digital scarcity, 177, 199–200
dinar, 28–29
Diocletian, 26, 28
direct exchange, 1
ducat, 30

easy money, 5
easy money trap, 5
Ehrlich, Paul, 195
Ethereum, 254

Federal Reserve, 49, 51, 59, 120, 125
fiat money, *see* government money
Finney, Hal, 209, 223, 252

Fisher, Irving, 124
florin, 30
fractional reserve banking, 113, 124, 161, 206,
   209
Friedman, Milton, 121–123, 125, 140, 155

Galbraith, John Kenneth, 155
GDP, 130–131
General Agreement on Trade and Tariffs, 58
gold, 17, 19–22, 23–24, 82, 85–89, 155, 214
gold standard, 19, 31–32, 35–40, 250
government money, 9, 37, 41–43, 51, 62, 66–70,
   87–89, 181
Great Depression, 49–53, 124–125

hard money, 5
hashing, 191, 248
Hayek, Friedrich, 47, 72, 106–107, 126
Hoover, Herbert, 49–50
hyperinflation, 48, 62–63, 66–67

Impossible Trinity, 128, 131
indirect exchange, 2
inflation, 26–27, 44–45, 48–51, 60–61, 81, 118,
   138–139
interest rates, 80, 112–119, 145, 157
International Monetary Fund, 57–58, 120

Julius Caesar, 25

Keynes, John Maynard, 51–52, 54–56, 71,
   82–83, 91–92, 95, 117, 131, 137–139, 143,
   153, 155
Kremer, Michael, 196

Lips, Ferdinand, 27

malinvestments, 145
marginal utility, 84
market demand, 19
marshmallow experiment, see Stanford
   Marshmallow Experiment
medium of exchange, 2
Menger, Carl, 3, 34
Merkle tree, 175
Merkle, Ralph, 175
Michelangelo, 100
Mischel, Walter, 77
Mises, Ludwig von, 36, 38, 70, 109–111,
   116–117, 135, 142, 145, 182
Monetarism, 121, 124, 137, 140
monetary demand, 19
monetary nationalism, 47, 213

Nakamoto, Satoshi, 142, 171, 212, 223, 252
Nero, 25
New Deal, 50
New Liberty Standard, 182

Newton, Isaac, 31
Nixon, Richard, 60–61

O'Keefe, David, 12–13

peer-to-peer network, 192
price elasticity of supply, 24
prices, 106–111, 119
proof-of-work, 171–172, 218–219
public key cryptography, 191, 217

Rai stones, 9, 11–13, 174
recession, 36, 91–92, 116–124, 138–140
Renaissance, 29–30
reserve currency, 37–39, 56, 206–210
Roman empire, 25
Roosevelt, Franklin Delano, 49–51
Rothbard, Murray, 34, 49, 79, 116, 126,
   143, 204
Rothko, Mark, 102
Royal Mint, 31

salability, 3
Samuelson, Paul, 55, 158–159
Satoshi, see Nakamoto, Satoshi
satoshis, 175, 179, 181, 198
savings, 35, 83, 90–93, 114, 143, 153, 163
scarcity, 110–114, 177, 193–195, 199
Schwartz, Anna, 121–123, 125
seashells, 14
silver, 17, 22–23, 30–33
Simon, Julian, 193, 195
smart contracts, 265–267
socialism, 109–111, 118
solidus, 26, 28–29, 212
sound money, 7, 30, 34, 43, 70–71, 73, 89–90,
   119, 146, 150, 153, 165, 249–251
Stanford Marshmallow Experiment, 77, 143–144
state theory of money, 136–137
stock-to-flow ratio, 5–6, 23, 155, 199
store of value, 4, 193, 208
Switzerland, 37, 90, 119

time preference, 7, 74–80, 143

unit of account, 8, 212–216
unsound money, 25, 38, 71, 90, 102, 115, 119,
   127, 145–163

Wales, Jimmy, 106
war, 145–149
White, Harry Dexter, 56
Wikipedia, 106
World War I, 41, 43–46
World War II, 53–55

Yap, 9, 11–13, 174